ENGLISH RENAISSANCE POETRY

ENGLISH RENAISSANCE POETRY

A COLLECTION OF SHORTER POEMS
FROM SKELTON TO JONSON

Edited by
JOHN WILLIAMS

The Norton Library
W·W·NORTON & COMPANY·INC·
NEW YORK

W. W. Norton & Company, Inc. also publishes *The Norton
Anthology of English Literature*, edited by M. H. Abrams et al;
The Norton Anthology of Poetry, edited by Arthur M. Eastman
et al; *World Masterpieces*, edited by Maynard Mack et al; *The
Norton Reader*, edited by Arthur M. Eastman et al; *The Norton
Facsimile of the First Folio of Shakespeare*, prepared by Charlton
Hinman; *The Norton Anthology of Modern Poetry*, edited by
Richard Ellmann and Robert O'Clair; and the *Norton Critical
Editions*.

Library of Congress Cataloging in Publication Data
Williams, John Edward, 1922–   ed.
    English Renaissance poetry; a collection of shorter
poems from Skelton to Jonson.
    (The Norton library)
    Reprint of the 1st ed. published by Doubleday, New
York.
    1. English poetry—Early modern (to 1700).
I. Title.
[PR1205.W55   1974]   821'.2'08   73-22163
ISBN 0-393-00726-X

Printed in the United States of America
2 3 4 5 6 7 8 9 0

CONTENTS

PREFACE

THREE PHASES OF
RENAISSANCE POETRY

I

The period from the beginning of the sixteenth century
to about 1630 is a crucial one in the history of English
poetry. For a little more than a hundred years, that most
sturdy and persistent of all literary forms, the short poem,
engaged the attentions of the best literary minds of the
century, and as a consequence underwent a series of trans-
formations that changed its nature to a degree not usually
recognized by the general reader. Caught in the tangled
history of that century, and sometimes obscured by it,
are some of the great poems in our language; implicit in
those poems, and in the criticism engendered by them, are
the essential questions of theory and practice that have
occupied historians and critics, as well as poets, for the
past three hundred and fifty years.

During this English Renaissance, the short poem passed
through three distinct but finally inseparable phases. The
earliest of these is the Native tradition, so called because
of its roots in the short English poem of the fourteenth
and fifteenth centuries and because of its dependence
upon a native medieval tradition of grammar and rhetoric;
the purest representatives of this tradition are such Tudor
and early Elizabethan poets as John Skelton, Sir Thomas
More, Sir Thomas Wyatt, Lord Vaux, George Gascoigne,
Barnabe Googe, George Turberville, and Sir Walter
Ralegh.

The intermediate tradition is the Petrarchan, so called because of its primary dependence upon the new Italian poetry of Francesco Petrarch and his followers in both Italy and France, and because of its secondary dependence upon the "new" Classical Latin, rather than Medieval Latin, as a normative literary language; this revival of interest in the more "eloquent" Latin writers started in Italy with Petrarch and his contemporaries and spread slowly throughout the continent during the fifteenth and sixteenth centuries. The best representatives of this tradition are such Elizabethans as Edmund Spenser, Sir Philip Sidney, Samuel Daniel, Thomas Campion, and the English Madrigalists.

The third phase is one to which it is difficult to attach a familiar label. It is the major tradition of English poetry, one which assimilates and completes the practices of the earlier phases, gathering the virtues of both and dispensing with the vices of either. Though early, Sir Thomas Wyatt in a few poems presages this tradition; but its best representatives are the major poets of the age, Fulke Greville, William Shakespeare, John Donne, and Ben Jonson.

The foregoing implies that there was a fairly conscious progression from one set of principles to another, from one method to another, throughout the century. That which follows will attempt to suggest the nature and implications of those principles and methods. But any real understanding of the progression must be gained, not by a mere rehearsal of the steps, but by a close examination of that which defines them and makes them possible— a body of great poetry that goes word by word, line by line, through the century, and beyond.

II

Around 1510, the humanist and Catholic martyr, Sir Thomas More, could speak unself-consciously, directly, almost colloquially, to both his subject and his audience, as if nothing separated them:

Whoso delighteth to proven and assay
Of wavering fortune the uncertain lot,
If that the answer please you not alway,
Blame ye not me; for I command you not
Fortune to trust, and eke full well ye wot
I have of her no bridle in my fist:
She runneth loose, and turneth where she list.

Similarly, a few years later, Wyatt could speak with a comparable straightforwardness and certainty:

If thou wilt mighty be, flee from the rage
Of cruel will, and see thou keep thee free
From the foul yoke of sensual bondáge . . .

And some fifty years after More had written his lines, George Gascoigne, perhaps the greatest poet of the purely Native tradition, was still able to speak to an audience of whose presence he was certain, in a tone familiar, blunt, and spontaneous:

The common speech is, spend and God will send;
But what sends he? A bottle and a bag,
A staff, a wallet, and a woeful end
For such as list in bravery so to brag.

These are examples of Native style; and though they were written by representatives of three different generations, by men of exceedingly different temperaments and persuasions, the examples have a great deal in common. All that they have in common will not be evident from these snippets, nor will all that they do not have in common. But a fairly careful reading of the whole poems of which these lines are the beginnings and a careful reading of other poems in the Native tradition will specify the following general observations.

The subject of the Native poem is usually broad and generic and of what we might call persistent human significance; the purpose to which the subject is put is instructive or informative or judicial. Almost always, the Native poet speaks from his own intelligence, as if he knew it existed; he feels no compulsion to mask himself, to assume a persona, to work from cunning, or to live in exile. Speaking from his own intelligence, he speaks to another intelligence, as if he knew that that, too, existed; he is a reasonable man, addressing with his own voice other reasonable men; and the tone of the voice tells us that he is confident of the existence of reasonable men in his audience. And since he is a reasonable man speaking to other reasonable men, his discourse is reasonably organized; he speaks in the accepted forms, forms that have traditionally organized the details of men's thought. That is to say, his discourse, which is the poem, is logical.

On the simplest level of structure, but not necessarily the lowest, the poem is additive and accretive, a kind of catalog of qualities or properties, the details of the poem being ordered by the mere presence of a subject that includes them; this ordering may be clumsy and mechanical, as it often is in Surrey, or it may be almost unbearably powerful, as it is in such a poem as Ralegh's *The Lie*. On a slightly more complex level, the poem, if it is brief, may be the elaboration of a single aphorism or proverb or maxim; if longer, it may be composed of a series of maxims, one maxim proceeding more or less necessarily from another. Several of Lord Vaux's poems are composed in this manner, as are other poems by other Native poets. Often a Native poem, especially if it is brief, is structured according to the demands of formal logic, in the shape of an enthymeme, a syllogism, a sorites, a dilemma, or whatever; sometimes, as in Turberville's brief epigram *Of a Rich Miser*, the lines themselves come very close to marking off the premises and conclusion; more often, the terms are more subtly disposed throughout the poem. But the characteristic structure of the Native poem, the structure in which nearly all the greatest poems of the phase are cast, is expository—that is, the method of sound discourse, in which an object, sensible or otherwise, is selected and dealt with in such a way that its various parts are examined in some detail and are rationally related, both to each other and to the object which they constitute.

This is the structure of the three poems that I have quoted; it is also the characteristic structure of the major phase, that which Ben Jonson used in his more ambitious poems and, with a few qualifications, the structure that John Donne elaborated in those poems of his that we most admire.

Since the Native poet is a reasonable man, and since he has organized his discourse as rationally as he is able, his tone will be appropriate to himself, to what he has to say, and to his audience. The rhetoric of his poem, then, will be subdued to his subject, determined by the substance of his poem, and by its own function, which is to give the appropriate value to that substance. Thus, if we read the Native poem passively or inattentively or insensitively—that is, if we read as if we were not mortals listening to another mortal—the style may seem flat, bare, almost lifeless. But if we *listen* to the poem, we shall hear beneath the emphatic stresses, beneath the bare and essential speech, the human cadence of the human voice, speaking to us as if we were alive.

III

Although the beginnings of Native poetry are dim, as are the true beginnings of any movement, the moment of its flourishing is clear. It is a long moment, one which extends from the beginning through the third quarter of the sixteenth century. And though the Petrarchan movement may have had its inception in the thirties, after Wyatt returned from Italy and began translating some of Petrarch's sonnets, it did not really take hold of the imaginations of any poets of talent until the late seventies or early eighties. Within twenty-five or thirty years, its course was run, though it left a mark on English poetry that was not to be removed.

Thus, it is not until the century is drawing to its close that we begin to get the first consistent and determined

revisions of Native practice. Here is a sonnet from Sir
Philip Sidney's sequence, *Astrophil and Stella:*

> With how sad steps, O Moon, thou climbst the skies!
> How silently, and with how wan a face!
> What, may it be that even in heavenly place
> That busy archer his sharp arrows tries?
> Sure, if that long-with-love-acquainted eyes
> Can judge of love, thou feel'st a lover's case:
> I read it in thy looks: thy languished grace,
> To me that feel the like, thy state descries.
> Then even of fellowship, O Moon, tell me,
> Is constant love deemed there but want of wit?
> Are beauties there as proud as here they be?
> Do they above love to be loved, and yet
> Those lovers scorn whom that love doth possess?
> Do they call virtue there ungratefulness?

Some ten or twelve years later, in the long *Epithalamion*
that celebrated his own marriage, Edmund Spenser wrote
to the Muses:

> Ye learnèd sisters, which have oftentimes
> Been to me aiding, others to adorn,
> Whom ye thought worthy of your graceful rimes,
> That even the greatest did not greatly scorn
> To hear their names sung in your simple lays,
> But joyed in their praise;
> And when ye list your own mishaps to mourn,
> Which death, or love, or fortune's wreck did raise,
> Your string could soon to sadder tenor turn,
> And teach the woods and waters to lament
> Your doleful dreariment. . . .

And at about the same time, in the forty-fifth of his son-
nets to *Delia,* Samuel Daniel addressed sleep:

> Care-charmer sleep, son of the sable night
>   Brother to death, in silent darkness born,
>   Relieve my languish and restore the light;
>   With dark forgetting of my care, return

And let the day be time enough to mourn
  The shipwreck of my ill-adventured youth;
  Let waking eyes suffice to wail their scorn
  Without the torment of the night's untruth.
Cease, dreams, the images of day-desires,
  To model forth the passions of the morrow;
  Never let rising sun approve you liars,
  To add more grief to aggravate my sorrow.
Still let me sleep, embracing clouds in vain,
And never wake to feel the day's disdain.

Just as the three examples of Native style quoted earlier had a great deal in common, so do these three examples of Petrarchan style. Typically, in these poems subject and theme have drawn so far apart that only by an act of rhetoric can they be reunited. Whether the poem deals explicitly with the moon, with the spirit of poetry, or with sleep, the thematic issue is remarkably similar; each poem attempts a definition of love, and attempts that definition by means that are suggestive and indirect. But the hidden definition is, essentially, quite simple: in Sidney's and Daniel's sonnets, it is the Petrarchan version of unfulfilled love, a version transformed by a mechanical and conventional Platonism that was the common equipment of most Petrarchan poets. Spenser's *Epithalamion* rejects the notion of love as unfulfillment but retains the Petrarchan convention of compliment to a lady who, however real she may be in fact, is only an ornament of the poem.

In such poetry as this, the audience to whom the Native poet addressed his poem has all but disappeared. In the Petrarchan tradition, poems are addressed to the Muses, to the moon, to sleep, to conventional ladies with curious names and identical persons, to highways, to joy, to life, to death—or to the air. No more do we hear the individual voice speaking, personally or impersonally, confident of a listener. The substance of the poem succumbs to its rhetoric, and the rhetoric celebrates itself.

It is a quality of style that most dramatically distinguishes the Petrarchan from the Native practice. Since Petrarchan style is usually supported only by the most perfunctory and conventional themes and subjects, the solidity, straightforwardness, and restraint of Native style is no longer evident; it has given way to an airy elegance, which does not so much support the substance of the poem as it decorates it, to a style distinguished by the ingenuity of its figures, a rapid association of details, a wordplay meant to dazzle rather than to inform, a diction that was faintly archaic and "literary" even in its own time, by an elaborate syntax, and by the varied and subtle rhythms resulting from the play of that syntax against the poetic line.

In Petrarchan practice, the rhetoric is very nearly the whole poem; to it, substance is subservient and structure incidental. Whatever structure the poem has tends to be verbal rather than architectural; for while many Petrarchan poems retain the grammatical form of logical structure, sometimes even of syllogistic structure, that form seldom is more than grammatical; and the details which might have specified the terms of the form are aspects of the rhetoric rather than aspects of the substance. In many ways, the procedure of the Petrarchan poet resembles that of the late Romantic, the Symbolist, and the "modern" poet; that is, the poet is more concerned with qualities and nuances than with relationships and definitions; more concerned with texture than with plot; more concerned with effect than with understanding; more concerned with affect than with objective accuracy.

There is a great deal of very bad poetry in both the Native and the Petrarchan traditions, although the "badness" of bad Native poetry is (or should be) immediately obvious, while the "badness" of Petrarchan poetry is much less so. But beyond the badness of individual poems, the methods of both schools have peculiar limitations and possibilities, a consideration of which is important if we are to understand the history of the poem as a changing form.

At its worst, Native poetry is platitudinous and empty, barren of feeling and emotion, and most painfully dull.

Sometimes the popular poetry, such as that of Thomas
Tusser, has what is to some the peculiarly primitive charm
of "bad" verse:

> Leave husbandry sleeping a while ye must do,
>   to learn of housekeeping a lesson or two:
> Whatever is sent thee, by travail and pain,
>   a time there is lent thee to render it again.
> Although ye defend it, unspent for to be,
>   another shall spend it, no thank unto thee.
> However we climb to accomplish the mind,
>   we have but a time, thereof profit to find.

If there is charm here, the charm is a result of the badness;
and the badness is simply the lack of an intelligence ade-
quate even to the simplest subject, a lack made obvious
by the plainness of the Native method. More frequently,
however, the badness is both pretentious and dull. Nearly
the whole of *The Mirror for Magistrates*, including the
once-admired "Induction" by Thomas Sackville, is written
in a manner more or less Native. Here are the beginning
lines of the "Induction":

> The wrathful winter, 'proaching on apace,
> With blustering blasts had all ybared the treen,
> And old Saturnus, with his frosty face
> With chilling cold had pierced the tender green;
> The mantles rent, wherein enwrappèd been
>   The gladsome groves that now lay overthrown,
>   The tapets torn, and every bloom down blown.

And some three hundred and fifty lines later:

> Great was her force, whom stone wall could not stay,
> Her tearing nails snatching at all she saw;
> With gaping jaws that by no means ymay
> Be satisfied from hunger of her maw,
> But eats herself as she that hath no law;
>   Gnawing, alas, her carcass all in vain,
>   Where you may count each sinew, bone, and vein.

On her while we thus firmly fixed our eyes,
That bled for ruth of such a dreary sight,
Lo, suddenly she shrieked in so huge wise
As made hell gates to shiver with the might;
Wherewith a dart we saw, how it did light
   Right on her breast, and therewithal, pale Death
   Enthrilling it, to reave her of her breath.

Because the intelligence of the poet is insufficient to his subject, and because his technique invites him to do so, all the details of the poem—from the simplest landscape to an ultimate act of physical and moral violence—are reduced to the same level of intensity. What might have been charmingly decorative in the Petrarchan style is simply annoying and crude in the bareness of plain style, and what might have been powerful though irrelevant is embarrassing and unbelievable. Even given a normative style, there is no relation discovered here between rhetoric and the value of the subject; the poem simply goes on, mechanically and dully, from detail to superfluous detail.

But even in the best Native poetry, such as that of Gascoigne, Googe, and Ralegh, there are certain technical limitations, although these are sometimes more theoretical than actual. Basically, these are limitations concerned with diction and syntax, with rhythm, and with the relationship between syntax and poetic line.

In the poetry of the Native tradition, the diction is deliberately plain, almost bare, and subservient to the substance or argument of the poem. The syntax moves toward simplicity, most units being straightforward and declarative, with relatively few qualifiers, interrupters, or displacements of syntactical units. Moreover, the poetic line, with its regular alternation of very light and very heavy stresses, tends to be equivalent to the syntactical unit, supporting it and giving it firmness and point, much in the way that the "heroic couplet" controlled and gave point to grammar and syntax in the eighteenth century. Now, given the firmness of structure, the well-disposed arguments or plots that we find in the best Native poetry,

this style and rhythm can be the instrument of a very
special kind of power. But minuteness, delicacy, precise
sensory accuracy, the shifting qualities of particulars—
these are not available, or not easily available, to the Na-
tive method. And when they are not available to literary
technique, their existence in our experience is peripheral
and imperfect.

The advance that the Petrarchan method made upon
English poetry, then, is precisely here. Although Sir Philip
Sidney in *The Defence of Poesie* gives perfunctory at-
tention to the medieval and classical precepts out of which
grew the Native practice, he is more vitally concerned
with a vision of the poet as "diviner, foreseer, or prophet"
and with poetry as a "sacred mystery," emerging from an
inspiration that is, in one sense or another, divine. And
a study of Sidney's verse tells us at once that the "sacred
mystery" manifested itself most genuinely in the texture,
in the surface, in the shimmering and sometimes unsub-
stantial film of the poem—that is to say, in the rhetoric.

In the best Petrarchan poetry, the rhythmic unit, which
is the poetic line, remains relatively firm, while the dis-
tinction between stressed and unstressed syllables becomes
fainter and fainter, and in some instances all but disap-
pears, as in these first two lines of one of Sidney's finest
poems:

Thou blind man's mark, thou fool's self-chosen snare,
Fond fancy's scum, and dregs of scattered thought. . . .

Both lines are perfectly iambic; but the difference in the
degree of accent among the stressed and unstressed syl-
lables is very slight indeed; in the two lines there are
only ten metrical stresses, but there are fifteen fairly heavy
speech accents. And more extreme examples could have
been chosen. Moreover, in the best of this poetry the
relationship between the syntactical unit and the poetic
line is a great deal more flexible and varied, with syntac-
tical units frequently running abruptly over the line and
completing themselves at odd and unexpected positions.
Because of this flexibility and freedom, the Petrarchan

poet ideally is able to get at subtle and complex qualities of experience that were unavailable to the technique of the Native poet. Minuteness, delicacy, sensory accuracy and richness, the shifting and strange qualities of particulars—for the first time they are consistently gotten at in English poetry. Both poetry and our lives are thus enriched.

But this perception of new qualities is gained at a substantial loss. In order to concentrate their energies upon the qualities of experience, upon nuances, shadings, and possibilities that had theretofore remained undiscovered and undisplayed, the Petrarchan poets felt it necessary to all but ignore the substance of the experience whence those qualities derived. And with disheartening frequency we come upon poem after poem in which a highly sophisticated technique is expended upon trivial and silly subject matters and themes. In the work of the best Petrarchans this, of course, is not altogether true. Sidney, and especially Thomas Campion, often hit upon subjects that are both moving and significant. Campion is the best of those Petrarchans who worked mainly in the song tradition, and some of his poems are among the purest and most gravely effective in our language; the Petrarchan loss is noticeable in remarkably few of his poems. But in other poets the loss is very real, and always damaging to one degree or another.

It was, then, the task of the poets of the major phase—Greville, Shakespeare, Donne, and Jonson—to recover this loss, to return to some of the essential practices of the Native tradition, yet to retain the richness made possible by the Petrarchan intercession.

IV

So far, I have discussed the "nativeness" of Native poetry and the "petrarchanism" of Petrarchan poetry as if those qualities had absolute significances within themselves. They have not, of course; they are important primarily insofar as they allow us to understand particular poems better, and secondarily insofar as they illuminate the progress and growth of the short poem in English. It should be clear that no poet is a purely Native poet and none a purely Petrarchan poet, at least in the generalized attributes that have been attached here to both those schools.

But given even this qualification, there are certain poets who do not fit very comfortably within the definitions—or, more exactly, who seem to strain outward beyond the limits implied by these definitions.

Though both Wyatt and Surrey introduced the Petrarchan mode to English poetry, neither of them is essentially a Petrarchan poet. Indeed, Wyatt's translations of Petrarch's poems habitually tame the rather violent Italian to a more restrained and generalized English speech. Wyatt's characteristic poems are poems of direct statement, with subdued rhetoric, a strong burden of meaning, and an unmistakable economy of technical means:

> Hate whom ye list, for I care not:
> Love whom ye list and spare not:
> Do what ye list and dread not:
> Think what ye list, I fear not. . . .

In such poems as this, Wyatt is squarely in the Native tradition.

But in a few others, such as *Blame not my lute* and the greater *They flee from me*, Wyatt appears to go beyond the limitations of both the Native and Petrarchan movements, and he resembles no one so much as the mature poets of the major phase, Ben Jonson and John Donne, presaging by some sixty or seventy years the reconciliation of the two movements even before the Petrarchan was really established. Despite these poems, however, Wyatt remains a Native poet, the Italianate practice being at the periphery of most of his work.

Likewise, Surrey is primarily a Native poet, though a lesser one; in some respects—perhaps because so many of his sonnets are direct paraphrases from the Italian, and because his structural powers are inferior to those of Wyatt—he seems to come somewhat nearer to the Petrarchans. I suspect that the Italianate quality comes from a couple of accidents: first, Surrey's limited powers as a poet did not allow him to have many subjects that were his own, and he therefore borrowed them from his Italian models; second, the weak structure of his poems allowed him a kind of freedom that was often his ruin, but a freedom that nevertheless reminds us of the quick shifts from detail to detail that we find in much Petrarchan poetry. But Surrey displays little of the technical virtuosity of the Petrarchan school; his meters are stiffer than those of the most native of Native poets, and his management of syntax against poetic line is usually dull and mechanical.

It is in the work of Fulke Greville that we find the first real and apparently conscious conflict between the Native and the Petrarchan practices.

Greville was an exact contemporary of Sir Philip Sidney; he was also his closest friend. The two began writing verse at about the same time; the models for their early verse were the same, and both were imbued with the fashionable neo-Platonism and intellectual Calvinism of the later decades of the sixteenth century. Greville's early poetry shows him to be a follower of the same Petrarchan mode that formed the practice of his friend, Sidney:

Cupid, thou naughty boy, when thou wert loathëd,
Naked and blind, for vagabonding noted,
Thy nakedness I in my reason clothëd,
Mine eyes I gave thee, so was I devoted. . . .

This early verse is not so skillful as that of his friend Sidney's, nor is its texture so luxuriant, its detail so dazzling; but its Petrarchism is obvious. Indeed, if the early poems in Greville's sequence, Caelica, were all we had, we would have to place Greville a great deal below Sidney, as indeed he has been placed by conventional 19th century criticism. But fortunately we have the later poems, which come down to us in a roughly chronological sequence, so that we can see Greville's growth over a period of some thirty years. Increasingly, as we read the sequence, we come to see that what we take to be flaws in the poems are caused not by Greville's ineptitude but by his discomfort in the Petrarchan mode. Gradually, the naughty Cupids disappear; the language becomes more generalized and direct; the structure of the poems becomes firmer, the style more powerful, the details less decorative—until, suddenly, about halfway through the sequence, we are aware that slowly, poem by poem, the strategy has been changing, and that the subjects have been growing more and more important. We have found such poems as *The nurse-life wheat*, the curiously anti-Petrarchan *Absence, the noble truce*; a little later, as we read such a poem as *You that seek what life is in death*, we realize that we have come a long way from the conventional Petrarchan poet that we began with. And when we get to *Caelica: 84*, Greville's farewell to Cupid, we realize that Greville is, as consciously as he can, bidding farewell not only to a subject but to a method. Thereafter occur the great poems of the mature Greville—*The earth with thunder torn, Wrapped up, O Lord, Down in the depth of mine iniquity*, and one of the most remarkable short poems of the century, *In night, when colors all to black are cast.*

In his *Life of Sidney*—a work that had a great deal to do with elevating Sidney's reputation at the expense of his own—Greville speaks of his own work in this manner: "For my own part, I found my creeping Genius more fixed upon the images of life than the images of wit, and therefore chose not to write to them on whose feet the ox had not already trod, as the proverb is, but to those only that are weather-beaten in the sea of this world, such as having lost sight of their gardens and groves, study to sail on a right course among rocks and quicksands." It was the immersion, for a while, in the Petrarchan method that allowed him to retain his sight of the gardens and groves; but it was his falling back upon the resources of earlier Native method that helped him to sail the right course among the rocks and quicksands.

While Greville was struggling in privacy with the loss

of his friend Sidney and with his own slow growth as a poet, at the height of the Petrarchan movement, and strongly moved by the practice of the Petrarchists, William Shakespeare composed his own sequence of sonnets. In many of these, Shakespeare appears simply as an exceedingly skillful Petrarchist, though with an intelligence and perceptivity clearly superior to that of most of his contemporaries. But here and there, sometimes in a few lines, sometimes in a whole poem, we begin to note a recovery, a moving away from the purely ornate and decorative toward something that seems quite new.

Let me not to the marriage of true minds
Admit impediments. Love is not love
Which alters when it alteration finds,
Or bends with the remover to remove:
O no! it is an ever fixëd mark,
That looks on tempests and is never shaken;
It is the star to every wandering bark,
Whose worth's unknown, although his height be taken.
Love's not Time's fool, though rosy lips and cheeks
Within his bending sickle's compass come;
Love alters not with his brief hours and weeks,
But bears it out even to the edge of doom.
    If this be error and upon me proved,
    I never writ, nor no man ever loved.

Except for the broken and abrupt rhythm of the first sentence, the poem opens as straightforwardly, directly, and economically as any Native poem might; indeed, the whole first quatrain is admirably direct, though the subdued play upon "alter" and "remove" reminds us of Petrarchan practice. But after the direct statement of the first quatrain, from the near-metaphorical "bends" in the fourth line, the poem skitters through a series of figures as fanciful as any found in the purest Petrarchist, though Shakespeare's control over them is superior to that of any of the more ornate Petrarchists, save perhaps Sidney in his best poems. The figures culminate in the Elizabethan commonplace of Time as a sickle, though the epithet

"bending" mitigates the triteness somewhat, partly be-
cause it echoes "bends" in the fourth line and takes on
some of the early force of that conception. Then at the
end, the poem reverts to the convention in which it began,
that of direct and generalized statement; but the gener-
alized language in the last four lines of the poem has,
as it were, passed through the shifting and figurative fire
of the six middle lines of the poem, and by that passing
has been transformed; especially around lines eleven and
twelve clings a richness like an echo or an afterglow, a
richness not really implicit in the lines themselves. If we
have not here the greatest of poetry, we nevertheless have
the beginnings of a method which will lead to the greatest
of poetry.

There is in the poetry of John Donne some of the harsh-
ness of sound, roughness of diction, and straightforward
familiarity that we have already seen in much of the po-
etry of the Native tradition:

> Busy old fool, unruly sun,
> Why dost thou thus
Through windows and through curtains call on us? . . .

For God's sake, hold your tongue and let me love! . . .

On the other hand, there is also some of the fancifulness
and artificial elegance of the Petrarchan tradition:

> Our hands were firmly cementéd
> With a fast balm which thence did spring;
> Our eye-beams twisted and did thread
> Our eyes upon one double string. . . .

Donne's effort to reconcile the opposing tendencies of
the Native and Petrarchan traditions is a great deal more
obvious than Shakespeare's; but except for the straight-
forwardness of some of his lines, a frequent roughness of
diction and harshness of speech, and his attempt to sug-
gest by poetic means the uncertainty of speech-rhythms,
he appears to have worked mainly within the Petrarchan
tradition, which is hyperbolic, violent, decorative, and

metaphorical, even though his temperament is quite remote from what we might expect in a Petrarchan poet. Many of his poems are deliberate parodies of Petrarchan subjects and conventions; many others, such as the Holy Sonnets, clearly are not. But between these lies a very large body of poetry, the body for which Donne is most famous, in which the two traditions are in violent conflict, a clash which reflects, no doubt, another struggle within Donne's own mind. But because of Donne's uncertainty in the matter, his reader must often remain unsure whether Petrarchism is being parodied or whether it is being seriously employed for serious ends.

It is here, in the not fully resolved conflict between Native and Petrarchan practice, that Donne achieves the "originality" that has been so overvalued by so many readers and critics. Actually, Donne offers very little that is new to the technique of English poetry. He seems "original" in the popular critical sense of that word only if we are ignorant of the two traditions out of which his practice grew, or if we refuse to recognize his use of the two traditions. Some of Donne's greatest successes, as well as some of his most dramatic failures, are made possible by this collision; and the fact that some of his greatest lines are found in some of his worst poems is evidence of the strength of that collision. Donne is truly original precisely where he should be, in his excellence as a poet, which is an excellence that, in a number of poems, surmounts the limitations of schools or movements, not by ignoring their implications but by understanding them.

If we come to Ben Jonson directly from William Shakespeare, especially if we have not appreciated the revision upon Petrarchist practice that Shakespeare performed and his indebtedness to the native tradition, it may seem that we are stepping over a line that separates one kind of poetry from another, a line resembling the one between the poetry of, let us say, Samuel Daniel and Barnabe Googe. Whereas Shakespeare most obviously uses the Petrarchan practice as a point of departure, Ben Jonson uses the Native practice, and that body of older classical theory out of which the Native practice grew.

Jonson's triumph is his style. It is the first in English lyric poetry that is really capable of comprehending the extreme range and diversity of human experience, without falsifying that experience or doing violence to it. It is a style capable of minor wit and malice, as in this brief epigram *To Doctor Empiric:*

> When men a dangerous disease did 'scape
> Of old, they gave a cock to Aesculape.
> Let me give two, that doubly am got free,
> From my disease's danger, and from thee.

It is capable of the delicate and sensual minor music of the song:

> Slow, slow, fresh fount, keep time with my salt tears;
>   Yet slower, yet; O faintly gentle springs;
> List to the heavy part the music bears,
>   Woe weeps out her division when she sings:
>   Droop herbs and flowers;
>   Fall grief in showers;
>   Our beauties are not ours.
>   O, I could still,
> Like melting snow upon some craggy hill,
>   Drop, drop, drop, drop,
> Since nature's pride is now a withered daffodil.

It is capable of the most moving and personal of utterances:

> Farewell, thou child of my right hand, and joy;
>   My sin was too much hope of thee, loved boy.
> Seven years thou wert lent to me, and I thee pay,
>   Exacted by thy fate, on the just day. . . .

It is a style that can be light and playful:

> Kiss me, sweet: the wary lover
> Can your favors keep, and cover,
> When the common courting jay
> All your bounties will betray. . . .

When the occasion demands, it can be savage and indignant:

> Ask not to know this man. If fame should speak
>   His name in any metal, it would break.
> Two letters were enough the plague to tear
>   Out of his grave, and poison every ear.
> A parcel of court-dirt, a heap, a mass
>   Of all vice hurled together, there he was,
> Proud, false, and treacherous, vindictive, all
>   That thought can add, unthankful, the lay-stall
> Of putrid flesh alive! of blood, the sink!
>   And so I leave to stir him, lest he stink.

And in the very best poems, it can move with quiet dignity and a grave profundity:

> Good and great God, can I not think of Thee,
>   But it must straight my melancholy be?
> Is it interpreted in me disease,
>   That, laden with my sins, I seek for ease?
> O, be thou witness, that the reins dost know
>   And hearts of all, if I be sad for show;
> And judge me after, if I dare pretend
>   To aught but grace, or aim at other end. . . .

There is in Jonson none of the mannered roughness and harshness that we find increasingly in Native style, and that we find in Donne; there is on the other hand none of the mannered artificiality and archaism of the Petrarchan style. The direct economy of Native style is retained, and the fluid subtlety potential in Petrarchan style is refined.

This style is nowhere better displayed than in three of Jonson's greatest poems: *To Heaven*, the first lines of which are quoted above, *To the World: A Farewell for a Gentlewoman*, and the *Elegy* beginning "Though Beauty be the mark of praise."

A study of this *Elegy* is especially instructive. It has a subject that would have delighted the most Petrarchan of poets, celebrating as it does a more or less Platonic con-

ception of human love. It is a poem of some power, and
it will move all but the most sentimental and insensitive
readers.

Yet there is not a conceit, nor even a developed figure
in the entire poem; there is not a concrete image; there
is not a roughness or flaw of rhythm; there is no "dramatic"
structure. The development is straightforward and deliber-
ate, the language is abstract and generalized, and the
structure is informally expository. The poem is as rich and
subtle and powerful as we could want it; but the richness
and subtlety and power proceed from the poet, not from
the accidental properties of his subject or his language.
The language is designed to demonstrate the intellectual
and emotional powers of the poet, after that language
has made those powers possible.

It is, finally, a language that has passed from the stark-
ness and bareness of outer reality through the dark, luxuri-
ant jungle of the self and has emerged from that journey
entire and powerful. It is the style with which English
poetry has had most seriously to contend for the past three
hundred and fifty years.

V

According to the view that I have been attempting to
define, the significance of the Petrarchist movement—de-
spite its occasional dramatic popularity, despite its affini-
ties with the Romantic movement of the late eighteenth
and early nineteenth centuries, and hence its lodgment in
literary history—has been widely misunderstood. It is not
in the main tradition of English poetry; it was an eccentric
movement away from the Native tradition that began with
Skelton, More, and their medieval predecessors, and it is
at once an enrichment and a decay of that tradition. In-
deed the best work within the Petrarchan movement is
that which either draws back a bit from the full implica-
tions that lie before the principles of the movement, or
(like the best work of the Madrigalists and Thomas Cam-

pion) tactfully sublimates the potentialities of the method to deliberately minor themes.

If the Petrarchan movement displaced the Native movement, it did not do so as a villain displacing a rightful ruler. The displacement, or something like it, was inevitable. The Native movement was far from exhausted when it was displaced; indeed, the method has had its followers in nearly every poetic generation since the beginning of the seventeenth century, the most notable in recent years being, perhaps, Thomas Hardy. But the method had taken the language as far as it could, given the principles out of which it worked; some of the great poems in our tongue had been composed according to its principles; and in even such a fine poet as George Gascoigne, we begin to see the method degenerating, mannerism overriding the native power of the style.

Even though we may think of Spenser's *Faerie Queene* as the great and monstrous monument to Petrarchism, we must finally admit that the Petrarchan movement produced no sustained body of poetry as great as that of the Native movement, however fine some Petrarchan poems might be. But we would be foolish to regret wholly the displacement that took place around 1580.

For the displacement was temporary; it became a reconciliation, and finally a marriage. And if the marriage was not an altogether harmonious one, few marriages are. It has lasted through several centuries; and if it still has not reached a perfect balance and accord, that is perhaps all to the good. It is still alive, and we are still trying to work it out.

VI

This collection does not attempt to be inclusive, nor does it attempt to be statistically representative of a little of everything, good, bad, or indifferent, in the period to which it is devoted; it is not designed to illustrate a theory of literary history, though obviously a theory has been derived from it. No such theory of literature will be very valuable if it is based on second- or third-rate works of art, especially if the second- or third-rate is confused with the excellent. Therefore, the poems were chosen on the basis of their literary merit, and on no other.

This anthology is designed for both the general reader and the more specialized student of Renaissance poetry. To the latter especially a note of explanation about the text is due. In all instances I have used the best and most readily available modern editions of the poets whose work is represented; I have not gone very far beyond these sources, or attempted systematically to collate editions, or to compare manuscript versions with printed versions. I am not a textual critic, and such work is beyond my competence. I have relied upon the editors of the various poets for my readings of the poems, though occasionally I have preferred a variant reading to an established one.

Samuel Johnson, in his *Preface to Shakespeare*, notes that "our ancestors were accustomed to so much negligence of English printers, that they could very patiently endure it." But the modern reader cannot, nor is there any very good reason why he should try. There may be some advantages, especially to the textual specialist, in offering an edition with "original" spellings and punctuation; but there are many more disadvantages, not the least of which is the likelihood that such an edition will offer the carelessness of a semiliterate typesetter rather than the intention of an author. But aside from that, the old, irregular spelling and punctuation give a spurious archaism to poems that were modern in their time, and that are best read today as if they were poems rather than literary specimens. I have, therefore, modernized spellings and punctuation freely; and to those words whose use has atrophied or whose meaning has shifted, I have appended brief glosses.

The biographical information included in the notes on the various poets has been taken from a number of sources. When there were standard or authoritative biographies available, I of course relied on those works; when there were no such works available, I sometimes had to make choices among conflicting data, especially in the matter of birth and death dates. In some instances my choices may eventually prove to be wrong; but they were made upon the best evidence available to me at the time.

Excepting only the drama written by Shakespeare, the short poem is the most important literary form of the age; I have, therefore, devoted this collection to it. Though a few of the poems in this book appear incidentally in plays, novels, and masques, they are complete in themselves, as are all the other poems. I have not included snippets or excerpts from longer works.

VII

The past two decades have seen a marked increase of critical interest in the poetry of the English Renaissance, an interest not, perhaps, so dramatic as an earlier concern for "metaphysical" poetry, but one which in the long run may be more substantial. A number of valuable new authoritative editions have appeared, notable among them William A. Ringler's recent *The Poems of Sir Philip Sidney* (New York: 1962) and Geoffrey Bullough's *The Poems and Dramas of Fulke Greville* (New York: 1945); the Muse's Library has given the general reader inexpensive new editions of Wyatt, Ralegh, and Drayton; and Alan Swallow, in his *Men of the Renaissance* series, has made widely available for the first time in many years the work of such poets as Thomas, Lord Vaux, and Barnabe Googe. Among the dozens of critical essays that should concern the student of the period, of especial importance are J. V. Cunningham's "Phoenix and the Turtle" and "Logic and the Lyric" in *Tradition and Poetic Structure* (Denver: 1960), and Alan Swallow's three studies of literary method, as well as his essays on Skelton, Wyatt, and Surrey, in *Editor's Essays of Two Decades* (Denver: 1961). And two very recent books by younger critics—John Thompson's *The Founding of English Metre* (New York:

1961) and Wesley Trimpi's *Ben Jonson's Poems: A Study of the Plain Style* (Stanford: 1962)—attest to the continuing vitality and growth of this interest.

No one has been more responsible for this increase of critical activity than the poet and critic, Yvor Winters. His essay, "The 16th Century Lyric in England," which appeared in the magazine *Poetry,* February, March, April, 1939, has had an influence far out of proportion to its general circulation; since its appearance, nearly all informed criticism of the short poem of the period has had, in one way or another, to take account of the theories and judgments enunciated in it. It should be clear to all that this anthology is deeply indebted to that pioneering essay, and to other aspects of the subject upon which Winters has touched in his other critical works: neither this work, nor the interest which occasioned it, would have been possible without Winters' efforts.

John Williams

JOHN SKELTON: 1460?–1529

Little is known of Skelton's life. His first extant work is an elegy on the death of Edward IV, written in 1483; by 1490 he was a scholar of international reputation. Erasmus called him the "light and ornament of English letters," and William Caxton spoke of him as a scholar, translator, and poet of great renown. But most of the works upon which Skelton's contemporary reputation rested have been lost. He took holy orders in 1498, after he had written his allegorical condemnation of public life, *The Bouge of Court*. In 1504 he retired to Norfolk as rector of Diss.

It is from this time that his real career as a poet starts. No longer is he the proper Latinate poet of the *Elegy to Edward*, or the conventional translator and scholar. He wrote *Phillip Sparrow* and *The Tunning of Elinour Rumming*, developing his distinctive short-lined rhythms and his peculiar, breathless tone. By 1512 Skelton was back in public life, at the court, where he was appointed King's Orator. He died at Westminster, leaving several children by a secret marriage.

Skelton's poetry had little direct influence in his own age, although such twentieth-century poets as Auden and Graves have acknowledged indebtedness. His work is primitive; but within the limits of that primitivism, it is—like the work of a greater modern poet whom he curiously resembles, William Carlos Williams—always skillful and frequently moving. Historically, Skelton's poetry represents the persistence of both a native popular folk tradition and the short-lined accentual Latin verse of the late medieval period in the English language.

TEXT:

The Complete Poems of John Skelton, edited by Phillip Henderson (1948).

WOEFULLY ARRAYED

> Woefully arrayed,
> My blood, man,
> For thee ran,
> It may not be nayed:
> My body blo and wan,
> Woefully arrayed.

Behold me, I pray thee, with all thy whole reason,
And be not so hard-hearted, and for this encheason,
Sith I for thy soul's sake was slain in good season,
Beguiled and betrayëd by Judas' false treason:
> Unkindly entreated,
> With sharp cord sore freted,
> The Jewës me threted:
They mowëd, they grinnëd, they scornëd me,
Condemnëd to death, as thou mayest see,
> Woefully arrayed.

Thus naked am I nailëd, O man, for thy sake!
I love thee, then love me; why sleepest thou? awake!
Remember my tender heart-root for thee brake,
With painës my veinës constrainëd to crake:
> Thus tuggëd to and fro,
> Thus wrappëd all in woe,
> Whereas never man was so,
Entreated thus in most cruel wise,
Was like a lamb offered in sacrifice,
> Woefully arrayed.

Of sharp thorn I have worn a crown on my head,
So painëd, so strainëd, so rueful, so red,
Thus bobbëd, thus robbëd, thus for thy love dead,
Unfeignëd I deignëd my blood for to shed:

blo: livid.
wan: without light, i.e., blood.
encheason: cause.

mowëd: mocked.
bobbëd: pummeled.

My feet and handës sore
The sturdy nailës bore:
What might I suffer more
Than I have done, O man, for thee?
Come when thou list, welcome to me,
          Woefully arrayed.

Of recórd thy good Lord I have been and shall be:
I am thine, thou art mine, my brother I call thee.
Thee love I entirely—see what is befallen me!
Sore beating, sore threating, to make thee, man, all free:
      Why art thou unkind?
      Why hast not me in mind?
      Come yet and thou shalt find
Mine endless mercy and grace—
See how a spear my heart did race,
          Woefully arrayed.

Dear brother, no other thing I of thee desire
But give me thine heart free to reward mine hire:
I wrought thee, I bought thee from eternal fire:
I pray thee array thee toward my high empire
      Above the orient,
      Whereof I am regent,
      Lord God omnipotent,
With me to reign in endless wealth:
Remember, man, thy soulës health.

          Woefully arrayed,
            My blood, man,
            For thee ran,
          It may not be nayed:
           My body blo and wan,
          Woefully arrayed.

race: cut, slash.

UPON A DEAD MAN'S HEAD

Your ugly token
My mind hath broken
From worldly lust:
For I have discussed
We are but dust,
And die we must.
　　It is general
To be mortal:
I have well espied
No man may him hide
From Death hollow-eyed,
With sinews wyderëd,
With bonës shyderëd,
With his worm-eaten maw,
And his ghastly jaw
Gasping aside,
Naked of hide,
Neither flesh nor fell.
　　Then, by my counsel,
Look that ye spell
Well this gospel:
For whereso we dwell
Death will us quell
And with us mell.
　　For all our pampered paunches
There may no fraunchis,
Nor worldly bliss,
Redeem us from this:
Our days be dated
To be checkmated

wyderëd: withered.　　　　　*mell*: mingle.
shyderëd: splintered.　　　　*fraunchis*: immunity.
fell: skin.

With draughtës of death
Stopping our breath:
Our eyen sinking,
Our bodies stinking,
Our gummës grinning,
Our soulës brinning.
To whom, then, shall we sue,
For to have rescue,
But to sweet Jesu
On us then for to rue?
    O goodly Child
Of Mary mild,
Then be our shield!
That we be not exiled
To the dyne dale
Of bootless bale,
Nor to the lake
Of fiendës black.
    But grant us grace
To see thy Face,
And to purcháse
Thine heavenly place,
And thy paláce
Full of soláce
Above the sky
That is so high:
Eternally
To behold and see
The Trinity!
    Amen.

Myrres vous y.

draughtës: moves or attacks in chess; also, a pun on breathing or drinking in something.
brinning: burning.
dyne dale: dark pit.
bootless: hopeless, irremediable.

bale: evil; also, consuming fire.
lake: play or sport.
Myrres vous y: view yourself therein.

MY DARLING DEAR, MY DAISY FLOWER

With lullay, lullay, like a child,
Thou sleepest too long, thou art beguiled.

My darling dear, my daisy flower,
   Let me, quod he, lie in your lap.
Lie still, quod she, my paramour,
   Lie still, hardëly, and take a nap.
   His head was heavy, such was his hap,
All drowsy dreaming, drowned in sleep,
That of his love he took no keep.
   With hey lullay, lullay, like a child,
   Thou sleepest too long, thou art beguiled.

With ba, ba, ba! and bas, bas, bas!
   She cherished him both cheek and chin,
That he wist never where he was:
   He had forgotten all deadly sin.
   He wanted wit her love to win:
He trusted her payment and lost all his pay;
She left him sleeping and stole away.
   With hey lullay, lullay, like a child,
   Thou sleepest too long, thou art beguiled.

The rivers rough, the waters wan,
   She sparëd not to wet her feet;
She waded over, she found a man
     That halsëd her heartily and kissed her sweet:
     Thus after her cold she caught a heat.
My love, she said, routeth in his bed;
Ywis he hath an heavy head.
   With hey lullay, lullay, like a child,
   Thou sleepest too long, thou art beguiled.

hardëly: by all means.   *routeth:* snores or belches.
wist: knew.   *Ywis:* indeed.
halsëd: embraced.

What dreamest thou, drunkard, drowsy pate?
   Thy lust and liking is from thee gone;
Thou blinkard blowbowl, thou wakest too late,
   Behold thou liest, luggard, alone!
   Well may thou sigh, well may thou groan,
To deal with her so cowardly:
Ywis, pole hatchet, she bleared thine eye.

TO MISTRESS ANNE

Mistress Anne,
I am your man,
As you may well espy.
If you will be
Content with me,
I am your man.

But if you will
Keep company still
With every knave that comes by,
Then you will be
Forsaken of me,
That am your man.

But if you fain,
I tell you plain,
If I presently shall die,
I will not such
As loves too much,
That am your man.

For if you can
Love every man
That can flatter and lie,
Then are ye
No match for me,
That am your man.

pole hatchet: lit., poleax; i.e.,
  blockhead, hatchet face, etc.

For I will not take
No such kind of make
(May all full well it try!),
But off will ye cast
At any blast,
That am your man.

TO MISTRESS MARGERY WENTWORTH

With marjoram gentle,
  The flower of goodlihead,
Embroidered the mantle
  Is of your maidenhead.
Plainly I cannot glose;
  Ye be, as I divine,
The pretty primrose,
  The goodly columbine.
With marjoram gentle,
  The flower of goodlihead,
Embroidered the mantle
  Is of your maidenhead.
Benign, courteous, and meek,
  With wordës well devised;
In you, who list to seek,
  Be virtues well comprised.
With marjoram gentle,
  The flower of goodlihead,
Embroidered the mantle
  Is of your maidenhead.

L'ENVOY: TO HIS BOOK

Go, little quair,
Demean you fair;
Take no despair,

make: mate, mistress.   *demean*: comport.
quair: quire; i.e., book.

Though I you wrate
After this rate
In English letter;
So much the better
Welcome shall ye
To some men be;
For Latin works
Be good for clerks;
Yet now and then
Some Latin men
May haply look
Upon your book,
And so proceed
In you to read,
That so indeed
Your fame may spread
In length and bread.
But then I dread
Ye shall have need
You for to speed
To harness bright,
By force of might,
Against envy
And obloquy;
And wote ye why?
Not for to fight
Against despite,
Nor to derain
Battle again
Scornful disdain,
Nor for to chide,
Nor for to hide
You cowardly;
But courteously

wrate: wrote.
rate: standard; also a pun on "cost" or "expense."
wote: know.

derain battle again: justify, vindicate, maintain in combat against.

That I have penned
For to defend,
Under the banner
Of all good manner,
Under protection
Of sad correction,
With toleration
And supportation
Of reformation,
If they can spy
Circumspectly
Any word defacëd
That might be 'rasëd,
Else ye shall pray
Them that ye may
Continue still
With their good will.

SIR THOMAS MORE: 1478-1535

Born in London, More was educated at St. Antony's
School and Canterbury College, later consolidated with
Christ Church College, Oxford, where he knew Thomas
Linacre and William Grocyn. After leaving Oxford, he
studied law in London, and seriously considered taking
holy orders. But he chose the practice of law, in which he
was quite successful; he was elected to Parliament in 1504,
and became an undersheriff of London six years later. Dur-
ing Erasmus's several visits to England, the two men got
to be close friends. As More became better known to
Henry VIII, he was given increasingly important appoint-
ments; in 1529 he was appointed Lord Chancellor, which
post he resigned in 1532 because of a difference with
Henry regarding the divorce from Queen Catherine. Hav-
ing refused to take an oath vesting the succession in the
issue of Anne Boleyn, he was beheaded in July 1535. Four
hundred years later, More was canonized by Pius XI.

Best known as the great Humanist author of *Utopia*,
More was also a valuable public servant, a classical scholar,
and a patron of learning. Though not a great poet, he has
been consistently undervalued, partly because the Native
movement as a whole has been undervalued. Most of
More's verse was written when he was a very young man;
his best work is his Latin epigrams, but his contribution
to English verse is of some significance. In such a poem as
To Them that Seek Fortune, written long before the ad-
vent of Wyatt and Surrey, he presages the re-establishment
of iambic pentameter as the normal English poetic line.

TEXT:

The English Works of Sir Thomas More, edited by W. E.
  Campbell and A. W. Reed (1931).

THE PAGEANTS OF THOMAS MORE

Childhood

I am called Childhood. In play is all my mind
To cast a quoit, a cock-stele, and a ball;
A top can I set, and drive it in his kind.
But would to God these hateful bookës all
Were in a fire burnt to powder small;
Then might I lead my life always in play,
Which life God send me to mine ending day.

Manhood

Manhood I am; therefore I me delight
To hunt and hawk, to nourish up and feed
The greyhound to the course, the hawk to the flight,
And to bestride a good and lusty steed.
These things become a very man, indeed,
Yet thinketh this boy his peevish game sweeter;
But what no force, his reason is no better.

Venus and Cupide

Whoso ne knoweth the strength, power, and might
Of Venus and me, her little son Cupíde,
Thou Manhood shalt a mirror be of right,
By us subduëd for all thy great pride.
No fiery dart pierceth thy tender side;
Now thou which erst despisëd children small
Shall wax a child again and be my thrall.

cock-stele: a stick for throwing   game often played at Shrove-
    at a cock tied to a post, a   tide.

Age

Old Age am I, with lockës thin and hoar—
Of our short life, the last and best part.
Wise and discreet, the public weal, therefore,
I help to rule, to my labor and smart.
Therefore, Cupíde, withdraw thy fiery dart;
Chargeable matters shall of love oppress
The childish game and idle business.

Death

Though I be foul, ugly, lean, and mis-shape,
Yet there is none in all this worldë wide
That may my power withstandë or escape;
Therefore, sage father, greatly magnified,
Descend from your chair, set apart your pride,
Witsafe to lend—though it be to your pain—
To me, a fool, some of your wise brain.

Fame

Fame I am callëd, marvel you nothing,
Though I with tongues am compassëd all round;
For in voice of people is my chief living.
O cruel death, thy power I confound;
When thou a noble man hast brought to ground,
Maugry thy teeth, to live cause him shall I,
Of people in perpetual memory.

witsafe: vouchsafe.   *maugry:* despite.

Time

I whom thou seest with horyloge in hand
Am naméd Time, the lord of every hour;
I shall in space destroy both sea and land.
O simple fame, how darest thou man honoúr,
Promising of his name, an endless flower,
Who may in the world have a name eternal,
When I shall in process destroy the world and all.

Eternity

Me needeth not to boast; I am Eternity.
The very name signifieth well
That mine empire infinite shall be.
Thou, mortal Time, every man can tell
Art nothing else but the mobility
Of sun and moon changing in every degree.
When they shall leave their course, thou shalt be brought,
For all thy pride and boasting, into nought.

THOMAS MORE TO THEM THAT SEEK FORTUNE

Whoso delighteth to proven and assay
Of wavering fortune the uncertain lot,
If that the answer please you not alway,
Blame ye not me; for I command you not
Fortune to trust, and eke full well ye wot
I have of her no bridle in my fist:
She runneth loose, and turneth where she list.

horyloge: a timepiece.

The rolling dice in whom your luck doth stand,
With whose unhappy chance ye be so wroth,
Ye know yourself came never in mine hand.
Lo, in this pond be fish and froggës both.
Cast in your net; but be you lief or loath,
Hold you content as fortune list assign:
For it is your own fishing and not mine.

And though in one chance fortune you offend,
Grudge not thereat, but bear a merry face:
In many another she shall it amend.
There is no man so far out of her grace
But he sometime hath comfort and soláce;
Ne none again so far forth in her favor
That is full satisfied with her behaviour.

Fortune is stately, solemn, proud, and high,
And richesse giveth, to have servíce therefore.
The needy beggar catcheth an halfpenný,
Some man a thousand pound; some less, some more.
But for all that she keepeth ever in store
From every man some parcel of his will,
That he may pray therefor, and serve her still.

Some man hath good, but children hath he none;
Some man hath both, but he can get none health;
Some hath all three, but up to honor's throne
Can he not creep, by no manner of stealth.
To some she sendeth children, riches, wealth,
Honor, worship, and reverence all his life;
But yet she pincheth him with a shrewd wife.

Then forasmuch as it is fortune's guise
To grant no man all things that he will axe,
But as herself list order and devise,
Doth every man his part divide and tax,
I counsel you each one, truss up your packs
And take no thing at all, or be content
With such reward as fortune hath you sent.

list: desires, wishes to.

All thingës in this book that ye shall read
Do as ye list; there shall no man you bind
Them to believe as surely as your creed;
But notwithstanding, certës in my mind,
I durst well swear, as true ye shall them find,
In every point, each answer by and by,
As are the judgments of Astronomy.

from THE TWELVE WEAPONS OF
SPIRITUAL BATTLE

This Life a Dream and Shadow

This wretched life, the trust and confidence
Of whose continuance maketh us bold to sin,
Thou perceivest well by experience;
Since that hour in which it did begin,
It holdeth on the course and will not lin,
But fast it runneth on and passen shall
As doth a dream, or shadow on the wall.

Eternal Reward, Eternal Pain

Thou seest this world is but a thoroughfare,
See thou behave thee wisely with thine host;
Hence must thou needs depart naked and bare,
And after thy desert look to what cost
Thou art conveyed at such time as thy ghost
From this wretched carcase shall dissever:
Be it joy or pain, endure it shall for ever.

lin: cease.

The Peace of a Good Mind

Why lovest thou so this brittle worldë's joy?
Take all the mirth, take all the fantasies,
Take every game, take every wanton toy,
Take every sport that men can thee devise;
And among them all, on warrantise,
Thou shalt no pleasure comparáble find
To the inward gladness of a virtuous mind.

from THE TWELVE PROPERTIES OR CONDITIONS OF A LOVER

The First Property

The first point is to love but one alone,
And for that one all other to forsake:
For whoso loveth many loveth none.
The flood that is in many channels, take
In each of them, shall feeble streamës make:
The love that is divided among many
Uneath sufficeth that any part have any.

So thou that hast thy love set unto God,
In thy remembrance this imprint and grave:
As He in sovereign dignity is odd,
So will He in love no parting fellows have.
Love Him, therefore, with all that He thee gave:
For body, soul, wit, cunning, mind and thought,
Part will He none, but either all or naught.

warrantise: warranty, guar-   uneath: scarcely.
    antee.   odd: unique.

The Seventh Property

There is no page or servant, most or least,
That doth upon his love attend and wait;
There is no little worm, no simple beast,
Ne none so small a trifle or conceit,
Lace, girdle, point, or proper glovë strait,
But that if to his love it have been near,
The lover hath it precious, lief and dear.

So every relic, image or pictúre
That doth pertain to God's magnificence,
The lover of God should with all busy cure
Have it in love, honoúr and reverence,
And specially give them pre-eminence
Which daily done His blessed body wurche,
The quick relics, the ministers of His Church.

The Eleventh Property

Diversely passioned is the lover's heart:
Now pleasant hope, now dread and grievous fear,
Now perfect bliss, now bitter sorrow smart;
And whether his love be with him or elsewhere,
Oft from his eyes there falleth many a tear,—
For very joy, when they together be;
When they be sundered, for adversity.

Like affections feeleth eke the breast
Of God's lover in prayer and meditation:
When that his love liketh in him rest
With inward gladness of pleasant contemplation,
Out break the tears for joy and delectation;
And when his love list eft to part him fro,
Out break the tears again for pain and woe.

cure: care.   wurche: performs.
done: gift.   eft: afterward.

SIR THOMAS WYATT: 1503?–42

Wyatt entered St. John's College, Cambridge, in 1516, and took the degree of M.A. in 1520. Before he was twenty-five, he was sent on missions to France and Italy by Henry VIII. He was knighted in 1536, and imprisoned the same year because of a quarrel with the Duke of Suffolk. Wyatt was probably a lover of Anne Boleyn, before Anne became the wife of Henry VIII; certainly this suspicion was attached to his name, and it might have had something to do with Wyatt's ups and downs at court. In 1541 he was imprisoned on a charge of treason, supposedly committed while he was ambassador to Spain; but he acquitted himself and was unconditionally pardoned. His fortunes bettered swiftly after his release, and in 1542 he was a member of Parliament and Commander of the Fleet; on a trip to meet the Spanish ambassador, he fell suddenly ill and died at Sherborne in Dorset.

The first significant publication of Wyatt's poems was in *Tottel's Miscellany*, 1557, where he appeared with Surrey and a number of other lesser poets. Tottel's butchering of the texts is well known; it was not until early in this century that a decent text of Wyatt was available, that of A. K. Foxwell. For many years, and even into the twentieth century, Surrey was thought a better poet than Wyatt; but recently critical opinion has dramatically reversed that judgment so that, ironically, Wyatt now is in danger of being overvalued. Most of Wyatt's poems are minor, though many of them are nearly perfectly executed; and his best work is squarely in the Native tradition, many of his verse forms being borrowed from medieval English poetry rather than Italian or French. Though it is doubtful that Wyatt's "skillfully varied rhythms" were

produced so consciously as most modern scholars and
critics would have us believe, Wyatt's contributions to
English prosody are nevertheless of great significance.

TEXT:

The Poems, two volumes, edited by A. K. Foxwell (1913).
The Collected Poems of Sir Thomas Wyatt, edited by
    Kenneth Muir (1948).
Some Poems of Sir Thomas Wyatt, edited by Alan Swal-
    low (1949).

WHOSO LIST TO HUNT

Whoso list to hunt, I know where is an hind,
    But as for me, alas, I may no more.
    The vain travail hath wearied me so sore,
    I am of them that farthest cometh behind.
Yet may I by no means my wearied mind
    Draw from the Deer, but as she fleeth afore
Fainting I follow. I leave off therefore,
    Since in a net I seek to hold the wind.
Who list her hunt (I put him out of doubt)
    As well as I may spend his time in vain.
    And, graven with diamonds, in letters plain
There is written her fair neck round about:
    "*Noli me tangere,* for Caesar's I am,
    And wild for to hold, though I seem tame."

IT MAY BE GOOD

It may be good, like it who list,
    But I do doubt: who can me blame?
For oft assured yet have I missed,
    And now again I fear the same.
    The windy words, the eye's quaint game,
Of sudden change maketh me aghast:
For dread to fall I stand not fast.

Alas! I tread an endless maze
  That seeketh to accord two contraries;
And hope still and nothing haze,
  Imprisonëd in liberties;
    As one unheard, and still that cries;
Always thirsty, and yet nothing I taste;
For dread to fall I stand not fast.

Assured, I doubt I be not sure;
  And should I trust to such surety
That oft hath put the proof in ure
  And never hath found it trusty?
    Nay, sir, in faith it were great folly.
And yet my life thus I do waste;
For dread to fall I stand not fast.

MADAM, WITHOUTEN MANY WORDS

Madam, withouten many words,
  Once I am sure ye will or no;
And if ye will, then leave your bourdes,
  And use your wit and show it so.

And with a beck ye shall me call;
  And if of one that burneth alway
Ye have any pity at all,
  Answer him fair with yea or nay.

If it be yea, I shall be fain;
  If it be nay, friends as before;
Ye shall another man obtain,
  And I mine own, and yours no more.

haze: hazard, chance.   *bourdes:* jests.
ure: use.

THEY FLEE FROM ME

They flee from me, that sometime did me seek
With naked foot, stalking in my chamber.
I have seen them gentle, tame, and meek
    That now are wild, and do not remember
    That sometime they put themselves in danger
To take bread at my hand; and now they range
Busily seeking with a continual change.

Thankëd be fortune it hath been otherwise
    Twenty times better; but once, in speciál,
In thin array, after a pleasant guise,
    When her loose gown from her shoulders did fall,
    And she me caught in her arms long and small,
Therewith all sweetly did me kiss,
And softly said, "Dear heart, how like you this?"

It was no dream: I lay broad waking.
    But all is turnëd, through my gentleness,
Into a strange fashion of forsaking;
    And I have leave to go of her goodness,
    And she also to use newfangleness.
But since that I so kindly am served,
I would fain know what she hath deserved.

MY LUTE AWAKE

My lute awake! perform the last
Labor that thou and I shall waste,
    And end that I have now begun:
For when this song is sung and past,
    My lute be still, for I have done.

As to be heard where ear is none,
As lead to grave in marble stone,
   My song may pierce her heart as soon.
Should we then sigh, or sing, or moan?
   No, no, my lute, for I have done.

The rocks do not so cruelly
Repulse the waves continually
   As she my suit and affectión,
So that I am past remedy;
   Whereby my lute and I have done.

Proud of the spoil that thou hast got
Of simple hearts thorough Love's shot,
   By whom, unkind, thou hast them won:
Think not he hath his bow forgot,
   Although my lute and I have done.

Vengeance shall fall on thy disdain
That makest but game on earnest pain;
   Think not alone under the sun
Unquit to cause thy lovers plain;
   Although my lute and I have done.

Perchance thee lie withered and old
The winter nights that are so cold,
   Plaining in vain unto the moon;
Thy wishes then dare not be told:
   Care then who list, for I have done.

And then may chance thee to repent
The time that thou hast lost and spent
   To cause thy lovers sigh and swoon:
Then shalt thou know beauty but lent,
   And wish and want as I have done.

unquit: unrequited.
plain: complain.

Now cease, my lute: this is the last
Labor that thou and I shall waste
    And ended is that we begun.
Now is this song both sung and past:
    My lute be still, for I have done.

I HAVE SOUGHT LONG

I have sought long with steadfastness
    To have had some ease of my great smart;
But nought availeth faithfulness
    To grave within your stony heart.

But hap and hit, or else hit not,
    As uncertain as is the wind,
Right so it fareth by the shot
    Of Love, alas, that is so blind.

Therefore I played the fool in vain,
    With pity when I first began
Your cruel heart for to constrain,
    Since love regardeth no doleful man.

But of your goodness, all your mind
    Is that I should complain in vain.
This is the favor that I find:
    Ye list to hear how I can plain.

But though I plain to please your heart,
    Trust me, I trust to temper it so
Not for to care which do revert:
    All shall be one in wealth or woe.

For fancy ruleth, though right say nay,
    Even as the goodman kissed his cow;
None other reason can ye lay
    But as who sayeth, "I reck not how."

hap: chance.

TAGUS, FAREWELL

Tagus, farewell, that westward with thy streams
   Turns up the grains of gold already tried;
With spur and sail for I go seek the Thames,
   Gaynward the sun that show'th her wealthy pride,
And to the town which Brutus sought by dreams
   Like bended moon doth lend her lusty side.
My King, my country, alone for whom I live,
Of mighty love the wings for this me give.

IS IT POSSIBLE

Is it possible
That so high debate,
So sharp, so sore, and of such rate,
Should end so soon and was begun so late?
Is it possible?

Is it possible
So cruel intent,
So hasty heat and so soon spent,
From love to hate, and thence for to relent?
Is it possible?

Is it possible
That any may find
Within one heart so diverse mind,
To change or turn as weather and wind?
Is it possible?

Is it possible
To spy it in an eye
That turns as oft as chance on die?
The truth whereof can any try?
Is it possible?

gaynward: against.

It is possible
For to turn so oft,
To bring that lowest that was most aloft,
And to fall highest, yet to light soft;
It is possible.

All is possible,
Who so list believe;
Trust therefore first, and after preve,
As men wed ladies by license and leave:
All is possible.

AND WILT THOU LEAVE ME THUS?

And wilt thou leave me thus?
Say nay, say nay, for shame,
To save thee from the blame
Of all my grief and grame,
And wilt thou leave me thus?
Say nay, say nay!

And wilt thou leave me thus
That hath loved thee so long
In wealth and woe among?
And is thy heart so strong
As for to leave me thus?
Say nay, say nay!

And wilt thou leave me thus,
That hath given thee my heart
Never for to depart
Neither for pain nor smart:
And wilt thou leave me thus?
Say nay, say nay!

preve: prove.

And wilt thou leave me thus
And have no more pitý
Of him that loveth thee?
Alas, thy cruelty!
And wilt thou leave me thus?
  Say nay, say nay!

IT WAS MY CHOICE

It was my choice, it was no chance
  That brought my heart in others' hold,
Whereby it hath had sufferance
  Longer, perdie, than Reason would;
Since I it bound where it was free,
  Methinks, iwis, of right it should
    Accepted be.

Accepted be without refuse,
  Unless that Fortune have the power
All right of love for to abuse;
  For, as they say, one happy hour
May more prevail than right or might;
  If fortune then list for to lour,
    What vaileth right?

What vaileth right if this be true?
  Then trust to chance and go by guess;
Then who so loveth may well go sue
  Uncertain Hope for his redress.
Yet some would say assuredly
  Thou mayst appeal for thy release
    To fantasy.

iwis: indeed.

To fantasy pertains to choose:
　　All this I know, for fantasy
First unto love did me induce;
　　But yet I know as steadfastly
That if love have no faster knot,
　　So nice a choice slips suddenly:
　　　　It lasteth not.

It lasteth not that stands by change.
　　Fancy doth change; fortune is frail;
Both these to please the way is strange.
　　Therefore me thinks best to prevail:
There is no way that is so just
　　As truth to lead, though t'other fail,
　　　　And thereto trust.

FORGET NOT YET

Forget not yet the tried intent
Of such a truth as I have meant;
My great travail so gladly spent
　　　　Forget not yet!

Forget not yet when first began
The weary life ye know, since whan
The suit, the service, none tell can;
　　　　Forget not yet!

Forget not yet the great assays,
The cruel wrong, the scornful ways,
The painful patience in denays,
　　　　Forget not yet!

Forget not yet, forget not this,
How long ago hath been, and is,
The mind that never meant amiss,
　　　　Forget not yet!

Forget not then thine own approved,
The which so long hath thee so loved,
Whose steadfast faith yet never moved;
    Forget not this!

BLAME NOT MY LUTE

Blame not my lute, for he must sound
    Of these or that as liketh me;
For lack of wit the lute is bound
    To give such tunes as pleaseth me.
Though my songs be somewhat strange,
And speaks such words as touch thy change,
    Blame not my lute.

My lute, alas, doth not offend,
    Though that perforce he must agree
To sound such tunes as I intend
    To sing to them that heareth me;
Then though my songs be somewhat plain,
And toucheth some that use to feign,
    Blame not my lute.

My lute and strings may not deny,
    But as I strike they must obey;
Break not them then so wrongfully,
    But wreak thyself some wiser way;
And though the songs which I indite
Do quit thy change with rightful spite,
    Blame not my lute.

Spite asketh spite, and changing change,
    And falsëd faith must needs be known;
The fault so great, the case so strange,
    Of right it must abroad be blown;
Then since that by thine own desert
My songs do tell how true thou art,
    Blame not my lute.

Blame but the self that hast misdone
And well deservëd to have blame;
Change thou thy way, so evil begone,
And then my lute shall sound that same;
But if till then my fingers play
By thy desert their wonted way,
   Blame not my lute.

Farewell, unknown! for though thou break
My strings in spite with great disdain,
Yet have I found out, for thy sake,
Strings for to string my lute again.
And if, perchance, this foolish rime
Do make thee blush at any time,
   Blame not my lute.

PERDIE, I SAID IT NOT

Perdie, I said it not,
 Nor never thought to do;
As well as I ye wot
 I have no power thereto.
And if I did, the lot
 That first did me enchain
Do never slack the knot
 But straight it to my pain.

And if I did, each thing
 That may do harm or woe
Continually may wring
 My heart whereso I go;
Report may always ring
 Of shame of me for aye,
If in my heart did spring
 The word that ye do say.

If I said so, each star
    That is in heaven above
May frown on me to mar
    The hope I have in love;
And if I did, such war
    As they brought unto Troy,
Bring all my life afar
    From all this lust and joy.

And if I did so say,
    The beauty that me bound
Increase from day to day
    More cruel to my wound,
With all the moan that may
    To plaint may turn my song;
My life may soon decay
    Without redress, by wrong.

If I be clear from thought,
    Why do ye then complain?
Then is this thing but sought
    To turn me to more pain.
Then that that ye have wrought
    Ye must it now redress;
Of right therefore ye ought
    Such rigor to repress.

And as I have deserved,
    So grant me now my hire;
Ye know I never swerved;
    Ye never found me liar.
For Rachel have I served
    (For Leah cared I never),
And her I have reserved
    Within my heart for ever.

WHAT SHOULD I SAY

What should I say
    Since faith is dead,
And truth away
    From you is fled?
    Should I be led
With doubleness?
Nay, nay, mistress!

I promised you,
    And you promised me,
To be as true
    As I would be;
    But since I see
Your double heart,
Farewell, my part!

Though for to take
    It is not my mind
But to forsake,
    I am not blind;
    And as I find,
So will I trust.
Farewell, unjust!

Can ye say nay?
    But you said
That I alway
    Should be obeyed;
    And thus betrayed—
Ere that I wist—
Farewell, unkissed!

HATE WHOM YE LIST

Hate whom ye list, for I care not:
Love whom ye list and spare not:
Do what ye list and dread not:
Think what ye list, I fear not:
For as for me, I am not,
But even as one that recks not
Whether ye hate or hate not:
For in your love I dote not:
Wherefore I pray you forget not,
But love whom ye list; for I care not.

DISDAIN ME NOT

Disdain me not without desert,
  Nor leave me not so suddenly,
Since well ye wot that in my heart
  I mean no thing but honesty:
    Disdain me not.

Refuse me not without cause why,
  Nor think me not to be unjust,
Since that by lot of fantasy
  The careful knot needs knit I must:
    Refuse me not.

Mistrust me not, though some there be
  That fain would spot my steadfastness;
Believe them not, seeing that ye see
  The proof is not as they express.
    Mistrust me not.

Forsake me not till I deserve,
  Nor hate me not till I offend,
Destroy me not till that I swerve;
  For since you know what I intend,
    Forsake me not.

Disdain me not, being your own;
　Refuse me not that am so true;
Mistrust me not till all be known;
　Forsake me never for no new:
　　Disdain me not.

WITHIN MY BREAST

Within my breast I never thought it gain
Of gentle mind the freedom for to lose;
Nor in my heart sank never such disdain
To be a forger, faults for to disclose;
Nor I can not endure the truth to glose,
To set a gloss upon an earnest pain;
Nor I am not in number one of those
That list to blow retreat to every train.

YOUR LOOKS SO OFTEN CAST

Your looks so often cast,
　Your eyes so friendly rolled,
Your sight fixëd so fast,
　Always one to behold:
　Though hide it fain ye would,
It plainly doth declare
　Who hath your heart in hold,
And where good will ye bear.

Fain would ye find a cloak
　Your burning fire to hide:
Yet both the flame and smoke
　Breaks out on every side.
　Ye can not love so guide
That it no issue win;
　Abroad needs must it glide,
That burns so hot within.

For cause your self do wink
   Ye judge all other blind,
And secret it you think
   Which every man doth find.
   In waste oft spend ye wind
Your self in love to quit:
   For agues of that kind
Will show who hath the fit.

Your sighs you fetch from far,
   And all to wry your woe;
Yet are ye ne'er the narre:
   Men are not blinded so.
   Deeply oft swear ye no,
But all those oaths are vain
   So well your eye doth show
Who put your heart to pain.

Think not, therefore, to hide
   That still itself betrays;
Nor seek means to provide
   To dark the sunny days.
   Forget those wonted ways;
Leave off such frowning cheer;
   There will be found no stays
To stop a thing so clear.

SPEAK THOU AND SPEED

Speak thou and speed, where will or power ought help'th;
Where power doth want, will must be won by wealth.
For need will speed, where will works not his kind,
And gain, thy foes, thy friends shall cause thee find.
For, suit and gold, what do not they obtain?
Of good and bad the tryers are these twain.

wry: turn aside.   *narre*: nearer.

IF THOU WILT MIGHTY BE

If thou wilt mighty be, flee from the rage
   Of cruel will, and see thou keep thee free
From the foul yoke of sensual bondáge;
     For though thy empire stretch to Indian sea,
     And for thy fear trembleth the farthest Thylee,
If thy desire have over thee the power,
Subject then art thou and no governoúr.

If to be noble and high thy mind be movëd,
   Consider well thy ground and thy beginning;
For he that hath each star in heaven fixëd,
     And gives the Moon her horns and her eclipsing,
     Alike hath made thee noble in his working,
So that wretched no way thou may be,
Except foul lust and vice do conquer thee.

All were it so thou had a flood of gold
   Unto thy thirst, yet should it not suffice;
And though with Indian stones, a thousandfold
     More precious than can thy self devise,
     Ychargëd were thy back, thy covetise
And busy biting yet should never let
Thy wretched life, ne do thy death profét.

SATIRE 3: TO SIR FRANCIS BRIAN

A spending hand that alway poureth out
   Had need to have a bringer in as fast,
   And on the stone that still doth turn about
There groweth no moss. These proverbs yet do last.

Thylee: Thule.   *profet:* profit.
let: prevent.

Reason hath set them in so sure a place
That length of years their force can never waste.
When I remember this, and eke the case
Wherein thou stands, I thought forthwith to write,
Brian, to thee who knows how great a grace
In writing is to counsel man the right:
To thee, therefore, that trots still up and down
And never rests, but running day and night
From realm to realm, from city, street, and town.
Why dost thou wear thy body to the bones
And mightst at home sleep in thy bed of down
And drink good ale so nappy for the nones,
Feed thyself fat and heap up pound by pound?
Likest thou not this? No, why? For swine so groans
In sty, and chaw the turds moulded on the ground,
And drivel on pearls, the head still in the manger,
Then of the harp the ass to hear the sound.
So sacks of dirt be filled up in the cloister
That serves for less than do these fatted swine.
Though I seem lean and dry, without moisture,
Yet will I serve my prince, my lord and thine;
And let them live to feed the paunch that list,
So I may live to feed both me and mine.
By God, well said! But what and if thou wist
How to bring in as fast as thou dost spend,
That would I learn. And it shall not be missed
To tell thee how. Now hark what I intend.
Thou knowest well, first, whoso can seek to please
Shall purchase friends where truth shall but offend:
Flee, therefore, truth: it is both wealth and ease.
For though that truth of every man hath praise,
Full near that wind goeth truth in great misease.
Use virtue as it goeth nowadays,
In word alone to make thy language sweet,
And of the deed yet do not as thou says,
Else be thou sure thou shalt be far unmeet
To get thy bread, each thing is now so scant.

unmeet: unable.

Seek still thy profit upon thy bare feet,
Lend in nowise, for fear that thou do want,
   Unless it be as to a dog a cheese,
   By which return be sure to win a cant
Of half at least: it is not good to lese.
   Learn at Kitson, that in a long white coat
   From under the stall without lands or fees
Hath leapt into the shop, who knoweth by rote
   This rule that I have told thee here before.
   Sometime, also, rich age beginneth to dote:
See thou when there thy gain may be the more,
   Stay him by the arm whereso he walk or go,
   Be near alway and, if he cough too sore,
When he hath spit, tread out and please him so.
   A diligent knave that picks his master's purse
   May please him so that he withouten mo
Executor is, and what is he the worse?
   But if so chance you get nought of the man,
   The widow may for all thy charge deburse
A rivelled skin, a stinking breath. What then?
   A toothless mouth shall do thy lips no harm.
   The gold is good, and though she curse or ban,
Yet where thee list thou mayst lie good and warm.
   Let the old mule bite upon the bridle
   Whilst there do lie a sweeter in thine arm.
In this also see you be not idle:
   Thy niece, thy cousin, thy sister or thy daughter,
   If she be fair, if handsome be her middle,
If thy better hath her love besought her,
   Advance his cause and he shall help thy need:
   It is but love, turn it to a laughter.
But ware I say, so gold thee help and speed,
   That in this case thou be not so unwise
   As Pandar was in such a like deed:

cant: portion or share.
lese: lose.
Kitson: the reference is uncer-
   tain; it probably indicates
the shop of Anthony Kit-
son, a wealthy bookseller of
   Wyatt's time.
deburse: disburse.

For he, the fool of conscience, was so nice
   That he no gain would have for all his pain.
   Be next thyself, for friendship bears no price.
Laughst thou at me? Why, do I speak in vain?
   —No, not at thee, but at thy thrifty jest.
   Wouldst thou I should, for any loss or gain,
Change that for gold that I have ta'en for best
   Next godly things, to have an honest name?
   Should I leave that, then take me for a beast!—
Nay, then farewell, and if thou care for shame
   Content thee then with honest poverty,
   With free tongue what thee mislikes to blame,
And for thy truth sometime adversity:
   And therewithal this thing I shall thee give—
   In this world now, little prosperity,
And coin to keep as water in a sieve.

AN EPITAPH OF SIR THOMAS GRAVENER,
KNIGHT

   Under this stone there lieth at rest
      A friendly man, a worthy knight,
   Whose heart and mind was ever pressed
      To favor truth, to further right.

   The poor's defence, his neighbor's aid,
      Most kind always unto his kin,
   That stint all strife that might be stayed,
      Whose gentle grace great love did win.

   A man that was full earnest set
      To serve his prince at all assays:
   No sickness could him from that let,
      Which was the shortening of his days.

let: prevent, hinder.

His life was good, he died full well,
   The body here, the soul in bliss;
With length of words why should I tell,
   Or farther show that well known is?—
Since that the tears of more and less
Right well declare his worthiness.

THOMAS, LORD VAUX: 1510-56

Vaux was educated at Cambridge, and succeeded to the Barony of Harrowden in 1523. Like Wyatt and Surrey, Vaux devoted his public life to the service of King Henry VIII. Although his career in court was not so distinguished as that of his better known contemporaries, he nevertheless was important enough to accompany Cardinal Wolsey upon a mission to France; a few years later he was in the company that went with Henry to Calais while Wyatt was Marshal of Calais. He took his seat in the House of Lords in 1531, and was made Knight of the Bath in 1533.

Though none of Vaux's work was printed in his lifetime, his reputation was considerable. This reputation was almost certainly based upon poems that have not come down to us; fewer than twenty poems can be very definitely attributed to Vaux, some of which appeared first in *Tottel's Miscellany* and some of which appeared, in 1576, in *The Paradise of Dainty Devices*. Were it not for the meagerness of this body of work, Vaux's reputation would probably be much larger; but those few poems that we do have are remarkable in themselves and good examples of Native style.

TEXT:

Miscellanies of the Fuller Worthies' Library, vol. iv, edited by A. B. Grosart (1884).

The Poems of Lord Vaux, edited by Larry P. Vonalt (1960).

ON THE INSTABILITY OF YOUTH

When I look back and in myself behold
The wandering ways that youth could not descry,
And mark the fearful course that youth did hold,
And mette in mind each step youth strayed awry,
 My knees I bow, and from my heart I call,
 O Lord, forget these faults and follies all.

For now I see how void youth is of skill;
I see also his prime time and his end;
I do confess my faults and all my ill,
And sorrow sore for that I did offend.
 And with a mind repentant of all crimes
 Pardon I ask for youth, ten thousand times.

The humble heart hath daunted the proud time,
Eke wisdom hath given ignorance a fall,
And wit hath taught what folly could not find,
And age hath youth her subject and her thrall,
 Therefore I pray, O Lord of life and truth;
 Pardon the faults committed in my youth.

Thou that didst grant the wise king his request,
Thou that in whale, Thy prophet didst preserve,
Thou that forgavest the wounding of Thy breast,
Thou that didst save the thief in state to starve,
 Thou only God, the Giver of all Grace,
 Wipe out of mind the path of youth's vain race.

Thou that by power to life didst raise the dead,
Thou that of Grace restorest the blind to sight,
Thou that for love, Thy life and love out bled,
Thou that of favor madest the lame go right,
 Thou that canst heal and help in all assays,
 Forgive the guilt that grew in youth's vain ways.

mette: measure.

And now since I, with faith and doubtless mind,
Do fly to Thee by prayer to appease Thy ire,
And since that Thee, I only seek to find,
And hope by faith to attain my just desire,
   Lord, mind no more youth's error and unskill,
   And able age, to do Thy holy will.

NO PLEASURE WITHOUT SOME PAIN

How can the tree but waste and wither away
That hath not sometime comfort of the sun?
How can that flower but fade and soon decay
That always is with dark clouds over-run?
   Is this a life? Nay, death you may it call
   That feels each pain, and knows no joy at all.

What foodless beast can live long in good plight?
Or is it life where senses there be none?
Or what availeth eyes without their light?
Or else a tongue to him that is alone?
   Is this a life? Nay, death you may it call
   That feels each pain and knows no joy at all.

Whereto serve ears if that there be no sound?
Or such a head where no device doth grow?
But all of plaints, since sorrow is the ground,
Whereby the heart doth pine in deadly woe?
   Is this a life? Nay, death you may it call
   That feels each pain and knows no joy at all.

OF A CONTENTED MIND

When all is done and said, in the end thus shall you find,
He most of all doth bathe in bliss that hath a quiet mind:
And, clear from worldly cares, to deem can be content
The sweetest time in all his life in thinking to be spent.

device: the faculty of devising
   or inventing.

The body subject is to fickle fortune's power,
And to a million of mishaps is casual every hour:
And death in time doth change it to a clod of clay;
Whenas the mind, which is divine, runs never to decay.

Companion none is like unto the mind alone;
For many have been harmed by speech; through thinking,
        few or none.
Fear oftentimes restraineth words, but makes not thoughts
        to cease;
And he speaks best that hath the skill when for to hold
        his peace.

Our wealth leaves us at death; our kinsmen at the grave;
But virtues of the mind unto the heavens with us we have.
Wherefore, for virtue's sake, I can be well content
The sweetest time of all my life to deem in thinking spent.

HE RENOUNCETH ALL THE EFFECTS OF
LOVE

Like as the hart, that lifteth up his ears
To hear the hound that hath him in the chase,
Doth cast the wind in dangers and in fears
With flying foot to pass away apace,
So must I fly of love, the vain pursuit,
Whereof the gain is lesser than the fruit.

And I also must loathe those leering looks,
Where love doth lurk still with a subtle sleight,
With painted mocks, and inward hidden hooks,
To trap by trust that lieth not in wait—
The end whereof, assay it whoso shall,
Is sugared smart, and inward bitter gall.

And I also must fly such Circian songs
Wherewith that Circe, Ulysses did enchant;
These wily wits, I mean, with filèd tongues
That hearts of steel have power to daunt,

Whoso as hawk that stoopeth to their call
For most desert receiveth least of all.

But woe to me that first beheld those eyes,
The trap wherein I say that I was tane:
An outward salve which inward me destroys,
Whereto I run as rat unto her bane—
As to the fish sometime it doth befall
That with the bait doth swallow hook and all.

Within my breast, wherewith I daily fed
The vain repast of amorous hot desire,
With loitering lust so long that hath me fed
Till he hath brought me to the flaming fire.
In time, as Phoenix ends her care and carks,
I make the fire and burn myself with sparks.

THE AGED LOVER RENOUNCETH LOVE

I loathe that I did love,
    In youth that I thought sweet,
As time requires for my behove,
    Methinks they are not meet.

My lusts they do me leave,
    My fancies all be fled,
And tract of time begins to weave
    Grey hairs upon my head.

For age with stealing steps
    Hath clawed me with his clutch,
And lusty life away she leaps,
    As there had been none such.

My Muse doth not delight
    Me as she did before;
My hand and pen are not in plight
    As they have been of yore.

tane: taken.   *carks:* troubles.

For reason me denies
  This youthly idle rhyme;
And day by day to me she cries,
  "Leave off these toys in time."

The wrinkles in my brow,
  The furrows in my face,
Say, limping age will hedge him now
  Where youth must give him place.

The harbinger of death,
  To me I see him ride;
The cough, the cold, the gasping breath
  Doth bid me to provide

A pickaxe and a spade,
  And eke a shrouding sheet,
A house of clay for to be made
  For such a guest most meet.

Methinks I hear the clerk
  That knolls the careful knell,
And bids me leave my woeful work,
  Ere nature me compel.

My keepers knit the knot
  That youth did laugh to scorn,
Of me that clean shall be forgot
  As I had not been born.

Thus must I youth give up,
  Whose badge I long did wear;
To them I yield the wanton cup
  That better may it bear.

Lo, here the barëd skull,
  By whose bald sign I know
That stooping age away shall pull
  Which youthful years did sow.

For beauty with her band
   These crooked cares hath wrought,
And shippëd me into the land
   From whence I first was brought.

And ye that bide behind,
   Have ye none other trust:
As ye of clay were cast by kind,
   So shall ye waste to dust.

HENRY HOWARD, EARL OF SURREY: 1517?–47

Educated by the learned tutor, John Clerk, Surrey early
had a knowledge of Latin, Italian, Spanish, and French.
As a boy he was a close friend of the Duke of Richmond,
an illegitimate son of Henry VIII, and stayed with him at
Windsor Palace. Surrey was one of Henry's retainers, and
led an active life at court, taking part in several naval and
military engagements against France. In 1546, he was ar-
rested and charged with treason, probably because either
he or his father had too strongly pressed a family claim
upon the succession of Henry VIII, who was then in his
last illness. In January 1547, he was beheaded on Tower
Hill, where a little more than ten years before Sir Thomas
More had met a like fate.

The recent reaction against Surrey has been extreme;
whereas nineteenth- and early twentieth-century academic
taste merely put Wyatt in an inferior position to Surrey,
modern taste has almost refused to read Surrey at all.
He certainly is not so fine a poet as Wyatt, and the things
for which he is "historically important"—the blank verse
translation of a part of the *Aeneid*, the close imitations
of Italian and French sonnets—are almost worthless as
pieces of art. But here and there one will find startlingly
direct and clear lines, and a few of his poems are very
fine.

TEXT:

The Poems of Henry Howard, Earl of Surrey, edited by
   Frederick Morgan Padelford (1928).

THE SOOTE SEASON

The soote season, that bud and bloom forth brings,
With green hath clad the hill and eke the vale;
The nightingale with feathers new she sings;
The turtle to her make hath told her tale.
Summer is come, for every spray now springs:
The hart hath hung his old head on the pale;
The buck in brake his winter coat he flings;
The fishes float with new-repairèd scale;
The adder all her slough away she slings;
The swift swallow pursueth the fliës smale;
The busy bee her honey now she mings;
Winter is worn that was the flowers' bale.
And thus I see among these pleasant things,
Each care decays, and yet my sorrow springs.

WHEN YOUTH HAD LED

When youth had led me half the race
That Cupid's scourge did make me run,
I lookèd back to meet the place
From whence my weary course begun.

And then I saw how my desire
By ill guiding had let my way:
Whose eyes, too greedy of their hire,
Had lost me many a noble prey.

For when in sighs I spent the day,
And could not cloak my grief by game,
Their boiling smoke did still bewray
The fervent rage of hidden flame.

soote: sweet, soft.   mings: mingles, mixes.
make: mate.   let: hinder, prevent.

And when salt tears did bain my breast,
Where Love his pleasant trains had sown,
The bruit thereof my fruit oppressed,
Ere that the blooms were sprung and blown.

And where mine eyes did still pursue
The flying chase that was their quest,
Their greedy looks did oft renew
The hidden wound within my breast.

When every look these cheeks might stain,
From deadly pale to flaming red,
By outward signs appearèd plain
The woe wherewith my heart was fed.

But all too late Love learneth me
To paint all kind of colors new,
To blind their eyes that else should see
My sparkled cheeks with Cupid's hue.

And now the covert breast I claim
That worships Cupid secretly
And nourisheth his sacred flame
From whence no blazing sparks do fly.

ALAS, SO ALL THINGS NOW

Alas, so all things now do hold their peace,
Heaven and earth disturbèd in no thing:
The beasts, the air, the birds their song do cease;
The nightès chare the stars about doth bring.
Calm is the sea, the waves work less and less.
So am not I, whom love, alas, doth wring,
Bringing before my face the great increase
Of my desires, whereat I weep and sing
In joy and woe, as in a doubtful ease.

bain: drench.   *chare:* chariot.

For my sweet thoughts sometime do pleasure bring;
But, by and by, the cause of my disease
Gives me a pang that inwardly doth sting,
When that I think what grief it is again
To live and lack the thing should rid my pain.

SO CRUEL PRISON

So cruel prison, how could betide, alas,
As proud Windsor, where I, in lust and joy,
With a king's son my childish years did pass,
In greater feast than Priam's sons of Troy,

Where each sweet place returns a taste full sour.
The large green courts, where we were wont to hove,
With eyes cast up unto the maiden's tower,
And easy sighs such as folk draw in love.

The stately sails, the ladies bright of hue,
The dances short, long tales of great delight,
With words and looks that tigers could but rue,
Where each of us did plead the other's right.

The palm-play, where, despoilëd for the game,
With dazëd eyes oft we by gleams of love
Have missed the ball, and got sight of our dame,
To bait her eyes which kept the leads above.

The gravelled ground, with sleeves tied on the helm;
On foaming horse, with swords and friendly hearts,
With chere as though the one should overwhelm,
Where we have fought and chasëd oft with darts.

betide: become a possession.
Windsor: the place where, in 1537, Surrey was confined for striking a courtier; he had spent his boyhood years there with his friend, the "king's son," the bastard Duke of Richmond.
hove: linger.
palm-play: a game like handball.
chere: care.

With silver drops the meads yet spread for ruth,
In active games of nimbleness and strength,
Where we did strain, trailëd by swarms of youth,
Our tender limbs, that yet shot up in length.

The secret groves, which oft we made resound
Of pleasant plaint and of our ladies' praise,
Recording soft what grace each one had found,
What hope of speed, what dread of long delays.

The wild forest, the clothëd holt with green,
With reins availed and swift y-breathëd horse,
With cry of hounds and merry blasts between,
Where we did chase the fearful hart aforce.

The void walls eke, that harbored us each night—
Wherewith, alas, reviveth in my breast
The sweet accord, such sleeps as yet delight,
The pleasant dreams, the quiet bed of rest,

The secret thoughts imparted with such trust,
The wanton talk, the divers change of play;
The friendship sworn, each promise kept so just,
Wherewith we passed the winter night away.

And with this thought the blood forsakes my face,
The tears berain my cheeks of deadly hue:
The which, as soon as sobbing sighs, alas,
Up-suppëd have, thus I my plaint renew:

"O place of bliss! renewer of my woes!
Give me accompt where is my noble fere
Whom in thy walls thou didst each night enclose,
To other lief, but unto me most dear."

fere: companion.

Echo, alas, that doth my sorrow rue,
Returns thereto a hollow sound of plaint.
Thus I, alone, where all my freedom grew,
In prison pine with bondage and restraint:

And with remembrance of the greater grief,
To banish the less, I find my chief relief.

WHEN RAGING LOVE

When raging love with extreme pain
Most cruelly distrains my heart;
When that my tears, as floods of rain,
Bear witness to my woeful smart;
When sighs have wasted so my breath
That I lie at the point of death—

I call to mind the navy great
That the Greeks brought to Troy town,
And how the boisterous winds did beat
Their ships, and rent their sails adown,
Till Agamemnon's daughter's blood
Appeased the gods, that them withstood:

And how that in those ten years' war
Full many a bloody deed was done,
And many a lord, that came full far
There caught his bane, alas, too soon,
And many a good knight overrun,
Before the Greeks had Helen won.

Then think I thus: "Sith such repair,
So long time war of valiant men,
Was all to win a lady fair,
Shall I not learn to suffer then,
And think my life well spent to be,
Serving a worthier wight than she?"

greater grief: Surrey's good   mer of 1536.
friend, the Duke of Rich-   distrains: oppresses.
mond, had died in the sum-

Therefore I never will repent,
But pains, contented, still endure;
For like as when, rough winter spent,
The pleasant spring straight draweth in ure,
So after raging storms of care,
Joyful at length may be my fare.

GIVE PLACE, YE LOVERS

Give place, ye lovers, here before
That spent your boasts and brags in vain;
My lady's beauty passeth more
The best of yours, I dare well sayen,
Than doth the sun the candle light,
Or brightest day the darkest night.

And thereto hath a troth as just
As had Penelope the fair;
For what she saith, ye may it trust,
As it by writing sealëd were:
And virtues hath she many mo
Than I with pen have skill to show.

I could rehearse, if that I would,
The whole effect of Nature's plaint
When she had lost the perfect mould,
The like to whom she would not paint:
With wringing hands how she did cry,
And what she said, I know it, I.

I know she swore with raging mind,
Her kingdom only set apart;
There was no loss by law of kind
That could have gone so near her heart.
And this was chiefly all her pain:
She could not make the like again.

ure: use.

Sith Nature thus gave her the praise
To be the chiefest work she wrought,
In faith, methink some better ways
On your behalf might well be sought
Than to compare, as ye have done,
To match the candle with the sun.

THE MEANS TO ATTAIN HAPPY LIFE

Martial, the things that do attain
The happy life be these, I find:
The riches left, not got with pain;
The fruitful ground, the quiet mind;
The equal friend, no grudge, no strife;
No charge of rule nor governance;
Without disease the healthful life;
The household of continuance;
The mean diet, no delicate fare;
True wisdom joined with simpleness;
The night dischargèd of all care,
Where wine the wit may not oppress;
The faithful wife, without debate;
Such sleeps as may beguile the night.
Contented with thine own estate,
Ne wish for death, ne fear his might.

LAID IN MY QUIET BED

Laid in my quiet bed, in study as I were,
I saw within my troubled head a heap of thoughts appear;
And every thought did show so lively in mine eyes,
That now I sighed, and then I smiled, as cause of thought
          did rise.
I saw the little boy in thought how oft that he
Did wish of God to 'scape the rod, a tall young man to be.
The young man, eke, that feels his bones with pains
          oppressed,
How he would be a rich old man, to live and lie at rest.

The rich old man that sees his end draw on so sore,
How he would be a boy again, to live so much the more.
Whereat full oft I smiled to see how all these three,
From boy to man, from man to boy, would chop and
    change degree.
And, musing thus, I think the case is very strange
That man from wealth, to live in woe, doth ever seek
    to change.
Thus thoughtful as I lay, I saw my withered skin,
How it doth show my dented jaws, the flesh was worn so
    thin;
And eke my toothless chaps, the gates of my right way
That opes and shuts as I do speak, do thus unto me say:
"Thy white and hoarish hairs, the messengers of age,
That show, like lines of true belief, that this life doth
    assuage,
Bid thee lay hand, and feel them hanging on thy chin—
The which do write two ages past, the third now coming in.
Hang up, therefore, the bit of thy young wanton time;
And thou that therein beaten art, the happiest life define."
Whereat I sighed, and said: "Farewell, my wonted joy!
Truss up thy pack, and trudge from me to every little boy,
And tell them thus from me: their time most happy is,
If, to their time, they reason had to know the truth of this."

chop: trade.

GEORGE GASCOIGNE: 1539?–77

Aside from a few dates and names, Gascoigne's biography is best contained in some of his finest poems—*Gascoigne's Woodmanship*, in the Dan Bartholmew poems, of which the *Dolorous Discourses* is one, in *The Green Knight's Farewell to Fancy*, in the several *Memories*, and elsewhere. Gascoigne was a student at Trinity College, Cambridge, and he studied law at Gray's Inn; from 1557 to 1559 he was a member of Parliament.

In virtually every calling that he followed, Gascoigne was a failure; he failed as a courtier, he failed as a gentleman farmer, he failed as a soldier—a series of defeats movingly explained and justified in his greatest poem, *Gascoigne's Woodmanship*. But he was perhaps the best-known English writer of his own day; he composed a blank verse tragedy, *Jocasta*, which was an adaptation of an Italian play; he wrote a comedy in prose, *Supposes*, again an adaptation, from Ariosto; he wrote a long satire in blank verse, *The Steel Glass*, a work for which he is, most unfortunately, best remembered; he wrote a fictional prose narrative, the *Adventures of Master F.J.*, the first narrative of its sort to appear in English; and he wrote the first important treatise on English prosody, *Certain Notes of Instruction*. His first book of poetry was *A Hundreth Sundrie Flowers*, which was reissued with additions and alterations in 1575 as *The Posies of George Gascoigne, Esquire*.

Gascoigne is certainly the most important poet of the purely Native movement and is one of the six or eight greatest poets of the century. His best work is found in his longer poems, where his powers of structure are best displayed. Though his diction is often harsh, it is deliberately so, as was that of a poet he resembles, John Donne; his poems move with a strange, rough dignity, and he is powerful in a way that no other poet of his century was. A valuable work upon his life is *George Gascoigne, Elizabethan Courtier, Soldier, and Poet*, by C. T. Prouty (1942).

TEXT:

The Complete Works of George Gascoigne, Vol. I, edited by John W. Cunliffe (1907).
George Gascoigne's Hundreth Sundrie Flowers, edited by C. T. Prouty, (1942).

THE PASSION OF A LOVER

I smile sometimes, although my grief be great,
To hear and see these lovers paint their pain,
And how they can in pleasant rimes repeat
The passing pangs which they in fancies feign.
But if I had such skill to frame a verse,
I could more pain than all their pangs rehearse.

Some say they find nor peace nor power to fight,
Which seemeth strange; but stranger is my state.
I dwell in dole, yet sojourn with delight;
Reposed in rest, yet wearied with debate.
For flat repulse might well appease my will,
But fancy fights to try my fortune still.

Some other say they hope, yet live in dread;
They freeze, they flame, they fly aloft, they fall;
But I nor hope with hap to raise my head
Nor fear to stoop, for why my gate is small.
Nor can I freeze, with cold to kill my heart,
Nor yet so flame, as might consume my smart.

How live I then, which thus draw forth my days?
Or tell me how I found this fever first?
What fits I feel? what distance? what delays?
What grief? what ease? what like I best? what worst?
These things they tell, which seek redress of pain;
And so will I, although I count it vain.

I live in love, even so I love to live
(Oh happy state, twice happy he that finds it);
But love to life this cognizance doth give,
This badge, this mark; to every man that minds it,
Love lendeth life, which, dying, cannot die,
Nor living live: and such a life lead I.

The sunny days which glad the saddest wights,
Yet never shine to clear my misty moon:
No quiet sleep, amid the moonshine nights,
Can close mine eyes, when I am woebegone;
Into such shades my peevish sorrow shrouds
That Sun and Moon are still to me in clouds.

And feverlike I feed my fancy still
With such repast as most impairs my health,
Which fever first I caught by wanton will
When coals of kind did stir my blood by stealth;
And gazing eyes in beauty put such trust
That love enflamed my liver all with lust.

My fits are like the fever-hectic fits,
Which one day quakes within and burns without,
The next day heat within the bosom sits,
And shivering cold the body goes about.
So is my heart most hot when hope is cold,
And quaketh most when I most heat behold.

Tormented thus without delays I stand,
All ways in one and evermore shall be,
In greatest grief when help is nearest hand,
And best at ease if death might make me free;
Delighting most in that which hurts my heart,
And hating change which might relieve my smart.

Yet you, dear dame, to whom this cure pertains,
Devise betimes some drams for my disease,
A noble name shall be your greatest gains,
Whereof be sure, if you will work mine ease,
And though fond fools set forth their fits as fast,
Yet grant with me that Gascoigne's passion passed.

A STRANGE PASSION OF A LOVER

Amid my bale I bathe in bliss;
I swim in heaven, I sink in hell;
I find amends for every miss,
And yet my moan no tongue can tell.
I live and love—what would you more?—
As never lover lived before.

I laugh sometimes with little lust;
So jest I oft and feel no joy;
Mine ease is builded all on trust,
And yet mistrust breeds mine annoy.
I live and lack, I lack and have;
I have and miss the thing I crave.

These things seem strange, yet are they true;
Believe me, sweet, my state is such
One pleasure which I would eschew
Both slakes my grief and breeds my grutch.
So doth one pain, which I would shoon,
Renew my joys where grief begun.

Then like the lark that passed the night
In heavy sleep with cares oppressed,
Yet when she spies the pleasant light,
She sends sweet notes from out her breast—
So sing I now because I think
How joys approach when sorrows shrink.

bale: torment.   *shoon:* show.
grutch: grudge.

And as fair Philomene again
Can watch and sing when others sleep,
And taketh pleasure in her pain,
To wray the woe that makes her weep,
So sing I now for to bewray
The loathsome life I lead alway.

The which to thee, dear wench, I write,
That knowest my mirth, but not my moan;
I pray God grant thee deep delight
To live in joys when I am gone.
I cannot live, it will not be;
I die to think to part from thee.

THE LULLABY OF A LOVER

Sing lullaby, as women do,
Wherewith they bring their babes to rest,
And lullaby can I sing too
As womanly as can the best.
With lullaby they still the child,
And if I be not much beguiled,
Full many wanton babes have I
Which must be stilled with lullaby.

First lullaby my youthful years;
It is now time to go to bed,
For crooked age and hoary hairs
Have won the haven within my head.
With lullaby, then, youth be still;
With lullaby content thy will;
Since courage quails and comes behind,
Go sleep, and so beguile thy mind.

bewray: reveal.

Next, lullaby my gazing eyes,
Which wonted were to glance apace.
For every glass may now suffice
To show the furrows in my face;
With lullaby then wink awhile,
With lullaby your looks beguile;
Let no fair face nor beauty bright
Entice you eft with vain delight.

And lullaby, my wanton will;
Let reason's rule now reign thy thought,
Since all too late I find by skill
How dear I have thy fancies bought;
With lullaby now take thine ease,
With lullaby thy doubts appease.
For trust to this: if thou be still,
My body shall obey thy will.

Eke lullaby, my loving boy,
My little Robin, take thy rest;
Since age is cold and nothing coy,
Keep close thy coin, for so is best;
With lullaby be thou content,
With lullaby thy lusts relent,
Let others pay which hath mo pence;
Thou art too poor for such expense.

Thus lullaby, my youth, mine eyes,
My will, my ware, and all that was.
I can no mo delays devise,
But welcome pain, let pleasure pass;
With lullaby now take your leave,
With lullaby your dreams deceive;
And when you rise with waking eye,
Remember then this lullaby.

GASCOIGNE'S PRAISE OF HIS MISTRESS

The hap which Paris had as due for his desert,
Who favored Venus for her face and scorned Minerva's
    art,
May serve to warn the wise that they no more esteem
The glistering gloss of beauty's blaze than reason should
    it deem.
Dan Priam's younger son found out the fairest dame
That ever trod on Troyan mold. What followed of the
    same?
I list not bruit her bale; let others spread it forth;
But for his part, to speak my mind, his choice was little
    worth.
My meaning is but this: who marks the outward show,
And never gropes for grafts of grace which in the mind
    should grow,
May chance upon such choice as trusty Troilus had,
And dwell in dole as Paris did, when he would fain be
    glad.
How happy then am I whose hap hath been to find
A mistress first that doth excel in virtues of the mind,
And yet therewith hath joined such favor and such grace
As Pandar's niece if she were here, would quickly give
    her place;
Within whose worthy breast Dame Bounty seeks to dwell,
And saith to beauty: yield to me, since I do thee excel;
Between whose heavenly eyes doth right remorse appear,
And pity placëd by the same doth much amend her cheer;
Who in my dangers deep did deign to do me good,
Who did relieve my heavy heart, and sought to save my
    blood;
Who first increased my friends and overthrew my foes,
Who loved all them that wished me well, and likëd none
    but those.

bruit her bale: report her
misery.

O Ladies, give me leave; I praise her not so far,
Since she doth pass you all as much as Titan stains a star.
You hold such servants dear, as able are to serve;
She held me dear when I, poor soul, could no good thing
    deserve.
You set by them that swim in all prosperity;
She set by me when as I was in great calamity.
You best esteem the brave and let the poorest pass;
She best esteemed my poor good will, all naked as it was.
But whither am I went? What humor guides my grain?
I seek to weigh the woolsack down with one poor pepper
    grain.
I seem to pen her praise that doth surpass my skill;
I strive to row against the tide, I hop against the hill.
Then let these few suffice: she Helen stains for hue,
Dido for grace, Cresside for cheer, and is as Thisbe true.
Yet if you further crave to have her name displayed,
Dame Favor is my mistress' name, Dame Fortune is her
    maid.

GASCOIGNE'S GOOD MORROW

You that have spent the silent night
In sleep and quiet rest,
And joy to see the cheerful light
That riseth in the east—
Now clear your voice, now cheer your heart,
Come help me now to sing;
Each willing wight come bear a part,
To praise the heavenly King.

And you whom care in prison keeps,
Or sickness doth suppress,
Or secret sorrow breaks your sleeps,
Or dolors do distress—
Yet bear a part in doleful wise,
Yea, think it good accord
And acceptáble sacrifice
Each spirit to praise the Lord.

The dreadful night with darksomeness
Had overspread the light,
And sluggish sleep with drowsiness
Had over-pressed our might—
A glass wherein we may behold
Each storm that stops our breath,
Our bed the grave, our clothes like mold,
And sleep like dreadful death.

Yet, as this deadly night did last
But for a little space,
And heavenly day now night is past
Doth show his pleasant face—
So must we hope to see God's face
At last in heaven on high,
When we have changed this mortal place
For immortality.

And of such haps and heavenly joys
As then we hope to hold,
All earthly sights, all worldly toys
Are tokens to behold.
The day is like the day of doom,
The sun, the Son of Man,
The skies the heavens, the earth the tomb
Wherein we rest till then.

The rainbow bending in the sky,
Bedecked with sundry hues,
Is like the seat of God on high,
And seems to tell these news:
That as thereby he promisèd
To drown the world no more,
So by the blood which Christ hath shed
He will our health restore.

The misty clouds that fall sometime
And overcast the skies
Are like to troubles of our time,
Which do but dim our eyes;

But as such dews are dried up quite
When Phoebus shows his face,
So are such fancies put to flight
Where God doth guide by grace.

The carrion crow, that loathsome beast,
Which cries against the rain,
Both for her hue and for the rest
The Devil resembleth plain:
And as with guns we kill the crow,
For spoiling our relief,
The Devil so must we overthrow
With gunshot of belief.

The little birds which sing so sweet
Are like the angels' voice,
Which render God his praises meet
And teach us to rejoice;
And as they more esteem that mirth
Than dread the night's annoy,
So must we deem our days on earth
But hell to heavenly joy.

Unto which joys for to attain
God grant us all his grace,
And send us after worldly pain
In heaven to have a place,
Where we may still enjoy that light
Which never shall decay;
Lord, for thy mercy, lend us might
To see that joyful day!

GASCOIGNE'S MEMORIES: II

The vain excess of flattering fortune's gifts
Envenometh the mind with vanity,
And beats the restless brain with endless drifts
To stay the staff of worldly dignity;
The beggar stands in like extremity.

Wherefore to lack the most and leave the least,
I count enough as good as any feast.

By too, too much Dan Croesus caught his death,
And bought with blood the price of glittering gold;
By too, too little many one lacks breath,
And starves in streets a mirror to behold:
So pride for heat, and poverty pines for cold.
Wherefore to lack the most and leave the least,
I count enough as good as any feast.

Store makes no sore: lo, this seems contrary,
And more the merrier is a proverb eke;
But store of sores may make a malady,
And one too many maketh some to seek,
When two be met that banquet with a leek:
Wherefore to lack the most and leave the least,
I count enough as good as any feast.

The rich man surfeiteth by gluttony,
Which feedeth still, and never stands content;
The poor again he pines for penury,
Which lives with lack when all and more is spent:
So too much and too little both be shent.
Wherefore to lack the most and leave the least,
I count enough as good as any feast.

The conqueror with uncontented sway
Doth raise up rebels by his avarice;
The recreant doth yield himself a prey
To foreign spoil by sloth and cowardice:
So too much and too little both be vice.
Wherefore to lack the most and leave the least,
I count enough as good as any feast.

shent: disgraced, shamed.

If so thy wife be too, too fair of face,
It draws one guest too many to thine inn;
If she be foul, and foilëd with disgrace,
In other pillows prickst thou many a pin:
So foul prove fools, and fairer fall to sin.
Wherefore to lack the most and leave the least,
I count enough as good as any feast.

And of enough, enough, and now no more,
Because my brains no better can devise;
When things be bad, a small sum maketh store,
So of such verse a few may soon suffice;
Yet still to this my weary pen replies
That I said last; and though you like it least,
It is enough and as good as a feast.

GASCOIGNE'S MEMORIES: III

The common speech is, spend and God will send;
But what sends he? A bottle and a bag,
A staff, a wallet, and a woeful end
For such as list in bravery so to brag.
Then if thou covet coin enough to spend,
Learn first to spare thy budget at the brink,
So shall the bottom be the faster bound;
But he that list with lavish hand to link
(In like expense) a penny with a pound,
May chance at last to sit aside and shrink
His harebrained head without Dame Dainty's door.
Hick, Hob, and Dick, with clouts upon their knee,
Have many times more goonhole groats in store
And change of crowns more quick at call than he,
Which let their lease and took their rent before.
For he that raps a royal on his cap,
Before he put one penny in his purse,

foilëd: polluted.
goonhole groats: small coins.
raps a royal on his cap: i.e., pays in gold coins for his hat.

Had need turn quick and broach a better tap,
Or else his drink may chance go down the worse.
I not deny but some men have good hap
To climb aloft by scales of courtly grace
And win the world with liberality;
Yet he that yerks old angels out apace
And hath no new to purchase dignity,
When orders fall, may chance to lack his grace;
For haggard hawks mislike an empty hand.
So stiffly some stick to the mercer's stall,
Till suits of silk have sweat out all their land;
So oft thy neighbors banquet in thy hall,
Till Davie Debet in thy parlor stand
And bids thee welcome to thine own decay.
I like a lion's looks not worth a leek
When every fox beguiles him of his prey;
What sauce but sorrow serveth him a week,
Which all his cates consumeth in one day?
First use thy stomach to a stand of ale,
Before thy Malmesey come in merchant's books,
And rather were for shift thy shirt of mail,
Than tear thy silken sleeves with tenter-hooks;
Put feathers in thy pillows great and small,
Let them be prinked with plumes, that gape for plumes;
Heap up both gold and silver safe in hooches,
Catch, snatch, and scratch for scrapings and for crumbs
Before thou deck thy hat on high with brooches.
Let first thine one hand hold fast all that comes,
Before that other learn his letting fly:
Remember still that soft fire makes sweet malt;
No haste but good, who means to multiply:
Bought wit is dear, and dressed with sour salt;
Repentance comes too late; and then say I,
Who spares the first and keeps the last unspent,
Shall find that sparing yields a goodly rent.

broach a better tap: i.e., find a
   better way.
angels: gold coins worth about
ten shillings.
cates: cakes.
hooches: chests, coffers.

GASCOIGNE'S MEMORIES: IV

1.   In haste, post haste, when first my wandering mind
Beheld the glistering court with gazing eye,
Such deep delights I seemed therein to find
As might beguile a graver guest than I.
The stately pomp of Princes and their peers
Did seem to swim in floods of beaten gold;
The wanton world of young delightful years
Was not unlike a heaven for to behold,
Wherein did swarm, for every saint, a Dame—
So fair of hue, so fresh of their attire,
As might excel Dame Cynthia for fame,
Or conquer Cupid with his own desire.
These and such like were baits that blazèd still
Before mine eye to feed my greedy will.

2.   Before mine eye to feed my greedy will,
Gan muster eke mine old acquainted mates,
Who helped the dish of vain delight to fill
My empty mouth with dainty delicates;   .
And foolish boldness took the whip in hand
To lash my life into this trustless trace,
Till all in haste I leaped aloof from land,
And hoist up soil to catch a courtly grace.
Each lingering day did seem a world of woe,
Till in that hapless haven my head was brought;
Waves of wanhope so tossed me to and fro
In deep despair to drown my dreadful thought:
Each hour a day, each day a year did seem,
And every year a world my will did deem.

3.   And every year a world my will did deem,
Till lo, at last to court now am I come,
A seemly swain that might the place beseem,
A gladsome guest embraced of all and some.

Not there content with common dignity,
My wandering eye in haste—yea, post, post, haste—
Beheld the blazing badge of bravery,
For want whereof I thought my self disgraced.
Then peevish pride puffed up my swelling heart
To further forth so hot an enterprise,
And comely cost began to play his part
In praising patterns of mine own devise.
Thus all was good that might be got in haste,
To prink me up, and make me higher placed.

4.   To prink me up and make me higher placed,
All came too late that tarried any time;
Pills of provision pleasëd not my taste;
They made my heels too heavy for to climb.
Me thought it best that boughs of boisterous oak
Should first be shred to make my feathers gay,
Till at the last a deadly dinting stroke
Brought down the bulk with edgetools of decay.
Of every farm I then let fly a lease
To feed the purse that paid for peevishness,
Till rent and all were fallen in such disease
As scarce could serve to maintain cleanliness.
The bough, the body, fine, farm, lease, and land—
All were too little for the merchant's hand.

5.   All were too little for the merchant's hand,
And yet my bravery bigger than his book:
But when this hot account was coldly scanned,
I thought high time about me for to look.
With heavy cheer I cast my head aback
To see the fountain of my furious race;
Compared my loss, my living, and my lack,
In equal balance with my jolly grace,
And saw expenses grating on the ground
Like lumps of lead to press my purse full oft,
When light reward and recompence were found
Fleeting like feathers in the wind aloft.
These thus compared, I left the court at large;
For why? The gains doth seldom quit the charge.

6.   For why? The gains doth seldom quit the charge;
And so say I, by proof too dearly bought.
My haste made waste, my brave and brainsick barge
Did float too fast to catch a thing of nought;
With leisure, measure, mean, and many mo,
I might have kept a chair of quiet state,
But hasty heads can not be settled so
Till crooked Fortune give a crabbed mate.
As busy brains must beat on tickle toys,
As rash invention breeds a raw device,
So sudden falls do hinder hasty joys;
And as swift baits do fleetest fish entice,
So haste makes waste; and therefore now I say,
No haste but good, where wisdom makes the way.

7.   No haste but good, where wisdom makes the way—
For proof whereof, behold the simple snail,
Who sees the soldier's carcass cast away,
With hot assault the castle to assail;
By line and leisure climbs the lofty wall
And wins the turret's top more cunningly
Than doughty Dick, who lost his life and all
With hoisting up his head too hastily.
The swiftest bitch brings forth the blindest whelps;
The hottest fevers coldest cramps ensue;
The nakedst need hath ever lastest helps:
With Neville, then, I find this proverb true:
That haste makes waste, and therefore still I say
No haste but good, where wisdom makes the way.

Neville: Alexander Neville, the young poet and translator; he was a friend of Barnabe Googe, and was probably at Gray's Inn with Gascoigne. Neville had given Gascoigne a Latin proverb, "whereupon he [Gascoigne] compiled these seven sonnets in sequence." See also note on p. 99.

THE CONSTANCY OF A LOVER

That selfsame tongue which first did thee entreat
To link thy liking with my lucky love,
That trusty tongue must now these words repeat:
I love thee still, my fancy cannot move.
That dreadless heart which durst attempt the thought
To win thy will with mine for to consent,
Maintains that vow which love in me first wrought:
I love thee still, and never shall repent.
That happy hand which hardily did touch
Thy tender body to my deep delight
Shall serve with sword to prove my passion such
As loves thee still, much more than it can write.
Thus love I still with tongue, hand, heart, and all,
And when I change, let vengeance on me fall.

DAN BARTHOLMEW'S DOLOROUS DISCOURSES

I have entreated care to cut the thread
Which all too long hath held my lingering life,
And here aloof now have I hid my head
From company thereby to stint my strife.
This solitary place doth please me best,
Where I may wear my willing mind with moan,
And where the sighs which boil out of my breast
May scald my heart, and yet the cause unknown.
All this I do, for thee my sweetest sour,
For whom of yore I counted not of care,
For whom with hungry jaws I did devour
The secret bait which lurkèd in the snare;
For whom I thought all foreign pleasures pain,
For whom, again, all pain did pleasure seem;
But only thine, I found all fancies vain;
But only thine, I did no dolors deem.

Such was the rage that whilom did possess
The privy corners of my mazëd mind,
When hot desire did count those torments less
Which gained the gaze that did my freedom bind.
And now, with care, I can record those days
And call to mind the quiet life I led
Before I first beheld thy golden rays,
When thine untruth yet troubled not my head.
Remember thou, as I cannot forget,
How I had laid both love and lust aside,
And how I had my fixëd fancy set
In constant vow forever to abide:
The bitter proof of pangs in pleasure past,
The costly taste, of honey mixed with gall;
The painted heaven which turned to hell at last;
The freedom feigned, which brought me but to thrall;
The lingering suit, well fed with fresh delays;
The wasted vows which fled with every wind;
The restless nights to purchase pleasing days;
The toiling days to please my restless mind.
All these, with more, had bruisëd so my breast
And graft such grief within my groaning heart,
That I had left Dame Fancy and the rest
To greener years, which might endure the smart.
My weary bones did bear away the scars
Of many a wound receivëd by disdain;
So that I found the fruit of all those wars
To be naught else but pangs of unknown pain.
And now mine eyes were shut from such delight,
My fancy faint, my hot desires were cold,
When cruel hap presented to my sight
Thy maiden's face, in years which were not old.
I think the Goddess of revenge devised
So to be wreaked on my rebelling will,
Because I had in youthful years despised
To taste the baits, which 'ticed my fancy still.
How so it were, God knows, I cannot tell;
But if I lie, you Heavens, the plague be mine;
I saw no sooner how delight did dwell

Between those little infant's eyes of thine
But straight a sparkling coal of quick desire
Did kindle flame within my frozen heart,
And yielding fancy softly blew the fire
Which since hath been the cause of all my smart.
What need I say? Thy self for me can swear
How much I tendered thee in tender years.
Thy life was then to me, God knows, full dear;
My life to thee is light, as now appears.
I loved thee first, and shall do to my last;
Thou flattered'st first, and so thou wouldst do still.
For love of thee full many pains I passed;
For deadly hate thou seekest me to kill.
I cannot now with manly tongue rehearse
How soon that melting mind of thine did yield;
I shame to write in this waymenting verse
With how small fight I vanquished thee in field.
But Caesar, he—which all the world subdued—
Was never yet so proud of victory,
Nor Hannibal, with martial feats endued,
Did so much please himself in policy
As I, poor I, did seem to triumph then,
When first I got the bulwarks of thy breast;
With hot alarms I comforted my men,
In foremost rank I stood before the rest
And shook my flag, not all to show my force,
But that thou mightst thereby perceive my mind;
Askaunces, lo, now could I kill thy corse,
And yet my life is unto thee resigned.
Well, let this pass; and think upon the joy,
The mutual love, the confidence, the trust,
Whereby we both abandonèd annoy
And fed our minds with fruits of lovely lust.
Think on the tithe, of kisses got by stealth
Of sweet embracings shortenèd by fear;
Remember that which did maintain our health;
Alas, alas, why should I name it here?

---

waymenting: lamenting.   *Askaunces:* as if saying.

And in the midst of all those happy days,
Do not forget the changes of my chance,
When in the depth of many wayward ways
I only sought what might thy state advance.
Thou must confess how much I cared for thee,
When of my self—I cared not for my self;
And when my hap was in mishaps to be,
Esteemed thee more than all the worldly pelf.
Mine absent thoughts did beat on thee alone
When thou hadst found a fond and newfound choice;
For lack of thee I sunk in endless moan,
When thou in change didst tumble and rejoice.
O mighty gods, needs must I honor you,
Needs must I judge your judgments to be just,
Because she did forsake him that was true,
And with false love did cloak a feignèd lust!
By high decrees you ordainèd the change
To light on such as she must needs mislike;
A meet reward for such as seek to range
When fancy's force their feeble flesh doth strike.
But did I then give bridle to thy fall?
Thou headstrong, thou, accuse me if thou can!
Did I not hazard love, yea, life and all,
To ward thy will from that unworthy man?
And when by toil I travailèd to find
The secret causes of thy madding mood,
I found naught else but tricks of Cressid's kind,
Which plainly proved that thou wert of her blood.
I found that absent Troilus was forgot
When Diomede had got both brooch and belt,
Both glove and hand, yea, heart and all, God wot,
When absent Troilus did in sorrows swelt.
These tricks, with more, thou knowst thyself I found,
Which now are needless here for to rehearse,
Unless it were to touch a tender wound
With corrosives my panting heart to perse.
But as the hound is counted little worth

perse: pierce.

Which giveth over for a loss or twain,
And cannot find the means to single forth
The stricken deer which doth in herd remain;
Or as the kindly spaniel which hath sprung
The pretty partridge for the falcon's flight
Doth never spare but thrusts the thorns among
To bring this bird yet once again to sight;
And though he know by proof—yea, dearly bought—
That seld or never, for his own avail,
This weary work of his in vain is wrought,
Yet spares he not, but labors tooth and nail,
So labored I to save thy wandering ship,
Which reckless then was running on the rocks;
And though I saw thee seem to hang the lip,
And set my great good will as light as flocks,
Yet hauled I in the mainsheet of thy mind
And stayed thy course by anchors of advice;
I won thy will into a better wind
To save thy ware, which was of precious price.
And when I had so harborèd thy bark
In happy haven, which safer was than Dover,
The Admiral, which knew it by the mark,
Straight challenged all, and said thou wert a rover.
Then was I first in thy behalf to plead;
Yea, so I did, the Judge can say no less;
And whiles in toil this loathsome life I lead,
Camest thou thyself the fault for to confess,
And down on knee before thy cruel foe
Didst pardon crave, accusing me for all,
And saidst I was the cause that thou didst so,
And that I spun the thread of all thy thrall.
Not so content, thou furthermore didst swear
That of thy self thou never meant to swerve—
For proof whereof thou didst the colors wear
Which might bewray what saint thou meant to serve.
And that thy blood was sacrificèd eke
To manifest thy steadfast, martyred mind,

bewray: betray, reveal.

Till I perforce, constrained thee for to seek
These raging seas, adventures there to find.
Alas, alas, and out alas for me,
Who am enforcëd thus for to repeat
The false reports and cloakëd guiles of thee
Whereon too oft my restless thoughts do beat.
But thus it was, and thus God knows it is—
Which when I found by plain and perfect proof
My musing mind then thought it not amiss
To shrink aside, lamenting all aloof,
And so to beat my simple shiftless brain
For some device that might redeem thy state.
Lo, here the cause for why I take this pain;
Lo, how I love the wight which me doth hate;
Lo, thus I lie and restless rest in Bath,
Whereas I bathe not now in bliss, perdie,
But boil in bale and scamble thus in scath,
Because I think on thine unconstancy.
And wilt thou know how here I spend my time
And how I draw my days in dolors still?
Then stay awhile; give ear unto my rime
So shalt thou know the weight of all my will.
When Titan is constrainëd to forsake
His leman's couch, and climbeth to his cart,
Then I begin to languish for thy sake;
And with a sigh, which may bewray my smart,
I clear mine eyes whom gum of tears has glued,
And up on foot I set my ghost-like corse;
And when the stony walls have oft renewed
My piteous plaints with echoes of remorse,
Then do I cry and call upon thy name,
And thus I say: Thou curst and cruel both,
Behold the man which taketh grief for game,
And loveth them which most his name do loathe.
Behold the man which ever truly meant,
And yet accused as author of thine ill;
Behold the man which all his life hath spent

scamble: make one's way.   *leman*: sweetheart, mistress.
scath: damage, sorrow.

To serve thy self and aye to work thy will;
Behold the man, which only for thy love
Did love himself, whom else he set but light;
Behold the man, whose blood for thy behove
Was ever pressed to shed itself outright.
And canst thou now condemn his loyalty?
And canst thou craft to flatter such a friend?
And canst thou see him sink in jeopardy?
And canst thou seek to bring his life to end?
Is this the right reward for such desart?
Is this the fruit of seed so timely sown?
Is this the price appointed for his part?
Shall truth be thus by treason overthrown?
Then farewell, faith, thou art no woman's fere.
And with that word I stay my tongue in time;
With rolling eyes I look about each where
Lest any man should hear my raving rime.
And all in rage, enragéd as I am,
I take my sheet, my slippers, and my gown,
And in the Bath from whence but late I came,
I cast myself in dolors there to drown.
There all alone I can myself convey
Into some corner where I sit unseen,
And to my self, there naked, can I say:
Behold these brawn-fallen arms which once have been
Both large and lusty, able for to fight;
Now are they weak, and wearishe God he knows,
Unable now to daunt the foul despite
Which is presented by my cruel foes.
Thy thighs are thin, my body lank and lean;
It hath no bombast now, but skin and bones:
And on mine elbow as I lie and lean,
I see a trusty token for the nonce.
I spy a bracelet bound about mine arm,
Which to my shadow seemeth thus to say:
Believe not me; for I was but a charm
To make thee sleep when others went to play.

fere: companion, mate.   *wearishe*: wizened, shriveled.

And as I gaze thus galded all with grief,
I find it fazëd almost quite in sunder.
Than think I thus: thus wasteth my relief,
And though I fade, yet to the world, no wonder.
For as this lace by leisure learns to wear,
So must I faint, even as the candle wasteth.
These thoughts, dear sweet, within my breast I bear;
And to my long home, thus my life it hasteth.
Herewith I feel the drops of sweltering sweat
Which trickle down my face, enforcëd so,
And in my body feel I likewise beat
A burning heart which tosseth to and fro.
Thus all in flames I cinder-like consume,
And were it not that wanhope lends me wind,
Soon might I fret my fancies all in fume,
And like a ghost my ghost his grave might find.
But freezing hope doth blow full in my face,
And cold of cares becomes my cordial,
So that I still endure that irksome place
Where sorrow seethes to scald my skin withal.
And when from thence or company me drives,
Or weary woes do make me change my seat,
Then in my bed my restless pains revives,
Until my fellows call me down to meat.
And when I rise, my corpse for to array,
I take the glass, sometimes; but not for pride,
For God he knows my mind is not so gay,
But for I would in comeliness abide.
I take the glass, wherein I seem to see
Such withered wrinkles and so foul disgrace
That little marvel seemeth it to me,
Though thou so well didst like the noble face.
The noble face was fair and fresh of hue,
My wrinkled face is foul and fadeth fast;
The noble face was unto thee but new,
My wrinkled face is old and clean outcast;

galded: galled.   *fazëd:* unraveled, worn
through.

The noble face might move thee with delight,
My wrinkled face could never please thine eye.
Lo, thus of crime I covet thee to quite,
And still accuse myself of surquidry,
As one that am unworthy to enjoy
The lasting fruit of such a love as thine;
Thus as I tickled still with every toy,
And when my fellows call me down to dine,
No change of meat provokes mine appetite,
Nor sauce can serve to taste my meats withal;
Then I devise the juice of grapes to dight,
For sugar and for cinnamon I call,
For ginger, grains, and for each other spice
Wherewith I mix the noble wine apace;
My fellows praise the depth of my devise,
And say it is as good as Ippocrace.
As Ippocrace, say I? And then I swelt,
My fainting limbs straight fall into a swown;
Before the taste of Ippocrace is felt,
The naked name in dolors doth me drown;
For then I call unto my troubled mind
That Ippocrace hath been thy daily drink,
That Ippocrace hath walked with every wind.
In bottles that were fillëd to the brink,
With Ippocrace thou banquetedst full oft,
With Ippocrace thou madst thyself full merry;
Such cheer had set thy new love so aloft
That old love now was scarcely worth a cherry.
And then again I fall into a trance;
But when my breath returns against my will,
Before my tongue can tell my woeful chance,
I hear my fellows how they whisper still.
One saith that Ippocrace is contrary
Unto my nature and complexión,
Whereby they judge that all my malady
Was long of that by alteratión.

quite: requite.   presumption.
surquidry: arrogance, pride,   *dight:* prepare, mix.

Another saith: No, no, this man is weak;
And for such weak, so hot things are not best.
Then at the last I hear no liar speak
But one which knows the cause of mine unrest,
And saith: This man is, for my life, in love;
He hath received repulse, or drunk disdain.
Alas, cry I; and ere I can remove,
Into a swown I soon return again.
Thus drive I forth, my doleful dining time,
And trouble others with my troubles still;
But when I hear the bell hath passëd prime,
Into the Bath I wallow by my will,
That there my tears, unseen, might ease my grief;
For though I starve, yet have I fed my fill;
In privy pangs I count my best relief.
And still I strive in weary woes to drench,
But when I plunge, then woe is at an ebb;
My glowing coals are all too quick to quench.
And I, too warm, am wrappëd in the web
Which makes me swim against the wishëd wave;
Lo, thus, dear wench, I lead a loathsome life,
And greedily I seek the greedy grave
To make an end of all these storms and strife;
But death is deaf, and hears not my desire,
So that my days continue still in dole,
And in my nights I feel the secret fire
Which close in embers coucheth like a coal,
And in the day hath been but rakëd up
With covering ashes of my company;
Now breaks it out and boils the careful cup
Which in my heart doth hang full heavily.
I melt in tears, I swelt in chilling sweat,
My swelling heart breaks with delay of pain,
I freeze in hope, yet burn in haste of heat,
I wish for death, and yet in life remain.
And when dead sleep doth close my dazzled eyes,
Then dreadful dreams my dolors do increase.
Methinks I lie awake in woeful wise
And see thee come, my sorrows for to cease.

Me seems thou sayest, my good, What meaneth this?
What ails thee thus to languish and lament?
How can it be that bathing all in bliss,
Such cause unknown disquiets thy content?
Thou dost me wrong to keep so close from me
The grudge or grief which grippeth now thy heart,
For well thou knowest I must thy partner be
In bale, in bliss, in solace, and in smart.
Alas, alas, these things I deem in dreams;
But when mine eyes are open and awake,
I see not thee, where with the flowing streams
Of brinish tears their wonted floods do make.
Thus as thou seest I spend both nights and days,
And for I find the world did judge me once
A witless writer of these lovers' lays,
I take my pen and paper for the nonce,
I lay aside this foolish riding rime.
And as my troubled head can bring to pass,
I thus bewray the torments of my time:
Bear with my Muse, it is not as it was.

GASCOIGNE'S WOODMANSHIP

My worthy Lord, I pray you wonder not
To see your woodman shoot so oft awry,
Nor that he stands amazèd like a sot
And lets the harmless deer, unhurt, go by.
Or if he strike a doe which is but carren,
Laugh not, good Lord, but favor such a fault;
Take will in worth, he would fain hit the barren;
But though his heart be good, his hap is naught.

My worthy Lord: Arthur, Lord Grey of Wilton, a patron and friend of both Spenser and Gascoigne. The occasion of this poem is a winter hunt at Grey's estate in Bedfordshire, shortly after Gascoigne had returned to England from the Spanish War. *carron:* carrion, i.e., a pregnant doe.

And therefore now I crave your Lordship's leave
To tell you plain what is the cause of this:
First, if it please your honor to perceive
What makes your woodman shoot so oft amiss,
Believe me, Lord, the case is nothing strange:
He shoots awry almost at every mark;
His eyes have been so usëd for to range,
That now, God knows, they be both dim and dark.
For proof he bears the note of folly now,
Who shot sometimes to hit Philosophy:
And ask you why? Forsooth, I make avow,
Because his wanton wits went all awry.
Next that, he shot to be a man of law,
And spent some time with learnëd Littleton;
Yet in the end he provëd but a daw,
For law was dark and he had quickly done.
Then could he wish Fitzherbert such a brain
As Tully had, to write the law by art,
So that with pleasure, or with little pain,
He might, perhaps, have caught a truant's part.
But all too late, he most misliked the thing
Which most might help to guide his arrow straight:
He winkëd wrong, and so let slip the string
Which cast him wide, for all his quaint conceit.
From thence he shot to catch a courtly grace,
And thought even there to wield the world at will;
But out, alas, he much mistook the place,
And shot awry at every rover still.
The blazing baits which draw the gazing eye,
Unfeathered there his first affectión;
No wonder then although he shot awry,
Wanting the feathers of discretión.

Littleton: Sir Thomas Little-
ton, a justice of the Com-
mon Pleas, author of the
famous *Littleton's Tenures.*
Fitzherbert: Sir Anthony Fitz-
herbert, a well-known bar-
rister, whose *La Grande
Abridgement* was the first
attempt to systematize the
whole of English law.
Tully: Cicero.

Yet more than them, the marks of dignity
He much mistook, and shot the wronger way,
Thinking the purse of prodigality,
Had been best mean to purchase such a prey.
He thought the flattering face which fleareth still
Had been full fraught with all fidelity,
And that such words as courtiers use at will
Could not have varied from the verity.
But when his bonnet, buttonëd with gold,
His comely cape, begarded all with gay,
His bombast hose, with linings manifold,
His knit silk stocks and all his quaint array,
Had picked his purse of all the Peter pence
Which might have paid for his promotión,
Then, all too late, he found that light expense
Had quite quenched out the court's devotión.
So that since then the taste of misery
Hath been always full bitter in his bit,
And why? Forsooth, because he shot awry,
Mistaking still the marks which others hit.
But now behold what mark the man doth find:
He shoots to be a soldier in his age;
Mistrusting all the virtues of the mind,
He trusts the power of his personage,
As though long limbs led by a lusty heart
Might yet suffice to make him rich again;
But flushing frays have taught him such a part
That now he thinks the wars yield no such gain.
And sure I fear, unless your lordship deign,
To train him yet into some better trade,
It will be long before he hit the vein,
Whereby he may a richer man be made.

---

fleareth: grins or grimaces fawningly, with a secondary implication of mocking or ridicule.

begarded all with gay: adorned with facings of bright, vari-colored materials.

Peter pence: formerly a tax due to the papal see; here, used to indicate money for bribery.

He cannot climb as other catchers can,
To lead a charge before himself be led;
He cannot spoil the simple sakeless man
Which is content to feed him with his bread;
He cannot pinch the painful soldier's pay,
And shear him out his share in ragged sheets;
He cannot stop to take a greedy prey
Upon his fellows groveling in the streets;
He cannot pull the spoil from such as pill,
And seem full angry at such foul offense,
Although the gain content his greedy will
Under the cloak of contrary pretence.
And nowadays the man that shoots not so
May shoot amiss, even as your woodman doth;
But then you marvel why I let them go,
And never shoot, but say farewell, forsooth.
Alas, my Lord, while I do muse hereon,
And call to mind my youthful years misspent,
They give me such a bone to gnaw upon
That all my senses are in silence pent.
My mind is rapt in contemplatión,
Wherein my dazzled eyes only behold
The black hour of my constellatión,
Which framëd me so luckless on the mold.
Yet therewithal I cannot but confess
That vain presumption makes my heart to swell,
For thus I think: not all the world, I guess,
Shoots bet than I; nay, some shoots not so well.
In Aristotle somewhat did I learn
To guide my manners all by comeliness,
And Tully taught me somewhat to discern
Between sweet speech and barbarous rudeness.
Old Parkins, Rastall, and Dan Bracten's books
Did lend me somewhat of the lawless Law;
The crafty courtiers with their guileful looks
Must needs put some experience in my maw.

sakeless: guiltless.
pill: pillage.
Parkins, Rastall, Bracten: Eng-lish jurists, authors of several important legal treatises.

Yet cannot these with many masteries mo
Make me shoot straight at any gainful prick,
Where some that never handled such a bow
Can hit the white, or touch it near the quick;
Who can nor speak nor write in pleasant wise,
Nor lead their life by Aristotle's rule,
Nor argue well on questions that arise,
Nor plead a case more than my Lord Mayor's mule,
Yet can they hit the marks that I do miss,
And win the mean which may the man maintain.
Now when my mind doth mumble upon this,
No wonder then although I pine for pain.
And whiles mine eyes behold this mirror thus,
The herd goeth by, and farewell, gentle does.
So that your Lordship quickly may discuss
What blinds mine eyes so oft, as I suppose.
But since my Muse can to my Lord rehearse
What makes me miss, and why I do not shoot,
Let me imagine in this worthless verse
If right before me, at my standing's foot
There stood a doe, and I should strike her dead,
And then she prove a carrion carcass too,
What figure might I find within my head
To 'scuse the rage which ruled me so to do?
Some might interpret by plain paraphrase
That lack of skill or fortune led the chance,
But I must otherwise expound the case;
I say Jehovah did this doe advance,
And made her bold to stand before me so,
Till I had thrust mine arrow to her heart,
That by the sudden of her overthrow
I might endeavor to amend my part,
And turn mine eyes that they no more behold
Such guileful marks as seem more than they be:
And though they glister outwardly like gold,
Are inwardly but brass, as men may see.

prick: target.

And when I see the milk hang in her teat,
Me thinks it saith, Old babe, now learn to suck,
Who in thy youth couldst never learn the feat
To hit the whites which live with all good luck.
Thus have I told, my Lord, God grant in season,
A tedious tale in rime, but little reason.

IN PRAISE OF A GENTLEWOMAN

If men may credit give to true reported fames,
Who doubts but stately Rome had store of lusty, loving
    dames?
Whose ears have been so deaf as never yet heard tell
How far the fresh Pompeia for beauty did excel?
And golden Marcus, he that swayed the Roman sword,
Bare witness of Bohemia, by credit of his word.
What need I more rehearse, since all the world did know
How high the floods of beauty's blaze within those walls
    did flow?
And yet in all that choice a worthy Roman knight—
Antonius, who conquerëd proud Egypt by his might—
Not all to please his eye, but most to ease his mind
Chose Cleopatra for his love, and left the rest behind.
A wondrous thing to read: in all his victory
He snapped but her for his own share, to please his
    fantasy.
She was not fair, God wot; the country breeds none bright;
Well may we judge her skin the foil, because her teeth
    were white.
Percase her lovely looks some praises did deserve,
But brown I dare be bold she was, for so the soil did serve.
And could Antonius forsake the fair in Rome
To love his nutbrown lady best, was this an equal doom?
I dare well say dames there did bear him deadly grudge;
His sentence had been shortly said, if Faustine had been
    judge.
For this I dare avow (without vaunt be it spoke):
So brave a knight as Anthony held all their necks in yoke.

I leave not Lucrece out, believe in her who list;
I think she would have liked his lure, and stoopëd to his
fist.
What moved the chieftain, then, to link his liking thus?
I would some Roman dame were here, the question to
discuss.
But I that read her life do find therein by fame
How clear her courtesy did shine in honor of her name.
Her bounty did excel, her truth had never peer,
Her lovely looks, her pleasant speech, her lusty loving
cheer.
And all the worthy gifts that ever yet were found,
Within this good Egyptian Queen did seem for to abound.
Wherefore he worthy was to win the golden fleece,
Which scorned the blazing stars in Rome to conquer such
a peace.
And she to quite his love, in spite of dreadful death,
Enshrined with snakes within his tomb, did yield her part-
ing breath.

Allegoria

If fortune favored him, then may that man rejoice,
And think himself a happy man by hap of happy choice.
Who loves and is beloved of one as good, as true,
As kind as Cleopatra was, and yet more bright of hue—
Her eyes as grey as glass, her teeth as white as milk,
A ruddy lip, a dimpled chin, a skin as smooth as silk.
A wight what could you more, that may content man's
mind,
And hath supplies for every want, that any man can find;
And may himself assure, when hence his life shall pass,
She will be stung to death with snakes, as Cleopatra was.

THE GREEN KNIGHT'S FAREWELL TO FANCY

Fancy (quoth he), farewell, whose badge I long did bear,
And in my hat full harebrainedly thy flowers did I wear.
Too late I find, at last, thy fruits are nothing worth;
Thy blossoms fall and fade full fast, though bravery bring
    them forth.
By thee I hoped always in deep delights to dwell,
But since I find thy fickleness, Fancy (quoth he), farewell.

Thou madst me live in love, which wisdom bids me hate;
Thou bleardst mine eyes and madst me think that faith
    was mine by fate.
By thee those bitter sweets did please my taste alway;
By thee I thought that love was light and pain was but
    a play.
I thought that beauty's blaze was meet to bear the bell,
And since I find myself deceived, Fancy (quoth he),
    farewell.

The gloss of gorgeous courts by thee did please mine eye;
A stately sight me thought it was to see the brave go by,
To see there feathers flaunt, to mark their strange device,
To lie along in ladies' laps, to lisp and make it nice;
To fawn and flatter both I likëd sometimes well,
But since I see how vain it is, Fancy (quoth he), farewell.

When court had cast me off, I toilëd at the plow;
My fancy stood in strange conceits; to thrive I wot not
    how:—
By mills, by making malt, by sheep, and eke by swine,
By duck and drake, by pig and goose, by calves and keep-
    ing kine,
By feeding bullocks fat, when price at markets fell;
But since my swains eat up my gains, Fancy (quoth he),
    farewell.

In hunting of the deer my fancy took delight;
All forests knew my folly still; the moonshine was my
    light.
In frosts I felt no cold; a sunburnt hue was best;
I sweat and was in temper still; my watching seemëd rest.
What dangers deep I passed, it folly were to tell;
And since I sigh to think thereon, Fancy (quoth he),
    farewell.

A fancy fed me once to write in verse and rime,
To wray my grief, to crave reward, to cover still my crime,
To frame a long discourse on stirring of a straw,
To rumble rime in raff and ruff, yet all not worth a haw;
To hear it said, There goeth the man that writes so well;
But since I see what poets be, Fancy (quoth he), farewell.

At music's sacred sound my fancies eft begun
In concords, discords, notes and clefts, in tunes of unison;
In hierarchies and strains, in rests, in rule and space,
In monochords and moving moods, in bourdons under
    bass.
In descants and in chants, I strainëd many a yell,
But since musicians be so mad, Fancy (quoth he),
    farewell.

To plant strange country fruits, to sow such seeds likewise,
To dig and delve for new found roots, where old might
    well suffice;
To prune the water-boughs, to pick the mossy trees—
Oh, how it pleased my fancy once!—to kneel upon my
    knees,
To graft a pippin stock when sap begins to swell;
But since the gains scarce quite the cost, Fancy (quoth
    he), farewell.

water-boughs: undergrowth.   *pippin:* young apple tree.

Fancy (quoth he), farewell, which made me follow drums,
Where powdered bullets serves for sauce to every dish
        that comes;
Where treason lurks in trust, where Hope all hearts be-
        guiles,
Where mischief lieth still in wait, when fortune friendly
        smiles;
Where one day's prison proves that all such heavens are
        hell,
And such I feel the fruits thereof; Fancy (quoth he),
        farewell.

If reason rule my thoughts, and God vouchsafe me grace,
Then comfort of philosophy shall make me change my
        race;
And fond I shall it find that fancy sets to show,
For weakly stands that building still which lacketh grace
        below.
But since I must accept my fortunes as they fell,
I say, God send me better speed; and, Fancy, now
        farewell!

BARNABE GOOGE: 1540–94

Googe studied at Oxford and Cambridge, where he pre-
pared himself for government service; he traveled in
France and Spain, after which he went into the service of
his kinsman, Lord Burghley. During the latter part of his
life he was a government official in Ireland, where he met
and became friendly with Edmund Spenser. Googe pub-
lished several translations, the most notable of which was
the violently anti-Catholic *Zodaicus Vitae* of Marcellus
Palingenius (i.e., Pietro Angelo Manzolli). His only vol-
ume of original poetry was *Eclogues, Epitaphs, and Son-
nets* published in 1563, when he was twenty-three years
old.

Googe's practice emerged from an intensively rhetori-
cal education, from a study of the best fifteenth-century
English poetry, and more immediately from the better
work in *Tottel's Miscellany*. He is a highly sophisticated
poet, whose tactics are quiet but strategic. Like many
others in the Native tradition, Googe has been entombed
in literary history because of an "introduction." In the
eight eclogues which make up nearly half of his book,
Googe "introduces" pastoral poetry into English. The ec-
logues, however, are feeble, perfunctory, and dull; his
finest work is in the briefer forms. An excellent intro-
duction to Googe is Alan Stephens's essay in *The Selected
Poems of Barnabe Googe*.

TEXT:

Eglogs, Epytaphes, and Sonettes, edited by Edward Arber
 (1871).
The Selected Poems of Barnabe Googe, edited by Alan
 Stephens (1961).

AN EPITAPH OF THE DEATH
OF NICHOLAS GRIMALD

Behold this fleeting world, how all things fade,
How every thing doth pass and wear away;
Each state of life, by common course and trade,
Abides no time, but hath a passing day.
For look, as life, that pleasant dame, hath brought
The pleasant years, and days of lustiness,
So death, our foe, consumeth all to naught,
Envying these, with dart doth us oppress;
And that which is the greatest grief of all,
The greedy gripe doth no estate respect,
But where he comes he makes them down to fall;
Ne stays he at the high sharp-witted sect.
For if that wit, or worthy eloquence,
Or learning deep, could move him to forbear,
O Grimald, then thou hadst not yet gone hence
But here had seen full many an aged year,
Ne had the muses lost so fine a flower,
Nor had Minerva wept to leave thee so;
If wisdom might have fled the fatal hour,
Thou hadst not yet been suffered for to go.
A thousand doltish geese we might have spared,
A thousand witless heads death might have found,
And taken them for whom no man had cared,
And laid them low in deep oblivious ground.
But fortune favors fools, as old men say,
And lets them live, and takes the wise away.

Nicholas Grimald: poet, Latin scholar, translator; predecessor to Googe.

gripe: a vulture; also, a slang term for miser or usurer.
sect: a class of persons.

TO DOCTOR BALE

Good agèd Bale, that with thy hoary hairs
Dost yet persist to turn the painful book,
O happy man that hast obtained such years
And leav'st not yet on papers pale to look,
Give over now to beat thy wearied brain,
And rest thy pen that long hath labored sore.
For aged men unfit sure is such pain,
And thee beseems to labor now no more;
But thou I think Don Plato's part will play:
With book in hand to have thy dying day.

TO MASTER EDWARD COBHAM

Old Socrates, whose wisdom did excel,
And passed the reach of wisest in his time,
Surmounted all that on the earth did dwell,
That craggy hills of virtue high did climb—
That Socrates, my Cobham, did allow
Each man in youth himself in glass to view,
And willed them oft to use the same—but how?
Not to delight in form of fading hue,
Nor to be proud thereof, as many be,
But for to strive by beauty of the mind
For to adorn the beauty he doth see.
If warlike form Dame Nature him assigned,
By virtuous life then countenance for to get
That shall deface the fairest of them all,
Such beauty as no age nor years will fret,
That flies with fame when fickle form doth fail.

Bale: John Bale (1495–1563), Bishop of Ossory, playwright, antiquary, historian of English literature, and Protestant polemicist.
painful: painstaking.

sore: strenuously.
Cobham: a brother of Henry Cobham, one of Queen Elizabeth's diplomats.
allow: sanction.

Thus much I say that here to thee present
My words, a glass for thee to look upon,
To thee whom God in tender years hath lent
A towardness that may be mused upon—
Such towardness as in more graver years
Doth sure a hope of greater things pretend.
Thy noble mind that to thy friends appears
Doth show the blood whereof thou dost descend;
The gentleness thou us'st unto all such
As smally have deserved good will of thee
Doth show the grace thou hast, that sure is much
As ever yet in any I did see.
Thy wit, as ripe as Nature well can give,
Declares a greater hope than all the rest
That shall remain to thee whilst thou dost live,
In desperate ills a medicine ever prest.
Thy good behavior of thyself in place
Wheresoever that thou chancest for to light,
So much both beauty, mind and wit doth grace
As well can be required of any wight.
What resteth now? But only God to praise
Of whom thou hast received these gifts of thine.
So shalt thou long live here with happy days,
And after death the starry skies shall climb.
Let naughty men say what they list to thee,
Trade thou thyself in serving Him above.
No sweeter service can devisëd be,
Whom if thou fear'st, and faithfully dost love,
Be sure no thing on earth shall thee annoy;
Be sure he will thee from each harm defend;
Be sure thou shalt long time thy life enjoy,
And after many years to have a blessëd end.

towardness: aptness, talent.   *resteth:* remains.
pretend: portend.   *naughty:* wicked.
prest: ready.   *trade:* school, exercise.
wight: person.

TO ALEXANDER NEVILLE

The little fish that in the stream doth fleet
With broad forth-stretchëd fins for his disport,
Whenas he spies the fish's bait so sweet,
In haste he hies, fearing to come too short;
But all too soon, alas, his greedy mind
By rash attempt doth bring him to his bane,
For where he thought a great relief to find,
By hidden hook the simple fool is ta'en.
So fareth man, that wanders here and there,
Thinking no hurt to happen him thereby;
He runs amain to gaze on beauty's cheer,
Takes all for gold that glisters in the eye,
And never leaves to feed by looking long
On beauty's bait, where bondage lies enwrapt,
Bondage that makes him sing another song,
And makes him curse the bait that him entrapped.
Neville, to thee that lovest their wanton looks:
Feed on the bait, but yet beware the hooks.

TO THE TRANSLATION OF PALINGENIUS

The labor sweet that I sustained in thee,
O Palingen, when I took pen in hand,
Doth grieve me now as oft as I thee see
But half hewed out before mine eyes to stand,
For I must needs (no help) a while go toil
In studies that no kind of muse delight,
And put my plow in gross untillëd soil
And labor thus with overwearied sprite;

Alexander Neville: (1544–
1614)—His translation of
Seneca's *Oedipus* appeared
in 1563.
fleet: swim.
Palingenius: Pietro Angelo

Manzolli, who wrote, un-
der the name "Marcellus
Palingenius," an anti-Roman
Catholic diatribe, *The Zo-
diac of Life*, which Googe
translated.

But if that God do grant me greater years
And take me not from hence before my time,
The muses nine, the pleasant singing feres,
Shall so inflame my mind with lust to rhyme
That, Palingen, I will not leave thee so,
But finish thee according to my mind.
And if it be my chance away to go,
Let some thee end that here remain behind.

OUT OF SIGHT, OUT OF MIND

The oftener seen, the more I lust,
The more I lust, the more I smart,
The more I smart, the more I trust,
The more I trust, the heavier heart,
The heavy heart breeds mine unrest;
Thy absence therefore like I best.

The rarer seen, the less in mind,
The less in mind, the lesser pain,
The lesser pain, less grief I find,
The lesser grief, the greater gain,
The greater gain, the merrier I;
Therefore I wish thy sight to fly.

The further off, the more I joy,
The more I joy, the happier life,
The happier life, less hurts annoy,
The lesser hurts, pleasure most rife;
Such pleasures rife shall I obtain
When distance doth depart us twain.

depart: separate.

A REFUSAL

Sith fortune favors not and all things backward go,
And sith your mind hath so decreed to make an end of
 woe,
Sith now is no redress, but hence I must away,
Farewell. I waste no vainer words. I hope for better day.

OF MISTRESS D.S.

Thy filëd words that from thy mouth did flow,
Thy modest look, with gesture of Diane,
Thy courteous mind, and all things framëd so
As answered well unto thy virtuous fame,
The gentleness that at thy hands I found
In stranger's house, all unacquainted I,
Good S—— hath my heart to thee so bound
That from thee can it not be forced to fly;
In pledge whereof, my service here I give,
If thou so wilt, to serve thee whilst I live.

OF MONEY

Give money me, take friendship whoso list,
For friends are gone come once adversity,
When moncy yet remaineth safe in chest,
That quickly can thee bring from misery;
Fair face show friends when riches do abound;
Come time of proof, farewell, they must away;
Believe me well, they are not to be found
If God but send thee once a lowering day.
Gold never starts aside, but in distress,
Finds ways enough to ease thine heaviness.

filëd words: a stock phrase for   *framëd:* disposed.
 smooth, neat language.

GOING TOWARDS SPAIN

Farewell, thou fertile soil that Brutus first out found
When he, poor soul, was driven clean from out his coun-
  try ground,
That northward lay'st thy lusty sides amid the raging seas,
Whose wealthy land doth foster up thy people all in ease,
While others scrape and cark abroad their simple food to
  get,
And silly souls take all for good that cometh to the net
Which they with painful pains do pinch in barren burn-
  ing realms,
While we have all without restraint among thy wealthy
  streams;
O blest of God, thou pleasant isle where wealth herself
  doth dwell,
Wherein my tender years I passed, I bid thee now farewell.
For fancy drives me forth abroad, and bids me take delight
In leaving thee and ranging far to see some stranger sight.
And, faith, I was not framëd here to live at home with
  ease,
But, passing forth for knowledge sake, to cut the foaming
  seas.

COMING HOMEWARD OUT OF SPAIN

O raging seas and mighty Neptune's reign
In monstrous hills that throwest thyself so high,
That with thy floods dost beat the shores of Spain,
And break the cliffs that dare thy force envy—

Brutus: legendary Trojan, de-
scendant of Aeneas, sup-
posed to have founded Lon-
don and become Britain's
first king.
lusty: massive.

cark: labor anxiously.
silly: unsophisticated, and, in
this instance, therefore de-
serving of compassion.
framëd: formed.

Cease now thy rage, and lay thine ire aside;
And thou that hast the governance of all,
O mighty God, grant weather, wind, and tide,
Till on my country coast our anchor fall.

GEORGE TURBERVILLE: 1540?–95?

Born in Dorsetshire, Turberville attended New College, Oxford. In London he resided in one of the Inns of Court; he became a secretary to the ambassador to Russia, and traveled to that country in 1568. In 1575 he acquired some property in Dorset, where he retired from public life.

Like Googe, Turberville began his literary career as a young man; in 1567, when he was in his middle twenties, he published three books, two of them translations of Ovid and Mantuanus, and the other his own *Epitaphs, Epigrams, Songs, and Sonnets*. As the title of this volume might indicate, Turberville was rather strongly influenced by Barnabe Googe, whose volume had appeared four years earlier. His work is, however, more minor in conception than that of Googe; his themes are most frequently very small, his poems minute and perfectly surfaced. His best poems are either witty or ironic or both; partly because of the perfection of their execution and the smallness of their themes, they remind one of the later Madrigalists, though the language and feeling of Turberville have a Native dryness unlike that of the later poets.

TEXT:

Epitaphs, Epigrams, Songs, and Sonnets, edited by J. P. Collier (1869).

TO THE ROVING PIRATE

Thou winst thy wealth by war,
   ungodly way to gain,
And in an hour, thy ship is sunk,
   goods drowned, the pirate slain.

The gun is all thy trust;
   it serves thy cruel foe;
Then brag not on thy cannon shot
   as though there were no mo.

TO ONE THAT HAD LITTLE WIT

I thee advise
If thou be wise
To keep thy wit
Though it be small:
'Tis rare to get
And far to fet,
'Twas ever yit
Dearest ware of all.

OF THE CLOCK AND THE COCK

Good reason thou allow
   one letter more to me
Than to the cock: for cocks do sleep
   when clocks do wake for thee.

fet: fetch.

THE LOVER EXHORTETH HIS
LADY TO TAKE TIME, WHILE TIME IS

Though brave your beauty be, and feature passing fair,
Such as Apelles to depaint might utterly despair,

Yet drowsy drooping Age, encroaching on apace,
With pensive plough will raze your hue, and Beauty's
    beams deface.

Wherefore in tender years how crooked Age doth haste
Revoke to mind, so shall you not your time consume in
    waste.

Whilst that you may, and youth in you is fresh and green,
Delight your self: for years do flit as fickle floods are seen;

For water slippëd by may not be called again,
And to revoke forepassëd hours were labor lost in vain.

Take time whilst time applies; with nimble foot it goes;
Nor to compare with passëd prime thy after age suppose.

The holts that now are hoar, both bud and bloom I saw;
I wore a garland of the briar that puts me now in awe.

The time will be when thou that dost thy friends defy
A cold and crooked beldam shalt in loathsome cabin lie;

Nor with such nightly brawls thy postern gate shall sound,
Nor roses strewn afront thy door in dawning shall be
    found.

brave: fine.   dance.
holts: woods.   *postern gate:* side entrance.
brawls: clamors; or, a type of

How soon are corpses, Lord, with filthy furrows filled?
How quickly Beauty, brave of late, and seemly shape is
        spilled?

Even thou that from thy youth to have been so, wilt
        swear;
With turn of hand in, all thy head shalt have gray pow-
        dered hair.

The snakes with shifted skins their loathsome age do way;
The buck doth hang his head on pale to live a longer day.

Your good without recure doth pass; receive the flower
Which if you pluck not from the stalk, will fall within
        this hour.

TO HIS LOVE, THAT SENT HIM A RING WHEREIN WAS GRAVED, "LET REASON RULE"

Shall Reason rule where Reason hath no right
Nor never had? shall Cupid lose his lands?
His claim? his crown? his kingdom? name of might?
No, Friend, thy ring doth will me thus in vain;
Reason and Love have ever yet been twain.

They are by kind of such contrary mold,
As one mislikes the other's lewd device:
What Reason wills Cupido never would;
Love never yet thought Reason to be wise.
To Cupid I my homage erst have done;
Let Reason rule the hearts that she hath won.

---

spilled: undone, ruined.   *by kind:* by nature.
way: send off.   *lewd:* plain, common.
hang his head: shed his horns.

THAT ALL THINGS ARE AS THEY ARE USED

Was never aught by Nature's art
    Or cunning skill so wisely wrought,
But Man by practice might convart
    To worser use than Nature thought.

Ne yet was ever thing so ill
    Or may be of so small a price,
But man may better it by skill,
    And change his sort by sound advice.

So that, by proof, it may be seen
    That all things are as is their use,
And man may alter Nature clean,
    And things corrupt by his abuse.

What better may be found than flame
    To Nature that doth succor pay?
Yet we do oft abuse the same
    In bringing buildings to decay.

For those that mind to put in use
    Their malice, moved to wrath and ire
To wreak their mischief, will be sure
    To spill and spoil thy house with fire.

So physic, that doth serve for ease,
    And to recure the grievëd soul,
The painful patient may disease
    And make him sick that erst was whole.

The true man and the thief are leeke,
    For sword doth serve them both, at need;
Save one by it doth safety seek
    And th' other of the spoil to speed.

leeke: likc.

As law and learning doth redress
　　That otherwise would go to wrack,
Even so it doth oft times oppress
　　And bring the true man to the rack.

Though poison pain the drinker sore
　　By boiling in his fainting breast,
Yet is it not refused therefore,
　　For cause sometime it breedeth rest,

And mixed with medicines of proof
　　According to Machaeon's art
Doth serve right well for our behoof
　　And succor sends to dying heart.

Yet these and other things were made
　　By Nature for the better use,
But we of custom take a trade
　　By wilful will them to abuse.

So nothing is by kind so void
　　Of vice, and with such virtue fraught,
But it by us may be annoyed,
　　And brought in tract of time to naught.

Again, there is not that so ill
　　Below the lamp of Phoebus' light,
But Man may better, if he will
　　Apply his wit to make it right.

Machaeon: son of Aesculapius,　　in the Trojan War.
　　and surgeon to the Greeks

TO AN OLD GENTLEWOMAN,
WHO PAINTED HER FACE

Leave off, good Beroe, now,
   to sleek thy shrivelled skin;
For Hecuba's face will never be
   as Helen's hue hath been.

Let beauty go with youth,
   renounce the glozing glass,
Take book in hand: that seemly rose
   is woxen withered grass.

Remove thy peacock's plumes,
   thou crank and curious dame:
To other trulls of tender years
   resign the flag of fame.

OF A RICH MISER

A miser's mind thou hast,
   thou hast a prince's pelf:
Which makes thee wealthy to thine heir,
   a beggar to thy self.

glozing: glossing; in this in-
   stance, flattering.

crank: lively, brisk, lusty.
trulls: trollops.

THAT NO MAN SHOULD WRITE
BUT SUCH AS DO EXCEL

Should no man write, say you, but such as do excel?
This fond device of yours deserves a Bable and a Bell;

Then one alone should do, or very few indeed:
For that in every Art there can but one alone exceed.

Should others idle be, and waste their age in vain,
That might perhaps in after time the prick and price
        attain?

By practice skill is got, by practice wit is won.
At games you see how many do to win the wager run.

Yet one among the moe doth bear away the Bell:
Is that a cause to say the rest, in running, did not well?

If none in physic should but only Galen deal,
No doubt a thousand perish would whom Physic now doth
        heal.

Each one his talent hath, to use at his devise,
Which makes that many men as well as one are counted
        wise.

For if that wit alone in one should rest and reign,
Then God the skulls of other men did make but all in
        vain.

Let each one try his force, and do the best he can,
For thereunto appointed were the hand and head of man.

Bable: mock-scepter carried by   *the prick*: the target (in arch-
    the Fool.   ery).
Bell: prize; also, part of Fool's   *price*: praise, honor.
    standard equipment.   *moe*: rest, others.

The poet Horace speaks against thy reason plain
Who says, 'tis somewhat to attempt, although thou not
      attain

The scope in every thing: to touch the highest degree
Is passing hard; to do the best, sufficing is for thee.

SIR EDWARD DYER: 1543–1607

Born in Somersetshire, Dyer probably attended Oxford. For most of his life, until the death of Queen Elizabeth, Dyer held minor posts at court; he was knighted in 1596. Dyer's life was spent quietly, and relatively few details of that life are known; he was a friend of Sidney and Greville, and in his own time he was well known as a poet. But only a handful of his poems have come down to us.

Though a friend of Sidney and Greville, he was eleven years older than either of them, and his poetry more purely represents the older tradition, with only a few awkward traces of the Italianate influence that marks all of Sidney's verse and some of Greville's. The fine elegy on Sidney may or may not be Dyer's; it has, and with some reason, been attributed to Greville. It is attributed here to Dyer only because Dyer's editor included it in the body of Dyer's work; the issue of its authorship is likely to remain unsettled.

TEXT:

At the Court of Queen Elizabeth: The Life and Lyrics of Sir Edward Dyer, edited by Ralph M. Sargent (1935).
"New Poems by Sir Edward Dyer," by B. M. Wagner, *Review of English Studies* (October, 1935).

FANCY, FAREWELL

Fancy, farewell, that fed my fond delight;
  Delight, adieu, the cause of my distress;
Distress, adieu, that dost me such despite;
  Despite, adieu, for death doth lend redress.

And death, adieu, for though I thus be slain,
    In thy despite I hope to live again.

Sweet heart, farewell. whose love hath wrought my woe;
    And farewell, woe, that wearied hast my wits;
And farewell, wit, which will bewitchëd so;
    And farewell, will, O full of frantic fits.
Franzy, farewell, whose force I feel too sore,
    And farewell, feeling, for I feel no more.

And life, adieu, that I have lived and loathed,
    And farewell, love, that makest me loathe my life;
Both love and life, farewell unto you both;
    Twixt hope and dread, farewell, all foolish strife.
Folly, farewell, which I have fancied so,
    And farewell, fancy, that first wrought my woe.

THE LOWEST TREES HAVE TOPS

The lowest trees have tops, the ant her gall,
The fly her spleen, the little spark his heat;
The slender hairs cast shadows, though but small,
And bees have stings, although they be not great;
    Seas have their source, and so have shallow springs:
    And love is love, in beggars and in kings.

Where waters smoothest run, there deepest are the fords;
The dial stirs, yet none perceives it move;
The firmest faith is found in fewest words;
The turtles do not sing, and yet they love;
    True hearts have ears and eyes, no tongues to speak:
    They hear and see, and sigh, and then they break.

turtles: i.e., turtledoves.

ELEGY ON THE DEATH OF SIDNEY

Silence augmenteth grief, writing increaseth rage,
Staled are my thoughts, which loved and lost the wonder
    of our age;
Yet quickened now with fire, though dead with frost ere
    now,
Enraged I write I know not what; dead, quick, I know not
    how.

Hard-hearted minds relent and rigor's tears abound,
And envy strangely rues his end, in whom no fault was
    found.
Knowledge her light hath lost, valor hath slain her knight,
Sidney is dead, dead is my friend, dead is the world's
    delight.

Place, pensive, wails his fall whose presence was her pride;
Time crieth out, My ebb is come; his life was my spring
    tide.
Fame mourns in that she lost the ground of her reports;
Each living wight laments his lack, and all in sundry sorts.

He was—woe worth that word!—to each well-thinking mind
A spotless friend, a matchless man, whose virtue ever
    shined;
Declaring in his thoughts, his life and that he writ,
Highest conceits, longest foresights, and deepest works of
    wit.

He, only like himself, was second unto none,
Whose death, though life, we rue and wrong, and all in
    vain do moan;
Their loss, not him, wail they that fill the world with cries;
Death slew not him, but he made death his ladder to the
    skies.

Now sink of sorrow I who live—the more the wrong!
Who wishing death, whom death denies, whose thread is
    all too long;
Who tied to wretched life, who looks for no relief,
Must spend my ever dying days in never ending grief.

Heart's ease and only I, like parallels, run on,
Whose equal length keep equal breadth and never meet
    in one;
Yet for not wronging him, my thoughts, my sorrow's cell,
Shall not run out, though leak they will for liking him so
    well.

Farewell to you, my hopes, my wonted waking dreams;
Farewell, sometimes enjoyed joy, eclipsëd are thy beams;
Farewell, self-pleasing thoughts which quietness brings
    forth;
And farewell, friendship's sacred league, uniting minds
    of worth.

And farewell, merry heart, the gift of guiltless minds,
And all sports which for life's restore variety assigns.
Let all that sweet is, void; in me no mirth may dwell:
Philip, the cause of all this woe, my life's content, fare-
    well!

Now rime, the son of rage, which art no kin to skill,
And endless grief, which deads my life, yet knows not
    how to kill,
Go seek that hapless tomb, which if ye hap to find,
Salute the stones that keep the limbs that held so good
    a mind.

MY MIND TO ME A KINGDOM IS

1

My mind to me a kingdom is;
Such perfect joy therein I find
That it excels all other bliss
That world affords or grows by kind:
    Though much I want which most would have,
    Yet still my mind forbids to crave.

2

No princely pomp, no wealthy store,
No force to win the victory,
No wily wit to salve a sore,
No shape to feed a loving eye—
    To none of these I yield as thrall.
    For why? My mind doth serve for all.

3

I see how plenty suffers oft
And hasty climbers soon do fall;
I see that those which are aloft
Mishap doth threaten most of all.
    They get with toil, they keep with fear;
    Such cares my mind could never bear.

4

Content I live, this is my stay:
I seek no more than may suffice,
I press to bear no haughty sway;
Look, what I lack my mind supplies.
   Lo, thus I triumph like a king,
    Content with that my mind doth bring.

5

Some have too much, yet still do crave;
I little have, and seek no more:
They are but poor, though much they have,
And I am rich with little store.
   They poor, I rich; they beg, I give;
    They lack, I leave; they pine, I live.

6

I laugh not at another's loss,
I grudge not at another's gain;
No worldly waves my mind can toss,
My state at one doth still remain.
   I fear no foe, I fawn no friend;
    I loathe not life, nor dread not end.

7

Some weigh their pleasure by their lust,
Their wisdom by their rage of will;
Their treasure is their only trust,
A cloakèd craft their store of skill.
   But all the pleasure that I find
    Is to maintain a quiet mind.

8

My wealth is health and perfect ease,
My conscience clear my chief defense;
I neither seek by bribes to please,
Nor by desert to breed offense.
  Thus do I live, thus will I die;
  Would all did so as well as I!

SIR WALTER RALEGH: 1552?–1618

Ralegh's career was a turbulent one. He was educated at
Oriel College, Oxford; and since his father was an un-
distinguished country gentleman, he had no ready entrance
into the world of affairs; yet by the time he was thirty,
after having fought as a soldier in the French wars of re-
ligion and in the Irish campaign, he was a favorite in the
court of Queen Elizabeth. For the rest of his life he was
in the thick of the political intrigue that animated the
court of Elizabeth; he explored Guiana, led a successful
expedition against Cadiz, was part of the government ap-
proved piracy against Spanish treasure ships—and after
Elizabeth's death, in the struggle for power that came with
the succession, he was imprisoned and brought to trial
upon the charge that he had conspired with Spain to bring
England under a Roman Catholic monarchy. The trial was
a mockery of justice. Condemned to death, he was spared
three days before the date set for his execution. He spent
the next thirteen years in prison, during which time he
began the *History of the World*, a work that was to account
for the events from the Creation to his own day. He was
released from prison in 1616 so that he could lead an
expedition to Guiana; but the conditions of his release
were impossible. He was ordered to plunder Guiana, then
Spanish territory, without giving offense to the Spaniards.
The expedition was a dismal failure; Ralegh returned to
England in 1618, and was beheaded the same year on the
old charge of conspiracy with the Spanish. He met his
death with great dignity, and won the sympathy of the
populace.

Ralegh was known to his contemporaries as one of the
best poets of his day; but few of his poems were published

in his lifetime, and he left no manuscript to be printed after his death. The most laborious scholarship has turned up only a most incomplete representation of his total work. Yet the poems we have show Ralegh to be a poet of considerable stature. In poetry as in life he went his own way. He was unaffected by the fashionable Petrarchism; he spoke directly and forcefully; and like the earlier Native poets, with whom he must be counted, he tended to speak personally and individually. Laconic, bitter, and defiant, his voice is one that strangely intimates the enigmatic loneliness of his life.

TEXT:

The Poems of Sir Walter Ralegh, edited by Agnes M. C. Latham (1951).

FAREWELL TO THE COURT

Like truthless dreams, so are my joys expired,
And past return are all my dandled days,
My love misled, and fancy quite retired:
Of all which past, the sorrow only stays.

My lost delights, now clean from sight of land,
Have left me all alone in unknown ways,
My mind to woe, my life in Fortune's hand:
Of all which past, the sorrow only stays.

As in a country strange without companion,
I only wail the wrong of death's delays,
Whose sweet spring spent, whose summer well nigh done;
Of all which past, the sorrow only stays:

Whom care forewarns, ere age and winter cold,
To haste me hence to find my fortune's fold.

CONCEIT BEGOTTEN BY THE EYES

Conceit begotten by the eyes
Is quickly born and quickly dies;
For while it seeks our hearts to have,
Meanwhile, there reason makes his grave;
For many things the eyes approve,
Which yet the heart doth seldom love.

For as the seeds in springtime sown
Die in the ground ere they be grown,
Such is conceit, whose rooting fails,
As child that in the cradle quails,
Or else within the mother's womb
Hath his beginning and his tomb.

Affection follows Fortune's wheels,
And soon is shaken from her heels;
For, following beauty or estate,
Her liking still is turned to hate;
For all affections have their change,
And fancy only loves to range.

Desire himself runs out of breath,
And, getting, doth but gain his death:
Desire nor reason hath nor rest,
And, blind, doth seldom choose the best:
Desire attained is not desire,
But as the cinders of the fire.

As ships in ports desired are drowned,
As fruit, once ripe, then falls to ground,
As flies that seek for flames are brought
To cinders by the flames they sought:
So fond desire when it attains,
The life expires, the woe remains.

And yet some poets fain would prove
Affection to be perfect love;
And that desire is of that kind,
No less a passion of the mind;
As if wild beasts and men did seek
To like, to love, to choose alike.

NATURE, THAT WASHED HER HANDS
IN MILK

Nature, that washed her hands in milk
And had forgot to dry them,
Instead of earth took snow and silk
At Love's request, to try them
If she a mistress could compose
To please Love's fancy out of those.

Her eyes he would should be of light,
A violet breath, and lips of jelly,
Her hair not black nor over-bright,
And of the softest down her belly:
As for her inside, he'd have it
Only of wantonness and wit.

At Love's entreaty, such a one
Nature made, but with her beauty
She hath framed a heart of stone,
So as Love, by ill destiny,
Must die for her whom Nature gave him,
Because her darling would not save him.

But Time, which Nature doth despise,
And rudely gives her love the lie,
Makes hope a fool and sorrow wise,
His hands doth neither wash nor dry,
But, being made of steel and rust,
Turns snow and silk and milk to dust.

The light, the belly, lips and breath,
He dims, discolors, and destroys,
With those he feeds (but fills not) Death
Which sometimes were the food of Joys:
Yea, Time doth dull each lively wit,
And dries all wantonness with it.

O cruel Time, which takes in trust
Our youth, our joys, and all we have,
And pays us but with age and dust;
Who in the dark and silent grave,
When we have wandered all our ways,
Shuts up the story of our days.

THE LIE

Go, Soul, the body's guest,
Upon a thankless arrant:
Fear not to touch the best;
The truth shall be thy warrant:
Go, since I needs must die,
And give the world the lie.

Say to the court, it glows
And shines like rotten wood;
Say to the church it shows
What's good, and doth no good:
If church and court reply,
Then give them both the lie.

Tell potentates, they live
Acting by others' action;
Not loved unless they give,
Not strong but by affection:
If potentates reply,
Give potentates the lie.

Tell men of high condition
That manage the estate,
Their purpose is ambition,
Their practice only hate:
And if they once reply,
Then give them all the lie.

Tell them that brave it most
They beg for more by spending,
Who, in their greatest cost,
Seek nothing but commending:
And if they make reply,
Then give them all the lie.

Tell zeal it wants devotion,
Tell love it is but lust;
Tell time it metes but motion,
Tell flesh it is but dust:
And wish them not reply,
For thou must give the lie.

Tell age it daily wasteth;
Tell honor how it alters;
Tell beauty how she blasteth;
Tell favor how it falters:
And as they shall reply,
Give every one the lie.

Tell wit how much it wrangles
In tickle points of niceness;
Tell wisdom she entangles
Herself in over-wiseness:
And when they do reply,
Straight give them both the lie.

Tell physic of her boldness;
Tell skill it is pretension;
Tell charity of coldness;
Tell law it is contention:

And as they do reply,
So give them still the lie.

Tell fortune of her blindness;
Tell nature of decay;
Tell friendship of unkindness;
Tell justice of delay:
And if they will reply,
Then give them all the lie.

Tell arts they have no soundness,
But vary by esteeming;
Tell schools they want profoundness,
And stand too much on seeming:
If arts and schools reply,
Give arts and schools the lie.

Tell faith it's fled the city;
Tell how the country erreth;
Tell manhood shakes off pity
And virtue least preferreth:
And if they do reply,
Spare not to give the lie.

So when thou hast, as I
Commanded thee, done blabbing
—Although to give the lie
Deserves no less than stabbing—
Stab at thee he that will,
No stab thy soul can kill.

ON THE CARDS AND DICE

Before the sixth day of the next new year,
Strange wonders in this kingdom shall appear.
Four kings shall be assembled in this isle,
Where they shall keep great tumult for a while.

Many men then shall have an end of crosses,
And many likewise shall sustain great losses.
Many that now full joyful are and glad,
Shall at that time be sorrowful and sad.
Full many a Christian's heart shall quake for fear,
The dreadful sound of trump when he shall hear.
Dead bones shall then be tumbled up and down,
In every city and in every town.
By day or night this tumult shall not cease,
Until an herald shall proclaim a peace,
An herald strange, the like was never born
Whose very beard is flesh, and mouth is horn.

SIR WALTER RALEGH TO HIS SON

Three things there be that prosper up apace
And flourish, whilst they grow asunder far;
But on a day, they meet all in one place,
And when they meet, they one another mar.
And they be these: the wood, the weed, the wag.
The wood is that which makes the gallow tree;
The weed is that which strings the hangman's bag;
The wag, my pretty knave, betokeneth thee.
Mark well, dear boy, whilst these assemble not,
Green springs the tree, hemp grows, the wag is wild;
But when they meet, it makes the timber rot,
It frets the halter, and it chokes the child.
　Then bless thee, and beware, and let us pray
　We part not with thee at this meeting day.

THE PASSIONATE MAN'S PILGRIMAGE

Give me my scallop-shell of quiet,
My staff of faith to walk upon,
My scrip of joy, immortal diet,
My bottle of salvatión,
My gown of glory, hope's true gage:
And thus I'll take my pilgrimage.

Blood must be my body's balmer;
No other balm will there be given,
Whilst my soul, like a white palmer,
Travels to the land of heaven,
Over the silver mountains
Where spring the nectar fountains.
And there I'll kiss
The bowl of bliss,
And drink my eternal fill
On every milken hill.
My soul will be a-dry before,
But after it will ne'er thirst more.

And by the happy blissful way
More peaceful pilgrims I shall see
That have shook off their gowns of clay
And go apparelled fresh like me.
I'll bring them first
To slake their thirst
And then to taste those nectar suckets
At the clear wells
Where sweetness dwells,
Drawn up by saints in crystal buckets.

And when our bottles and all we
Are filled with immortality,
Then the holy paths we'll travel,
Strewed with rubies thick as gravel;
Ceilings of diamonds, sapphire floors,
High walls of coral and pearly bowers.

From thence to heaven's bribeless hall,
Where no corrupted voices brawl,
No conscience molten into gold,
No forged accusers bought and sold,
No cause deferred, no vain-spent journey—
For there Christ is the King's Attorney,

Who pleads for all without degrees,
And He hath angels, but no fees.

When the grand twelve million jury
Of our sins and sinful fury
'Gainst our souls black verdicts give,
Christ pleads His death, and then we live,
Be Thou my speaker, taintless pleader,
Unblotted lawyer, true proceeder!
Thou movest salvation even for alms,
Not with a bribëd lawyer's palms.

And this is my eternal plea
To Him that made heaven, earth, and sea:
Seeing my flesh must die so soon
And want a head to dine next noon,
Just at the stroke, when my veins start and spread,
Set on my soul an everlasting head!
Then am I ready, like a palmer fit,
To tread those blest paths which before I writ.

WHAT IS OUR LIFE?

What is our life? A play of passion,
Our mirth the music of division;
Our mothers' wombs the tiring houses be,
Where we are dressed for this short comedy;
Heaven the judicious sharp spectator is
That sits and marks still who doth act amiss;
Our graves that hide us from the searching sun
Are like drawn curtains when the play is done.
Thus march we playing to our latest rest—
Only we die in earnest, that's no jest.

angels: lit., small coins; this is
a frequently found pun.

EVEN SUCH IS TIME

Even such is time, which takes in trust
Our youth, our joys, and all we have,
And pays us but with age and dust;
Who, in the dark and silent grave,
When we have wandered all our ways,
Shuts up the story of our days,
And from which earth and grave and dust,
The Lord shall raise me up, I trust.

EPITAPH ON THE EARL OF LEICESTER

Here lies the noble Warrior that never blunted sword;
Here lies the noble Courtier that never kept his word;
Here lies his Excellency that governed all the state;
Here lies the Lord of Leicester that all the world did hate.

LINES FROM CATULLUS

The sun may set and rise;
But we, contrariwise,
Sleep after our short light
One everlasting night.

EDMUND SPENSER: 1552–99

Spenser left Cambridge in 1578 to become secretary to the Bishop of Rochester; the following year he went into the service of Robert Dudley, Earl of Leicester; and in 1580 he became secretary to Lord Grey, Lord Deputy of Ireland. Though he made frequent visits to London, he remained in the Irish civil service for the rest of his life.

Spenser set out to make himself the best known poet in England, and he succeeded. Even before he entered Cambridge, he had translated Petrarch and du Bellay; and he worked largely within the forms and from the points of view that were most fashionable in his day. A thorough-going Petrarchist, he had a somewhat sentimental concern for the English language which manifested itself in a frequently inaccurate archaic diction; he was ardently nationalistic; and he acceded to the easy idealism of Renaissance neo-Platonism. His most famous work is, of course, *The Faerie Queen*, which is almost a monument to Petrarchan method. Highly elaborate, eloquent, repetitive, it is at once a medieval romance, an epic, and an allegory; yet its medievalism is fictitious and gothic, it has none of the brute power of the epic, and its allegory is unsure and inconsistent. The most persistent principle of its structure is its rhetoric, which is probably a principle insufficient to sustain a poem of nearly thirty-five thousand lines. Spenser's best poems are his two marriage poems; in these, the elaborate, formal, almost ritualistic rhetoric and syntax are used to meaningful advantage. And though both poems are overdecorated, the decoration is beautiful and often moving.

TEXT: *The Works of Edmund Spenser, A Variorum Edition*, edited by Edwin Greenlaw, et. al. *The Minor Poems*, vol. 2, edited by Charles G. Osgood and Henry G. Lotspeich (1947).

EPITHALAMION

Ye learnèd sisters, which have oftentimes
Been to me aiding, others to adorn,
Whom ye thought worthy of your graceful rimes,
That even the greatest did not greatly scorn
To hear their names sung in your simple lays,
But joyed in their praise;
And when ye list your own mishaps to mourn,
Which death, or love, or fortune's wreck did raise,
Your string could soon to sadder tenor turn,
And teach the woods and waters to lament
Your doleful dreariment.
Now lay those sorrowful complaints aside,
And having all your heads with garland crowned,
Help me mine own love's praises to resound,
Ne let the same of any be envíed:
So Orpheus did for his own bride,
So I unto my self alone will sing—
The woods shall to me answer, and my Echo ring.

Early, before the world's light-giving lamp
His golden beam upon the hills doth spread,
Having dispersed the night's uncheerful damp,
Do ye awake, and with fresh lustyhead,
Go to the bower of my belovèd love,
My truest turtle dove:
Bid her awake, for Hymen is awake,
And long since ready forth his mask to move,
With his bright tead that flames with many a flake,
And many a bachelor to wait on him,
In their fresh garments trim.
Bid her awake, therefore, and soon her dight,
For lo! the wishèd day is come at last,
That shall for all the pains and sorrows past,

learnèd sisters: the Muses of   *tead*: torch.
  poetry.   *dight*: dress.

Pay to her usury of long delight:
And whilst she doth her dight,
Do ye to her of joy and solace sing,
That all the woods may answer, and your echo ring.

Bring with you all the nymphs that you can hear,
Both of the rivers and the forests green,
And of the sea that neighbors to her near,
All with gay garlands goodly well beseen.
And let them also with them bring in hand
Another gay garlánd
For my fair love, of lilies and of roses,
Bound truelove-wise with a blue silk riband.
And let them make great store of bridal posies,
And let them eke bring store of other flowers
To deck the bridal bowers.
And let the ground whereas her foot shall tread,
For fear the stones her tender foot should wrong,
Be strewed with fragrant flowers all along,
And diapered like the discolorëd mead.
Which done, do at her chamber door await,
For she will waken straight;
The whiles do ye this song unto her sing,
The woods shall to you answer, and your echo ring.

Ye nymphs of Mulla, which with careful heed
The silver scaly trouts do tend full well,
And greedy pikes which use therein to feed,
(Those trouts and pikes all others do excel)
And ye likewise which keep the rushy lake,
Where none do fishes take,
Bind up the locks the which hang scattered light,
And in his waters, which your mirror make,
Behold your faces as the crystal bright,
That when you come whereas my love doth lie,
No blemish she may spy.
And eke ye lightfoot maids which keep the deer
That on the hoary mountain use to tower,
And the wild wolves, which seek them to devour,

With your steel darts do chase from coming near,
Be also present here
To help to deck her, and to help to sing,
That all the woods may answer, and your echo ring.

Wake now, my love, awake! for it is time:
The rosy Morn long since left Tithones' bed,
All ready to her silver coach to climb,
And Phoebus 'gins to show his glorious head.
Hark, how the cheerful birds do chant their lays,
And carol of love's praise!
The merry lark her matins sings aloft,
The thrush replies, the mavis descant plays,
The ousel shrills, the ruddock warbles soft,
So goodly all agree, with sweet consent,
To this day's merriment.
Ah! my dear love, why do ye sleep thus long,
When meeter were that ye should now awake,
To wait the coming of your joyous make,
And hearken to the birds' love-learnèd song,
The dewy leaves among?
For they of joy and pleasance to you sing,
That all the woods them answer, and their echo ring.

My love is now awake out of her dreams,
And her fair eyes, like stars that dimmèd were
With darksome cloud, now show their goodly beams
More bright than Hesperus his head doth rear.
Come now, ye damsels, daughters of delight,
Help quickly her to dight.
But first come ye, fair Hours, which were begot
In Jove's sweet paradise, of Day and Night,
Which do the seasons of the year allot,

Tithones: Tithonus, a mortal loved by the goddess of dawn, who was given immortality but not eternal youth, so that his immortality is spent in a state of senility.
mavis: a song thrush.
ruddock: robin redbreast.
Hours: i.e., the daughters of Jove.

And all that ever in this world is fair
Do make and still repair.
And ye three handmaids of the Cyprian Queen,
The which do still adorn her beauty's pride,
Help to adorn my beautifulest bride:
And as ye her array, still throw between
Some graces to be seen;
And as ye use to Venus, to her sing,
The whiles the woods shall answer, and your echo ring.

Now is my love all ready forth to come.
Let all the virgins therefore well await,
And ye fresh boys, that tend upon her groom,
Prepare your selves, for he is coming straight.
Set all your things in seemly good array,
Fit for so joyful day,
The joyfulst day that ever sun did see.
Fair Sun, show forth thy favorable ray,
And let thy lifeful heat not fervent be,
For fear of burning her sunshiny face,
Her beauty to disgrace.
O fairest Phoebus, father of the Muse,
If ever I did honor thee aright,
Or sing the thing that mote thy mind delight,
Do not thy servant's simple boon refuse,
But let this day, let this one day be mine,
Let all the rest be thine.
Then I thy sovereign praises loud will sing,
That all the woods shall answer, and their echo ring.

Hark how the minstrels 'gin to shrill aloud
Their merry music that resounds from far,
The pipe, the tabor, and the trembling croud,
That well agree withouten breach or jar.
But most of all the damsels do delight
When they their timbrels smite,

Cyprian Queen: Venus.   *croud:* violin.

And thereunto do dance and carol sweet,
That all the senses they do ravish quite,
The whiles the boys run up and down the street,
Crying aloud with strong confusëd noise,
As if it were one voice.
"Hymen, io Hymen, Hymen," they do shout,
That even to the heavens their shouting shrill
Doth reach, and all the firmament doth fill;
To which the people, standing all about,
As in approvance do thereto applaud,
And loud advance her laud,
And evermore they "Hymen, Hymen!" sing,
That all the woods them answer, and their echo ring.

Lo! where she comes along with portly pace,
Like Phoebe from her chamber of the east,
Arising forth to run her mighty race,
Clad all in white, that seems a virgin best.
So well it her beseems, that ye would ween
Some angel she had been.
Her long loose yellow locks like golden wire,
Sprinkled with pearl, and pearling flowers atween,
Do like a golden mantle her attire,
And being crownëd with a garland green,
Seem like some maiden queen.
Her modest eyes, abashëd to behold
So many gazers as on her do stare,
Upon the lowly ground affixëd are;
Ne dare lift up her countenance too bold,
But blush to hear her praises sung so loud,
So far from being proud.
Nathless do ye still loud her praises sing,
That all the woods may answer, and your echo ring.

Tell me, ye merchants' daughters, did ye see
So fair a creature in your town before,
So sweet, so lovely, and so mild as she,
Adorned with beauty's grace and virtue's store?

Her goodly eyes like sapphires shining bright,
Her forehead ivory white,
Her cheeks like apples which the sun hath ruddied,
Her lips like cherries charming men to bite,
Her breast like to a bowl of cream uncrudded,
Her paps like lilies budded,
Her snowy neck like to a marble tower,
And all her body like a palace fair,
Ascending up, with many a stately stair,
To honor's seat and chastity's sweet bower.
Why stand ye still, ye virgins, in amaze,
Upon her so to gaze,
Whiles ye forget your former lay to sing,
To which the woods did answer, and your echo ring?

But if ye saw that which no eyes can see,
The inward beauty of her lively spright,
Garnished with heavenly gifts of high degree,
Much more then would ye wonder at that sight,
And stand astonished like to those which read
Medusa's mazeful head.
There dwells sweet Love, and constant Chastity,
Unspotted Faith, and comely Womanhood,
Regard of Honor, and mild Modesty;
There Virtue reigns as queen in royal throne,
And giveth laws alone,
The which the base affections do obey
And yield their services unto her will;
Ne thought of thing uncomely ever may
Thereto approach to tempt her mind to ill.
Had ye once seen these, her celestial treasures,
And unrevealëd pleasures,
Then would ye wonder, and her praises sing,
That all the woods should answer, and your echo ring.

Open the temple gates unto my love,
Open them wide that she may enter in,
And all the posts adorn as doth behove,
And all the pillars deck with garlands trim,

spright: spirit.

For to receive this saint with honor due,
That cometh in to you.
With trembling steps and humble reverence,
She cometh in before the Almighty's view;
Of her, ye virgins, learn obedience,
When so ye come into those holy places,
To humble your proud faces.
Bring her up to the high altar, that she may
The sacred ceremonies there partake,
The which do endless matrimony make;
And let the roaring organs loudly play
The praises of the Lord in lively notes,
The whiles with hollow throats
The choristers the joyous anthem sing,
That all the woods may answer, and their echo ring.

Behold, whiles she before the altar stands,
Hearing the holy priest that to her speaks
And blesseth her with his two happy hands,
How the red roses flush up in her cheeks,
And the pure snow with goodly vermil stain,
Like crimson dyed in grain;
That even the angels, which continually
About the sacred altar do remain,
Forget their service and about her fly,
Oft peeping in her face, that seems more fair
The more they on it stare.
But her sad eyes, still fastened on the ground,
Are governëd with goodly modesty,
That suffers not one look to glance awry,
Which may let in a little thought unsound.
Why blush ye, love, to give to me your hand,
The pledge of all our band?
Sing, ye sweet angels, Allelujah sing,
That all the woods may answer, and your echo ring.

Now all is done; bring home the bride again,
Bring home the triumph of our victory,
Bring home with you the glory of her gain,
With joyance bring her and with jollity.

Never had man more joyful day than this,
Whom heaven would heap with bliss.
Make feast, therefore, now all this live-long day;
This day for ever to me holy is;
Pour out the wine without restraint or stay,
Pour not by cups, but by the belly full,
Pour out to all that wull,
And sprinkle all the posts and walls with wine,
That they may sweat, and drunken be withal.
Crown ye God Bacchus with a coronal,
And Hymen also crown with wreaths of vine;
And let the Graces dance unto the rest,
For they can do it best:
The whiles the maidens do their carol sing,
To which the woods shall answer, and their echo ring.

Ring ye the bells, ye young men of the town,
And leave your wonted labors for this day.
This day is holy; do ye write it down
That ye for ever it remember may.
This day the sun is in his chiefest height,
With Barnaby the bright,
From whence declining daily by degrees,
He somewhat loseth of his heat and light,
When once the Crab behind his back he sees.
But for this time it ill ordainèd was
To choose the longest day in all the year,
And shortest night, when longest fitter were;
Yet never day so long but late would pass.
Ring ye the bells to make it wear away,
And bonfires make all day,
And dance about them, and about them sing:
That all the woods many answer, and your echo ring.

wull: will.
Graces: three daughters of Jove, ladies in waiting to Venus.
Barnaby: St. Barnabas's day, which in Spenser's time fell on June 22.
Crab: Sign of the house of Cancer, out of which the sun moves in mid-June.

Ah! when will this long weary day have end,
And lend me leave to come unto my love?
How slowly do the hours their numbers spend!
How slowly does sad Time his feathers move!
Haste thee, O fairest planet, to thy home
Within the western foam:
Thy tirëd steeds long since have need of rest.
Long though it be, at last I see it gloom,
And the bright evening star with golden crest
Appear out of the east.
Fair child of beauty, glorious lamp of love,
That all the host of heaven in ranks dost lead,
And guidest lovers through the nightës dread,
How cheerfully thou lookest from above
And seemst to laugh atween thy twinkling light,
As joying in the sight
Of these glad many, which for joy do sing,
That all the woods them answer, and their echo ring!

Now cease, ye damsels, your delights forepast;
Enough is it that all the day was yours:
Now day is done, and night is nighing fast;
Now bring the bride into the bridal bowers.
The night is come, now soon her disarray,
And in her bed her lay;
Lay her in lilies and in violets,
And silken curtains over her display,
And odored sheets, and Arras coverlets.
Behold how goodly my fair love does lie,
In proud humility!
Like unto Maia, when as Jove her took
In Tempe, lying on the flowery grass,
Twixt sleep and wake, after she weary was
With bathing in the Acidalian brook.
Now it is night, ye damsels may be gone,
And leave my love alone,

Maia: daughter of Atlas, and   mother of Mercury.
with Jove as the father, the

And leave likewise your former lay to sing:
The woods no more shall answer, nor your echo ring.

Now welcome, night! thou night so long expected,
That long day's labor dost at last defray,
And all my cares, which cruel Love collected,
Hast summed in one, and cancellèd for aye:
Spread thy broad wing over my love and me,
That no man may us see,
And in thy sable mantle us enwrap,
From fear of peril and foul horror free.
Let no false treason seek us to entrap,
Nor any dread disquiet once annoy
The safety of our joy:
But let the night be calm and quietsome,
Without tempestuous storms or sad affray:
Like as when Jove with fair Alcmena lay,
When he begot the great Tirynthian groom;
Or like as when he with thy self did lie,
And begot Majesty,
And let the maids and youngmen cease to sing:
Ne let the woods them answer, nor their echo ring.

Let no lamenting cries nor doleful tears
Be heard all night within, nor yet without;
Ne let false whispers, breeding hidden fears,
Break gentle sleep with misconceivèd doubt.
Let no deluding dreams nor dreadful sights
Make sudden sad affrights;
Ne let house-fires nor lightning's helpless harms,
Ne let the Pouke nor other evil sprights,
Ne let mischievous witches with their charms,
Ne let hobgoblins, names whose sense we see not,
Fray us with things that be not.

Tirynthian groom: i.e., Hercu-
les, so called because he was
born at the city of Tiryns.

Pouke: i.e., Puck, before
Shakespeare's treatment
quite a formidable spirit.

Let not the shriek-owl nor the stork be heard,
Nor the night raven that still deadly yells,
Nor dammëd ghosts called up with mighty spells,
Nor grisly vultures make us once afeard:
Ne let the unpleasant choir of frogs still croaking
Make us to wish their choking.
Let none of these their dreary accents sing;
Ne let the woods them answer, nor their echo ring.

But let still Silence true night watches keep,
That sacred Peace may in assurance reign,
And timely Sleep, when it is time to sleep,
May pour his limbs forth on your pleasant plain,
The whiles an hundred little wingëd loves,
Like divers feathered doves,
Shall fly and flutter round about your bed,
And in the secret dark that none reproves,
Their pretty stealths shall work, and snares shall spread
To filch away sweet snatches of delight,
Concealed through covert night.
Ye sons of Venus, play your sports at will:
For greedy Pleasure, careless of your toys,
Thinks more upon her paradise of joys
Than what ye do, all be it good or ill.
All night, therefore, attend your merry play,
For it will soon be day:
Now none doth hinder you, that say or sing,
Ne will the woods now answer, nor your echo ring.

Who is the same which at my window peeps?
Or whose is that fair face that shines so bright?
Is it not Cynthia, she that never sleeps,
But walks about high heaven all the night?
O fairest goddess, do thou not envý
My love with me to spy:
For thou likewise didst love, though now unthought,
And for a fleece of wool, which privily
The Latmian shepherd once unto thee brought,
His pleasures with thee wrought.

Therefore to us be favorable now;
And sith of women's labors thou hast charge,
And generation goodly dost enlarge,
Incline thy will to effect our wishful vow,
And the chaste womb inform with timely seed,
That may our comfort breed:
Till which we cease our hopeful hap to sing,
Ne let the woods us answer, nor our echo ring.

And thou, great Juno, which with awful might
The laws of wedlock still dost patronize,
And the religion of the faith first plight
With sacred rites hast taught to solemnize,
And eke for comfort often callèd art
Of women in their smart,
Eternally bind thou this lovely band,
And all thy blessings unto us impart.
And thou, glad Genius, in whose gentle hand
The bridal bower and genial bed remain,
Without blemish or stain,
And the sweet pleasures of their love's delight
With secret aid dost succor and supply,
Till they bring forth the fruitful progeny,
Send us the timely fruit of this same night.
And thou, fair Hebe, and thou Hymen free,
Grant that it may so be.
Til which we cease your further praise to sing,
Ne any woods shall answer, nor your echo ring.

And ye high heavens, the temple of the gods,
In which a thousand torches flaming bright
Do burn, that to us wretched earthly clods
In dreadful darkness lend desirèd light,
And all ye powers which in the same remain,
More than we men can feign,

religion of the faith first plight: pledge of conjugal fidelity.
    i.e., the sanctity of the first

Pour out your blessing on us plenteously,
And happy influence upon us rain,
That we may raise a large posterity,
Which from the earth, which they may long possess
With lasting happiness,
Up to your haughty palaces may mount,
And for the guerdon of their glorious merit,
May heavenly tabernacles there inherit,
Of blessed saints for to increase the count.
So let us rest, sweet love, in hope of this,
And cease till then our timely joys to sing:
The woods no more us answer, nor our echo ring.

Song, made in lieu of many ornaments
With which my love should duly have been decked,
Which cutting off through hasty accidents,
Ye would not stay your due time to expect,
But promised both to recompense—
Be unto her a goodly ornament,
And for short time an endless monument.

PROTHALAMION

Calm was the day, and through the trembling air
Sweet-breathing Zephyrus did softly play
A gentle spirit, that lightly did delay
Hot Titan's beams, which then did glister fair,
When I (whom sullen care,
Through discontent of my long fruitless stay
In prince's court, and expectation vain
Of idle hopes, which still do fly away
Like empty shadows, did afflict my brain)
Walked forth to ease my pain
Along the shore of silver-streaming Thames;
Whose rutty bank, the which his river hems,
Was painted all with variable flowers,
And all the meads adorned with dainty gems

Fit to deck maidens' bowers,
And crown their paramours
Against the bridal day, which is not long:
Sweet Thames! run softly, till I end my song.

There in a meadow by the river's side
A flock of nymphs I chancëd to espy,
All lovely daughters of the flood thereby,
With goodly greenish locks all loose untied
As each had been a bride;
And each one had a little wicker basket
Made of fine twigs entrailëd curiously,
In which they gathered flowers to fill their flasket,
And with fine fingers cropped full feateously
The tender stalks on high.
Of every sort which in that meadow grew
They gathered some; the violet, pallid blue,
The little daisy that at evening closes,
The virgin lily and the primrose true,
With store of vermeil roses,
To deck their bridegrooms' posies
Against the bridal day, which was not long:
Sweet Thames! run softly, till I end my song.

With that I saw two swans of goodly hue
Come softly swimming down along the Lee;
Two fairer birds I yet did never see;
The snow which doth the top of Pindus strew
Did never whiter shew
Nor Jove himself, when he a swan would be
For love of Leda, whiter did appear;
Yet Leda was, they say, as white as he,
Yet not so white as these, nor nothing near;
So purely white they were
That even the gentle stream, the which them bare,
Seemed foul to them, and bade his billows spare
To wet their silken feathers, lest they might
Soil their fair plumes with water not so fair,

And mar their beauties bright,
That shone as Heaven's light,
Against their bridal day, which was not long:
Sweet Thames! run softly, till I end my song.

Eftsoons the nymphs, which now had flowers their fill,
Ran all in haste to see that silver brood
As they came floating on the crystal flood;
Whom when they saw, they stood amazèd still
Their wondering eyes to fill;
Them seemed they never saw a sight so fair
Of fowls so lovely that they sure did deem
Them heavenly born, or to be that same pair
Which through the sky draw Venus' silver team;
For sure they did not seem
To be begot of any earthly seed,
But rather angels, or of angels' breed;
Yet were they bred of summer's-heat, they say.
In sweetest season, when each flower and weed
The earth did fresh array;
So fresh they seemed as day,
Even as their bridal day, which was not long:
Sweet Thames! run softly, till I end my song.

Then forth they all out of their baskets drew
Great store of flowers, the honor of the field,
That to the sense did fragrant odors yield,
All which upon those goodly birds they threw
And all the waves did strew,
That like old Peneus' waters they did seem
When down along by pleasant Tempe's shore,
Scattered with flowers, through Thessaly they stream,
That they appear, through lilies' plenteous store,
Like a bride's chamber floor.
Two of those nymphs meanwhile two garlands bound
Of freshest flowers which in that mead they found,

summer's-heat: a pun on Som-   name.
    erset, the ladies' family   *Peneus:* a river in Thessaly.

The which presenting all in trim array,
Their snowy foreheads therewithal they crowned,
Whilst one did sing this lay
Prepared against that day,
Against their bridal day, which was not long:
Sweet Thames! run softly, till I end my song.

"Ye gentle birds! the world's fair ornament,
And heaven's glory, whom this happy hour
Doth lead unto your lovers' blissful bower,
Joy may you have, and gentle heart's content
Of your love's couplement;
And let fair Venus, that is queen of love,
With her heart-quelling son upon you smile,
Whose smile, they say, hath virtue to remove
All love's dislike, and friendship's faulty guile
For ever to assoil.
Let endless peace your steadfast hearts accord,
And blessèd plenty wait upon your board,
And let your bed with pleasures chaste abound,
That fruitful issue may to you afford,
Which may your foes confound,
And make your joys redound
Upon your bridal day, which is not long:
Sweet Thames! run softly, till I end my song."

So ended she; and all the rest around
To her redoubled that her undersong,
Which said their bridal day should not be long:
And gentle Echo from the neighbor ground
Their accents did resound.
So forth those joyous birds did pass along,
Adown the Lee that to them murmured low,
As he would speak but that he lacked a tongue,
Yet did by signs his glad affection show,
Making his stream run slow.
And all the fowl which in his flood did dwell
Gan flock about these twain, that did excel

assoil: set free.

The rest, so far as Cynthia doth shend
The lesser stars. So they, enrangëd well,
Did on those two attend,
And their best service lend
Against their wedding day, which was not long:
Sweet Thames! run softly, till I end my song.

At length they all to merry London came,
To merry London, my most kindly nurse,
That to me gave this life's first native source,
Though from another place I take my name,
An house of ancient fame:
There when they came whereas those bricky towers
The which on Thames' broad agëd back do ride,
Where now the studious lawyers have their bowers,
There whilom wont the Templar-knights to bide,
Till they decayed through pride;
Next whereunto there stands a stately place,
Where oft I gainëd gifts and goodly grace
Of that great lord, which therein wont to dwell,
Whose want too well now feels my friendless case.
But ah! here fits not well
Old woes, but joys to tell
Against the bridal day, which is not long:
Sweet Thames! run softly, till I end my song.

Yet therein now doth lodge a noble peer,
Great England's glory and the world's wide wonder,
Whose dreadful name late through all Spain did thunder,
And Hercules' two pillars standing near
Did make to quake and fear:
Fair branch of honor, flower of chivalry,
That fillest England with thy triumphs' fame,
Joy have thou of thy noble victory,
And endless happiness of thine own name
That promiseth the same!

shend: shame.   who had returned from the
whilom: formerly.   capture of Cadiz.
noble peer: the Earl of Essex,

That through thy prowess and victorious arms
Thy country may be freed from foreign harms,
And great Eliza's glorious name may ring
Through all the world, filled with thy wide alarms,
Which some brave Muse may sing
To ages following,
Upon the bridal day, which is not long:
Sweet Thames! run softly, till I end my song.

From those high towers this noble lord issuing,
Like radiant Hesper when his golden hair
In the ocean billows he hath bathëd fair,
Descended to the river's open viewing,
With a great train ensuing.
Above the rest were goodly to be seen
Two gentle knights of lovely face and feature,
Beseeming well the bower of any queen,
With gifts of wit and ornaments of nature
Fit for so goodly stature,
That like the twins of Jove they seemed in sight
Which deck the baldric of the heavens bright;
They two, forth pacing to the river's side,
Received those two fair brides, their love's delight;
Which, at the appointed tide,
Each one did make his bride,
Against their bridal day, which is not long:
Sweet Thames! run softly, till I end my song.

SONNETS FROM AMORETTI

25: How long shall this

How long shall this like dying life endure
And know no end of her own misery,
But waste and wear away in terms unsure,
Twixt fear and hope depending doubtfully?

Yet better were at once to let me die,
And show the last ensample of your pride,
Than to torment me thus with cruelty,
To prove your power, which I too well have tried.
But yet if in your hardened breast ye hide
A close intent at last to show me grace,
Then all the woes and wrecks which I abide
As means of bliss I gladly will embrace,
And wish that more and greater they might be,
That greater meed at last may turn to me.

53: *The panther, knowing that his spotted hide*

The panther, knowing that his spotted hide
Doth please all beasts, but that his looks them fray,
Within a bush his dreadful head doth hide,
To let them gaze whilst he on them may prey.
Right so my cruel fair with me doth play;
For with the goodly semblant of her hue
She doth allure me to mine own decay,
And then no mercy will unto me shew.
Great shame it is, thing so divine in view,
Made for to be the world's most ornament,
To make the bait her gazers to imbrue.
Good shames to be to ill an instrument;
But mercy doth with beauty best agree,
As in their Maker ye them best may see.

58: *By her that is most assured to her self*

Weak is the assurance that weak flesh reposeth
In her own power, and scorneth others' aid;
That soonest falls, when as she most supposeth
Her self assured, and is of nought afraid.
All flesh is frail, and all her strength unstayed,

meed: reward, gift.

Like a vain bubble blowen up with air:
Devouring time and changeful chance have preyed
Her glory's pride, that none may it repair.
Ne none so rich or wise, so strong or fair,
But faileth, trusting on his own assurance:
And he that standeth on the highest stair
Falls lowest; for on earth nought hath endurance.
Why then do ye, proud fair, misdeem so far,
That to yourself ye most assurèd are?

67: *Like as a huntsman*

Like as a huntsman, after weary chase,
Seeing the game from him escaped away,
Sits down to rest him in some shady place,
With panting hounds beguilèd of their prey—
So after long pursuit and vain assay,
When I all weary had the chase forsook,
The gentle deer returned the self-same way,
Thinking to quench her thirst at the next brook.
There she, beholding me with milder look,
Sought not to fly, but fearless still did bide:
Till I in hand her yet half trembling took,
And with her own good will her firmly tied.
Strange thing, me seemed, to see a beast so wild,
So goodly won, with her own will beguiled.

68: *Most glorious Lord of life*

Most glorious Lord of life, that on this day
Didst make thy triumph over death and sin,
And having harrowed hell, didst bring away
Captivity thence captive, us to win:
This joyous day, dear Lord, with joy begin,
And grant that we, for whom thou didest die,
Being with thy dear blood clean washed from sin,
May live forever in felicity:

And that thy love we weighing worthily,
May likewise love thee for the same again;
And for thy sake, that all like dear didst buy,
With love may one another entertain.
So let us love, dear love, like as we ought:
Love is the lesson which the Lord us taught.

88: *Since I have lacked the comfort*

Since I have lacked the comfort of that light,
The which was wont to lead my thoughts astray,
I wander as in darkness of the night,
Afraid of every danger's least dismay.
Ne aught I see, though in the clearest day,
When others gaze upon their shadows vain,
But the only image of that heavenly ray,
Whereof some glance doth in mine eye remain.
Of which beholding the idea plain,
Through contemplation of my purest part,
With light thereof I do my self sustain,
And thereon feed my love-affamished heart.
But with such brightness whilst I fill my mind,
I starve my body, and mine eyes do blind.

SIR PHILIP SIDNEY: 1554–86

When he was nine years old and a student at Shrewsbury School, Sidney met Fulke Greville, who was to become his lifelong friend and biographer. Sidney attended Oxford for four years; through the offices of his father and his uncle, the famous Earl of Leicester, he had a ready entree to court. He quickly became one of the favorites of Queen Elizabeth, who sent him on missions to France, Germany, Italy, Hungary, and the Netherlands. He and Greville and Edward Dyer were close literary associates, but they did not strongly influence each other's writings. Sidney was knighted in 1583, and was sent to the Netherlands as Governor of Flushing in 1585. The following year he died from a wound received in combat at the battle of Zutphen.

Nothing of Sidney's was published during his lifetime. He was well known as a poet during his brief years at court, but his real fame came after his death, partly as a result of the quality of his poetry and partly as a result of his personal legend. His *Defence of Poesie*, written in reply to the attack upon poetry and decadent drama by Stephen Gosson, is a compendium of the fashionable "new" literary thought of the later sixteenth century. The ideas in the *Defence* are gathered from those critics, Italian and Latin, most closely identified with the Petrarchan movement in Italy, and they are held together by Sidney's rhetoric and enthusiasm. Generally speaking, Sidney's best verse is found in his songs rather than in the more famous sonnets of Astrophil and Stella.

TEXT: *The Complete Works of Sir Philip Sidney*, in 4 vols., edited by A. Feuillerat (1912–26).
The Poems of Sir Philip Sidney, edited by William A. Ringler (1962).

SONNETS FROM ASTROPHIL AND STELLA

31: *With how sad steps*

With how sad steps, O Moon, thou climbst the skies!
How silently, and with how wan a face!
What, may it be that even in heavenly place
That busy archer his sharp arrows tries?
Sure, if that long-with-love-acquainted eyes
Can judge of love, thou feel'st a lover's case:
I read it in thy looks: thy languished grace,
To me that feel the like, thy state descries.
Then even of fellowship, O Moon, tell me,
Is constant love deemed there but want of wit?
Are beauties there as proud as here they be?
Do they above love to be loved, and yet
Those lovers scorn whom that love doth possess?
Do they call virtue there ungratefulness?

39: *Come, Sleep, O Sleep*

Come, Sleep, O Sleep, the certain knot of peace,
The baiting-place of wit, the balm of woe,
The poor man's wealth, the prisoner's release,
The indifferent judge between the high and low!
With shield of proof shield me from out the prease
Of those fierce darts Despair at me doth throw.
O make in me those civil wars to cease:
I will good tribute pay, if thou do so.
Take thou of me smooth pillows, sweetest bed,
A chamber deaf to noise and blind to light,
A rosy garland and a weary head:
And if these things, as being thine by right,
Move not thy heavy grace, thou shalt in me,
Livelier than elsewhere, Stella's image see.

prease: press or throng.

41: *Having this day my horse*

Having this day my horse, my hand, my lance
Guided so well that I obtained the prize,
Both by the judgment of the English eyes
And of some sent from that sweet enemy France;
Horsemen my skill in horsemanship advance,
Townfolks my strength; a daintier judge applies
His praise to sleight which from good use doth rise;
Some lucky wits impute it but to chance;
Others, because of both sides I do take
My blood from them who did excel in this,
Think Nature me a man-at-arms did make.
How far they shot awry! The true cause is,
Stella looked on, and from her heavenly face
Sent forth the beams which made so fair my race.

74: *I never drank of Aganippe well*

I never drank of Aganippe well,
Nor ever did in shade of Tempe sit,
And Muses scorn with vulgar brains to dwell;
Poor layman I, for sacred rites unfit.
Some do I hear of poets' fury tell,
But, God wot, wot not what they mean by it;
And this I swear by blackest brook of hell,
I am no pick-purse of another's wit.
How falls it then, that with so smooth an ease
My thoughts I speak, and what I speak doth flow
In verse, and that my verse best wits doth please?
Guess we the cause: What, is it thus? Fie, no.
Or so? Much less. How then? Sure thus it is:
My lips are sweet, inspired with Stella's kiss.

sleight: skill.   on Mount Helicon, sacred
Aganippe well: the fountain   to the Muses.

84: *Highway, since you*

Highway, since you my chief Parnassus be,
And that my Muse, to some ears not unsweet,
Tempers her words to trampling horses' feet
More oft than to a chamber-melody,
Now, blessëd you, bear onward blessëd me
To her where I my heart, safeliest, shall meet:
My Muse and I must you of duty greet
With thanks and wishes, wishing thankfully.
Be you still fair, honored by public heed,
By no encroachment wronged, nor time forgot,
Nor blamed for blood, nor shamed for sinful deed,
And, that you know I envy you no lot
Of highest wish, I wish you so much bliss,
Hundreds of years you Stella's feet may kiss!

ONLY JOY, NOW HERE YOU ARE

Only Joy, now here you are,
Fit to hear and ease my care.
Let my whispering voice obtain
Sweet reward for sharpest pain:
Take me to thee, and thee to me.
"No, no, no, no, my dear, let be."

Night hath closed all in her cloak,
Twinkling stars love-thoughts provoke,
Danger hence good care doth keep,
Jealousy itself doth sleep;
Take me to thee, and thee to me.
"No, no, no, no, my dear, let be."

Better place no wit can find,
Cupid's yoke to loose or bind;
These sweet flowers on fine bed too,
Us in their best language woo:

Take me to thee, and thee to me.
"No, no, no, no, my dear, let be."

This small light the moon bestows
Serves thy beams but to disclose,
So to raise my hap more high;
Fear not else, none can us spy:
Take me to thee, and thee to me.
"No, no, no, no, my dear, let be."

That you heard was but a mouse;
Dumb sleep holdeth all the house.
Yet asleep, methinks, they say,
"Young fools, take time while you may."
Take me to thee, and thee to me.
"No, no, no, no, my dear, let be."

Niggard Time threats, if we miss
This large offer of our bliss,
Long stay ere he grant the same:
Sweet, then, while each thing doth frame,
Take me to thee, and thee to me.
"No, no, no, no, my dear, let be.

Your fair mother is a-bed,
Candles out and curtains spread;
She thinks you do letters write;
Write, but first let me indite.
Take me to thee, and thee to me.
"No, no, no, no, my dear, let be."

Sweet, alas, why strive you thus?
Concord better fitteth us.
Leave to Mars the force of hands:
Your power in your beauty stands.
Take thee to me, and me to thee.
"No, no, no, no, my dear, let be."

Woe to me, and do you swear
Me to hate but I forbear?
Cursëd be my destines all
That brought me so high to fall.
Soon with my death I will please thee.
"No, no, no, no, my dear, let be."

O DEAR LIFE, WHEN SHALL IT BE?

O dear life, when shall it be
That mine eyes thine eyes may see,
And in them thy mind discover
Whether absence have had force
Thy remembrance to divorce
From the image of thy lover?

O if I myself find not
After parting aught forgot,
Nor debarred from beauty's treasure,
Let not tongue aspire to tell
In what high joys I shall dwell:
Only thought aims at the pleasure.

Thought, therefore, will I send thee
To take up the place for me:
Long I will not after tarry.
There, unseen, thou mayst be bold
Those fair wonders to behold
Which in them my hopes do carry.

Thought, see thou no place forbear;
Enter bravely everywhere;
Seize on all to her belonging.
But if thou wouldst guarded be,
Fearing her beams, take with thee
Strength of liking, rage of longing.

Think of that most grateful time
When my leaping heart will climb
In thy lips to have his biding,
There those roses for to kiss
Which do breathe a sugared bliss,
Opening rubies, pearls dividing.

Think of my most princely power
When I blessèd shall devour
With my greedy licorous senses
Beauty, music, sweetness, love,
While she doth against me prove
Her strong darts but weak defences.

Think, think of those dallyings
When with dovelike murmurings,
With glad moaning, passèd anguish,
We change eyes, and heart for heart
Each to other do impart,
Joying till joy makes us languish.

O my thought, my thoughts surcease!
Thy delights my woes increase:
My life melts with too much thinking.
Think no more, but die in me,
Till thou shalt revivèd be
At her lips, my nectar drinking.

WHO IS IT THAT THIS DARK NIGHT

"Who is it that this dark night
Underneath my window plaineth?"
It is one who from thy sight
Being, ah, exiled, disdaineth
Every other vulgar light.

"Why, alas, and are you he?
Be not yet those fancies changëd?"
Dear, when you find change in me,
Though from me you be estrangëd,
Let my change to ruin be.

"Well, in absence this will die;
Leave to see and leave to wonder."
Absence sure will help, if I
Can learn how myself to sunder
From what in my heart doth lie.

"But time will these thoughts remove;
Time doth work what no man knoweth."
Time doth as the subject prove;
With time still the affection groweth
In the faithful turtle dove.

"What if you new beauties see;
Will not they stir new affection?"
I will think they pictures be,
Image-like of saints' perfection,
Poorly counterfeiting thee.

"But your reason's purest light
Bids you leave such minds to nourish."
Dear, do reason no such spite;
Never doth thy beauty flourish
More than in my reason's sight.

"But the wrongs love bears will make
Love at length leave undertaking."
No, the more fools it do shake,
In a ground of so firm making
Deeper still they drive the stake.

"Peace, I think that some give ear;
Come no more lest I get anger."
Bliss, I will my bliss forbear,
Fearing, sweet, you to endanger;
But my soul shall harbor there.

"Well, begone, begone I say,
Lest that Argus' eyes perceive you."
O unjust is Fortune's sway,
Which can make me thus to leave you,
And from louts to run away.

WHAT TONGUE CAN HER PERFECTIONS TELL?

What tongue can her perfections tell
In whose each part all pens may dwell?
Her hair fine threads of finest gold,
In curlëd knots man's thought to hold,
But that her forehead says, "In me
A whiter beauty you may see."
Whiter indeed, more white than snow
Which on cold Winter's face doth grow:
That doth present those even brows
Whose equal line their angles bows;
Like to the Moon, when, after change,
Her hornëd head abroad doth range,
And arches be two heavenly lids,
Whose wink each bold attempt forbids.
For the black stars those spheres contain,
The matchless pair even praise doth stain;
No lamp whose light by Art is got,
No sun which shines and seeth not,
Can liken them, without all peer
Save one as much as other clear;
Which only thus unhappy be
Because themselves they cannot see.
Her cheeks with kindly claret spread,
Aurora-like new out of bed;
Or like the fresh queen-apple's side,
Blushing at sight of Phoebus' pride.

Argus: the legendary giant
with a hundred eyes.

Her nose, her chin, pure ivory wears,
No purer then the pretty ears,
So that therein appears some blood,
Like wine and milk that mingled stood;
In whose incirclets if ye gaze
Your eyes may tread a lover's maze,
But with such turns the voice to stray,
No talk untaught can find the way.
The tip no jewel needs to wear,
The tip is jewel of the ear.
But who those ruddy lips can miss,
Which, blessëd, still themselves do kiss?
Rubies, cherries, and roses new,
In worth, in taste, in perfect hue,
Which never part but that they show
Of precious pearl the double row;
The second sweetly-fencëd ward,
Her heavenly-dewëd tongue to guard,
Whence never word in vain did flow.
Fair under these doth stately grow
The handle of this pleasant work,
The neck, in which strange graces lurk:
Such be, I think, the sumptuous towers
Which skill doth make in princes' bowers.
So good assay invites the eye
A little downward to espy
The lively clusters of her breasts,
Of Venus' babe the wanton nests:
Like pommels round of marble clear,
Where azured veins well-mixed appear,
With dearest tops of porphyry.
Betwixt these two a way doth lie,
A way more worthy Beauty's fame
Than that which bears the milky name.
This leads unto the joyous field
Which only still doth lilies yield;

incirclets: i.e., curls.

But lilies such whose native smell
The Indian odors doth excel:
Waist it is called, for it doth waste
Men's lives until it be embraced.
There may one see, and yet not see,
Her ribs in white well armëd be,
More white than Neptune's foamy face
When struggling rocks he would embrace.
In these delights the wandering thought
Might of each side astray be brought,
But that her navel doth unite
In curious circle busy sight:
A dainty seal of virgin-wax,
Where nothing but impression lacks.
The belly, then, glad sight doth fill,
Justly entitled Cupid's hill,
A hill most fit for such a master,
A spotless mine of alabaster,
Like alabaster fair and sleek,
But soft and supple satin-like.
In that sweet seat the boy doth sport;
Loath I must leave his chief resort,
For such a use the world hath gotten
The best things still must be forgotten.
Yet never shall my song omit
Those thighs, for Ovid's song more fit,
Which flankëd with two sugared flanks,
Lift up her stately-swelling banks,
That Albion clives in whiteness pass,
With haunches smooth as looking-glass.
But, bow all knees! Now of her knees
My tongue doth tell what fancy sees,
The knots of joy, the gems of love,
Whose motion makes all graces move,
Whose bought incaved doth yield such sight
Like cunning painter shadowing white.

clives: cliffs.   *bought:* bend or curve; i.e., of
the knees.

The gartering-place, with child-like sign
Shows easy print in metal fine;
But there again the flesh doth rise
In her brave calves, like crystal skies,
Whose Atlas is a smallest small,
More white than whitest bone of whale.
There oft steals out that round clean foot,
This noble cedar's precious root,
In show and scent pale violets,
Whose step on earth all beauty sets.
But back unto her back, my Muse!—
Where Leda's swan his feathers mews,
Along whose ridge such bones are met,
Like comfits round in marchpane set.
Her shoulders be like two white doves,
Perching within square royal rooves,
Which leaded are with silver skin,
Passing the hate-spot ermelin.
And thence those arms derivèd are:
The phoenix' wings be not so rare
For faultless length and stainless hue.
Ah, woe is me, my woes renew;
Now course doth lead me to her hand,
Of my first love the fatal band,
Where whiteness doth forever sit:
Nature herself enameled it.
For there with strange compact doth lie
Warm snow, moist pearl, soft ivory;
There fall those sapphire-colored brooks,
Which conduit-like with curious crooks
Sweet islands make in that sweet land.
As for the fingers of the hand,
The bloody shafts of Cupid's war,
With amethysts they headed are:
Thus hath each part his beauty's part.
But how the Graces do impart

mews: molts or sheds.   *marchpane:* a fancy cake.
comfits: sweetmeats.   *ermelin:* ermine.

To all her limbs a special grace,
Becoming every time and place,
Which doth even beauty beautify,
And most bewitch the wretched eye:
How all this is but a fair inn
Of fairer guest which dwells within,
Of whose high praise and praiseful bliss
Goodness the pen, heaven paper is,
The ink immortal fame doth lend.
As I began so must I end:
No tongue can her perfections tell,
In whose each part all pens may dwell.

WHEN TWO SUNS DO APPEAR

When two suns do appear,
Some say it doth betoken wonders near,
    As prince's loss or change.
Two gleaming suns of splendor like I see,
    And seeing feel in me
Of prince's heart quite lost the ruin strange.
    But now each where doth range
With ugly cloak the dark envíous Night,
    Who, full of guilty spite,
Such living beams should her black seat assail,
Too weak for them our weaker sight doth vail.
    No, says fair Moon, my light
Shall bar that wrong, and though it not prevail
Like to my brother's rays, yet those I send
Hurt not the face which nothing can amend.

OFT HAVE I MUSED

Oft have I mused, but now at length I find
Why those that die, men say they do depart.
Depart!—a word so gentle, to my mind
Weakly did seem to paint Death's ugly dart.

But now the stars, with their strange course, do bind
Me one to leave, with whom I leave my heart:
I hear a cry of spirits faint and blind,
That, parting thus, my chiefest part I part.
Part of my life, the loathèd part to me,
Lives to impart my weary clay some breath:
But that good part, wherein all comforts be,
Now dead, doth show departure is a death—
Yea, worse than death: death parts both woe and joy:
From joy I part, still living in annoy.

THE NIGHTINGALE, AS SOON AS APRIL BRINGETH

The nightingale, as soon as April bringeth
Unto her rested sense a perfect waking,
While late bare earth, proud of new clothing, springeth,
Sings out her woes, a thorn her song-book making;
    And, mournfully bewailing,
    Her throat in tunes expresseth
    What grief her breast oppresseth
For Tereus' force on her chaste will prevailing.
O Philomela fair, O take some gladness,
That here is juster cause of plaintful sadness:
    Thine earth now springs, mine fadeth;
Thy thorn without, my thorn my heart invadeth.

Alas, she hath no other cause of anguish
But Tereus' love, on her by strong hand wroken,
Wherein she suffering, all her spirits languish,
Full womanlike complains her will was broken.
    But I, who, daily craving,
    Cannot have to content me,
    Have more cause to lament me,
Since wanting is more woe than too much having.

Tereus: the husband of Procne, who raped Philomela; out of pity, the gods turned Procne into a swallow and Philomela into a nightingale.

O Philomela fair, O take some gladness,
That here is juster cause of plaintful sadness:
   Thine earth now springs, mine fadeth;
Thy thorn without, my thorn my heart invadeth.

RING OUT YOUR BELLS

Ring out your bells, let mourning shows be spread;
For Love is dead.
All Love is dead, infected
With plague of deep disdain:
Worth, as nought worth, rejected,
And Faith fair scorn doth gain.
From so ungrateful fancy,
From such a female franzy,
From them that use men thus,
Good Lord, deliver us!

Weep, neighbors, weep! do you not hear it said
That Love is dead?
His death-bed, peacock's folly;
His winding-sheet is shame;
His will, false-seeming holy;
His sole executor blame.
From so ungrateful fancy,
From such a female franzy,
From them that use men thus,
Good Lord, deliver us!

Let dirge be sung and trentals rightly read,
For Love is dead.
Sir Wrong his tomb ordaineth
My mistress' marble heart,
Which epitaph containeth:
"Her eyes were once his dart."

trentals: masses for the dead.

From so ungrateful fancy,
From such a female franzy,
From them that use men thus,
Good Lord, deliver us!

Alas, I lie! rage hath this error bred.
Love is not dead.
Love is not dead, but sleepeth
In her unmatchëd mind,
Where she his counsel keepeth
Till due desert she find.
Therefore from so vile fancy,
To call such wit a franzy,
Who Love can temper thus,
Good Lord, deliver us!

WHO HATH HIS FANCY PLEASËD

Who hath his fancy pleasëd
With fruits of happy sight,
Let here his eyes be raisëd
On Nature's sweetest light:
A light which doth dissever
And yet unite the eyes,
A light which, dying never,
Is cause the looker dies.

She never dies, but lasteth
In life of lover's heart:
He ever dies that wasteth
In love his chiefest part.
Thus is her life still guarded
In never-dying faith:
Thus is his death rewarded,
Since she lives in his death.

Look, then, and die: the pleasure
Doth answer well the pain.
Small loss of mortal treasure,
Who may immortal gain.
Immortal be her graces,
Immortal is her mind:
They, fit for heavenly places,
This, heaven in it doth bind.

But eyes these beauties see not,
Nor sense that grace descries:
Yet eyes deprivëd be not
From sight of her fair eyes,
Which, as of inward glory
They are the outward seal,
So may they live still sorry,
Which die not in that weal.

But who hath fancies pleasëd
With fruits of happy sight,
Let here his eyes be raisëd
On Nature's sweetest light.

THOU BLIND MAN'S MARK

Thou blind man's mark, thou fool's self-chosen snare,
Fond fancy's scum, and dregs of scattered thought;
Band of all evils, cradle of causeless care;
Thou web of will, whose end is never wrought:
Desire! Desire! I have too dearly bought,
With price of mangled mind, thy worthless ware;
Too long, too long, asleep thou hast me brought,
Who should my mind to higher things prepare.
But yet in vain thou hast my ruin sought,
In vain thou mad'st me to vain things aspire,
In vain thou kindlest all thy smoky fire,
For Virtue hath this better lesson taught:
Within myself to seek my only hire,
Desiring nought but how to kill Desire.

LEAVE ME, O LOVE

Leave me, O love which reachest but to dust,
And thou, my mind, aspire to higher things.
Grow rich in that which never taketh rust:
Whatever fades but fading pleasure brings.
Draw in thy beams, and humble all thy might
To that sweet yoke where lasting freedoms be;
Which breaks the clouds and opens forth the light
That doth both shine and give us sight to see.
O take fast hold; let that light be thy guide
In this small course which birth draws out to death,
And think how evil becometh him to slide
Who seeketh heaven and comes of heavenly breath.
Then farewell, world! thy uttermost I see:
Eternal Love, maintain thy life in me.

FULKE GREVILLE: 1554-1628

Sidney's and Greville's careers were nearly parallel, though Greville attended Cambridge rather than Oxford. The two came to court at the same time, and both were favorites of Elizabeth. After Sidney's death Greville became one of the wealthiest and most influential men in England; after Elizabeth's death, he served James as Chancellor of the Exchequer. He was knighted in 1603, and in 1621 he was made first Baron Brooke. He was a generous literary patron; among the recipients of his aid were Samuel Daniel and William Davenant.

As the earlier poets Wyatt and Surrey were once paired by conventional scholarship and criticism, and Surrey preferred to Wyatt, so have Greville and Sidney been paired, and Sidney preferred to Greville. In recent years, however, Greville has been read more and more; and as he is read more, the depth and power of his work is more widely recognized, and the significance of his career is more accurately understood. Though he stands at the beginning of the Petrarchan movement, he is the first poet in whom the conflict between the earlier Native practice and the later Petrarchan practice becomes very meaningful. He wrote two verse dramas that show the influence of the French Senecans, and five very long verse treatises, as well as the *Life of Sidney*; but his final worth must rest upon *Caelica*, a sequence of short poems that shows his growth from a fairly skilled but conventional Petrarchan to the major poet who must be ranked with Jonson and Donne.

TEXT:

Poems and Dramas of Fulke Greville, in 2 vols., edited by Geoffrey Bullough (1945).

POEMS FROM CAELICA

7: *The world, that all contains*

The world, that all contains, is ever moving;
The stars within their spheres forever turned;
Nature, the queen of change, to change is loving;
And form to matter new is still adjourned.

Fortune, our fancy-God, to vary liketh;
Place is not bound to things within it placed;
The present time upon time passëd striketh;
With Phoebus' wandering course the earth is graced.

The air still moves, and by its moving cleareth;
The fire up ascends, and planets feedeth;
The water passeth on, and all lets weareth;
The earth stands still, yet change of changes breedeth.

Her plants, which summer ripes, in winter fade;
Each creature in unconstant mother lieth;
Man made of earth, and for whom earth is made,
Still dying lives, and living ever dieth.
    Only like fate sweet Myra never varies,
    Yet in her eyes the doom of all change carries.

12: *Cupid, thou naughty boy*

Cupid, thou naughty boy, when thou wert loathëd,
Naked and blind, for vagabonding noted,
Thy nakedness I in my reason clothëd,
Mine eyes I gave thee, so was I devoted.

Fie, Wanton, fie! who would show children kindness?
No sooner he into mine eyes was gotten
But straight he clouds them with a seeing blindness,
Makes reason wish that reason were forgotten.

From thence to Myra's eyes the Wanton strayeth,
Where, while I charge him with ungrateful measure,
So with fair wonders he mine eyes betrayeth,
That my wounds, and his wrongs, become my pleasure;
 Till for more spite to Myra's heart he flieth,
 Where living to the world, to me he dieth.

16: Fie, foolish earth

Fie, foolish Earth, think you the heaven wants glory
Because your shadows do your self benight?
All's dark unto the blind; let them be sorry;
The heavens in themselves are ever bright.

Fie, fond desire, think you that love wants glory
Because your shadows do your self benight?
The hopes and fears of lust may make men sorry,
But love still in her self finds her delight.

Then, Earth, stand fast; the sky that you benight
Will turn again, and so restore your glory;
Desire, be steady; hope is your delight,
An orb wherein no creature can be sorry,
 Love being placed above these middle regions,
 Where every passion wars itself with legions.

22: I, with whose colors

I, with whose colors Myra dressed her head;
I, that ware posies of her own hand-making;
I, that mine own name in the chimneys read,
By Myra finely wrought ere I was waking:
 Must I look on, in hope time coming may
 With change bring back my turn again to play?

I, that on Sunday at the church-stile found
A garland sweet, with true-love knots in flowers,
Which I to wear about mine arm was bound,
That each of us might know that all was ours:
    Must I now lead an idle life in wishes,
    And follow Cupid for his loaves and fishes?

I, that did wear the ring her mother left;
I, for whose love she gloried to be blamèd;
I, with whose eyes her eyes committed theft;
I, who did make her blush when I was namèd:
    Must I lose ring, flowers, blush, theft and go naked,
    Watching with sighs, till dead love be awakèd?

I, that when drowsy Argus fell asleep,
Like Jealousy o'erwatchèd with desire,
Was even warnèd modesty to keep,
While her breath, speaking, kindled Nature's fire:
    Must I look on a-cold, while others warm them?
    Do Vulcan's brothers in such fine nets arm them?

Was it for this that I might Myra see
Washing the water with her beauties, white?
Yet would she never write her love to me.
Thinks wit of change while thoughts are in delight?
    Mad girls must safely love, as they may leave;
    No man can print a kiss; lines may deceive.

29: *Faction, that ever dwells*

Faction, that ever dwells
In courts where wit excels,
    Hath set defiance;
Fortune and Love have sworn
That they were never born
    Of one alliance.

Cupid, that doth aspire
To be God of desire,
  Swears he gives laws,—
That where his arrows hit,
Some joy, some sorrow it,
  Fortune no cause.

Fortune swears weakest hearts,
The books of Cupid's arts,
  Turn with her wheel;
Senses themselves shall prove
Venture hath place in love;
  Ask them that feel.

This discord, it begot
Atheists, that honor not
  Nature, thought good;
Fortune should ever dwell
In courts, where wits excel;
  Love keep the wood.

Thus to the wood went I
With Love to live and die;
  Fortune's forlorn.
Experience of my youth
Thus makes me think the truth
  In desert born.

My saint is dear to me;
Myra herself is she,
  She fair and true;
Myra that knows to move
Passions of love with love:
  Fortune, Adieu.

38: *Caelica, I overnight was finely used*

Caelica, I overnight was finely used,
Lodged in the midst of paradise, your Heart;
Kind thoughts had charge I might not be refused;
Of every fruit and flower I had part.

But curious knowledge, blown with busy flame,
The sweetest fruits had down in shadows hidden;
And for it found mine eyes had seen the same,
I from my paradise was straight forbidden,—

Where that cur, Rumor, runs in every place,
Barking with care, begotten out of fear;
And glassy Honor, tender of Disgrace,
Stands Seraphin to see I come not there;
    While that fine soil, which all these joys did yield,
    By broken fence is proved a common field.

40: *The nurse-life wheat*

The nurse-life wheat, within his green husk growing,
Flatters our hope and tickles our desire,
Nature's true riches in sweet beauties showing,
Which set all hearts with labor's love on fire.

No less fair is the wheat when golden ear
Shows unto hope the joys of near enjoying;
Fair and sweet is the bud, more sweet and fair
The rose, which proves that time is not destroying.

Caelica, your youth, the morning of delight,
Enameled o'er with beauties white and red,
All sense and thoughts did to belief invite,
That love and glory there are brought to bed;
    And your ripe years' love-noon—he goes no higher—
    Turns all the spirits of Man into desire.

nurse-life: i.e., life-fostering.

45: *Absence, the noble truce*

Absence, the noble truce
Of Cupid's war,
Where, though desires want use,
They honored are,
Thou art the just protection
Of prodigal affection;
Have thou the praise.
When bankrupt Cupid braveth,
Thy mines his credit saveth
With sweet delays.

Of wounds which presence makes
With Beauty's shot,
Absence the anguish slakes,
But healeth not.
Absence records the stories
Wherein Desire glories,
Although she burn;
She cherisheth the spirits
Where Constancy inherits
And passions mourn.

Absence, like dainty clouds
On glorious-bright,
Nature's weak senses shrouds
From harming light.
Absence maintains the treasure
Of pleasure unto pleasure,
Sparing with praise;
Absence doth nurse the fire,
Which starves and feeds desire
With sweet delays.

Presence to every part
Of Beauty ties;
Where wonder rules the heart,
There pleasure dies.
Presence plagues mind and senses
With modesty's defences;
Absence is free.
Thoughts do in absence venter
On Cupid's shadowed center;
They wink and see.

But thoughts be not so brave
With absent joy;
For you with that you have
Your self destroy.
The absence which you glory
Is that which makes you sorry
And burn in vain;
For thought is not the weapon
Wherewith thoughts-ease men cheapen.
Absence is pain.

52: *Away with these self-loving lads*

Away with these self-loving lads,
Whom Cupid's arrow never glads;
Away, poor souls that sigh and weep,
In love of those that lie asleep.
    For Cupid is a meadow-God,
    And forceth none to kiss the rod.

Sweet Cupid's shafts, like destiny,
Do causeless good or ill decree;
Desert is born out of his bow,
Reward upon his wing doth go:
    What fools are they that have not known
    That Love likes no laws but his own.

venter: venture.

My songs they be of Cynthia's praise,
I wear her rings on holy days;
In every tree I write her name,
And every day I read the same.
  Where Honor Cupid's rival is,
  There miracles are seen of his.

If Cynthia crave her ring of me,
I blot her name out of the tree;
If doubt do darken things held dear,
Then well fare nothing once a year:
  For many run, but one must win;
  Fools only hedge the cuckoo in.

The worth that worthiness should move
Is love, that is the bow of love;
And love as well thee foster can
As can the mighty nobleman.
  Sweet saint, 'tis true, you worthy be,
  Yet without Love nought worth to me.

    56: *All my senses, like beacon's flame*

All my senses, like beacon's flame,
Gave alarum to desire
To take arms in Cynthia's name
And set all my thoughts on fire.
Fury's wit persuaded me
Happy love was hazard's heir;
Cupid did best shoot and see
In the night where smooth is fair.
Up I start believing well
To see if Cynthia were awake;
Wonders I saw, who can tell?
And thus unto myself I spake:
"Sweet God Cupid, where am I,
That by pale Diana's light
Such rich beauties do espy
As harm our senses with delight?

Am I borne up to the skies?
See where Jove and Venus shine,
Showing in her heavenly eyes
That desire is divine;
Look where lies the milken way,
Way unto that dainty throne,
Where, while all the Gods would play,
Vulcan thinks to dwell alone."
I gave reins to this conceit,
Hope went on the wheel of lust;
Fancy's scales are false of weight,
Thoughts take thought that go of trust.
I stepped forth to touch the sky,
I a God by Cupid dreams;
Cynthia, who did naked lie,
Runs away like silver streams,
Leaving hollow banks behind
Who can neither forward move,
Nor if rivers be unkind
Turn away or leave to love.
There stand I, like arctic pole,
Where Sol passeth o'er the line,
Mourning my benighted soul,
Which so loseth light divine.
There stand I like men that preach
From the execution place,
At their death content to teach
All the world with their disgrace.
He that lets his Cynthia lie
Naked on a bed of play
To say prayers ere she die,
Teacheth time to run away.
Let no love-desiring heart
In the stars go seek his fate:
Love is only Nature's art;
Wonder hinders love and hate.
    None can well behold with eyes
    But what underneath him lies.

69: *When all this All*

When all this All doth pass from age to age,
And revolution in a circle turn,
Then heavenly Justice doth appear like rage,
The caves do roar, the very seas do burn,
   Glory grows dark, the sun becomes a night,
   And makes this great world feel a greater might.

When Love doth change his seat from heart to heart,
And worth about the wheel of fortune goes,
Grace is diseased, desert seems overthwart,
Vows are forlorn, and truth doth credit lose,
   Chance then gives law, desire must be wise
   And look more ways than one, or lose her eyes.

My age of joy is past, of woe begun;
Absence my presence is, strangeness my grace;
With them that walk against me, is my sun;
The wheel is turned; I hold the lowest place.
   What can be good to me, since my love is,
   To do me harm, content to do amiss?

82: *You that seek what life is in death*

You that seek what life is in death,
Now find it air that once was breath:
New names unknown, old names gone,
Till time end bodies, but souls none.
   Reader! then make time, while you be,
   But steps to your eternity.

84: Farewell, sweet boy

Farewell, sweet boy; complain not of my truth;
Thy mother loved thee not with more devotion;
For to thy boy's play I gave all my youth;
Young master, I did hope for your promotion.

While some sought honors, princes' thoughts observing,
Many wooed Fame, the child of pain and anguish;
Others judged inward good a chief deserving;
I in thy wanton visions joyed to languish.

I bowed not to thy image for succession,
Nor bound thy bow to shoot reformëd kindness;
Thy plays of hope and fear were my confession,
The spectacles to my life was thy blindness.
    But, Cupid, now farewell; I will go play me
    With thoughts that please me less, and less betray me.

86: The earth with thunder torn

The earth with thunder torn, with fire blasted,
With waters drowned, with windy palsy shaken,
Cannot for this with heaven be distasted,
Since thunder, rain, and winds from earth are taken.
Man torn with love, with inward furies blasted,
Drowned with despair, with fleshly lustings shaken,
Cannot for this with heaven be distasted:
Love, fury, lustings out of man are taken.
Then, Man, endure thy self; those clouds will vanish;
Life is a top which whipping sorrow driveth;
Wisdom must bear what our flesh cannot banish;
The humble lead, the stubborn bootless striveth.
    Or Man, forsake thy self, to heaven turn thee;
    Her flames enlighten Nature, never burn thee.

88: *Man, dream no more*

Man, dream no more of curious mysteries,
As what was here before the world was made,
The first man's life, the state of Paradise,
Where heaven is, or hell's eternal shade:
    For God's works are like him, all infinite;
    And curious search but crafty sin's delight.

The flood that did, and dreadful fire that shall,
Drown and burn up the malice of the earth,
The divers tongues and Babylon's down-fall
Are nothing to the man's renewëd birth.
    First, let the law plough up thy wicked heart,
    That Christ may come, and all these types depart.

When thou hast swept the house that all is clear,
When thou the dust hast shaken from thy feet,
When God's All-might doth in thy flesh appear,
Then seas with streams above thy sky do meet:
    For goodness only doth God comprehend,
    Knows what was first, and what shall be the end.

97: *Eternal Truth, almighty, infinite*

Eternal Truth, almighty, infinite,
Only exilëd from man's fleshly heart
Where ignorance and disobedience fight,
In hell and sin, which shall have greatest part—
    When thy sweet mercy opens forth the light
Of Grace which giveth eyes unto the blind,
And with the law even plowest up our sprite
To faith, wherein flesh may salvation find,
    Thou bidst us pray; and we do pray to thee,
But as to power and God without us placed,
Thinking a wish may wear out vanity,
Or habits be by miracles defaced.

One thought to God we give, the rest to sin;
Quickly unbent is all desire of good;
True words pass out, but have no being within;
We pray to Christ, yet help to shed his blood.
  For while we say, "Believe!" and feel it not,
Promise amends, and yet despair in it,
Hear Sodom judged, and go not out with Lot,
Make Law and Gospel riddles of the wit,—
    We with the Jews even Christ still crucify,
    As not yet come to our impiety.

98: *Wrapped up, O Lord, in man's degeneration*

Wrapped up, O Lord, in man's degeneration,
The glories of thy truth, thy joys eternal,
Reflect upon my soul dark desolation,
And ugly prospects o'er the spirits infernal.
  Lord, I have sinned, and mine iniquity
  Deserves this hell; yet, Lord, deliver me.

Thy power and mercy never comprehended
Rest lively imaged in my conscience wounded;
Mercy to grace, and power to fear extended,
Both infinite; and I in both confounded.
  Lord, I have sinned, and mine iniquity
  Deserves this hell; yet, Lord, deliver me.

If from this depth of sin, this hellish grave,
And fatal absence from my Saviour's glory
I could implore His mercy, who can save,
And for my sins, not pains of sin, be sorry,—
  Lord, from this horror of iniquity
  And hellish grave, Thou wouldst deliver me.

99: *Down in the depth of mine iniquity*

Down in the depth of mine iniquity,
That ugly center of infernal spirits,
Where each sin feels her own deformity
In these peculiar torments she inherits—
   Deprived of human graces and divine,
   Even there appears this saving God of mine.

And in this fatal mirror of transgression,
Shows man as fruit of his degeneration,
The error's ugly infinite impression,
Which bears the faithless down to desperation.
   Deprived of human graces and divine,
   Even there appears this saving God of mine.

In power and truth, almighty and eternal,
Which on the sin reflects strange desolation,
With glory scourging all the spirits infernal,
And uncreated hell with unprivation—
   Deprived of human graces, not divine,
   Even there appears this saving God of mine.

For on this spiritual cross condemnëd lying
To pains infernal by eternal doom,
I see my Saviour for the same sins dying,
And from that hell I feared, to free me, come.
   Deprived of human graces, not divine,
   Thus hath his death raised up this soul of mine.

100: *In night, when colors all to black are cast*

In night, when colors all to black are cast,
Distinction lost, or gone down with the light,
The eye, a watch to inward senses placed,
Not seeing, yet still having power of sight,

Gives vain alarums to the inward sense,
Where fear, stirred up with witty tyranny,
Confounds all powers, and through self-offence
Doth forge and raise impossibility,

Such as in thick depriving darknesses
Proper reflections of the error be,
And images of self-confusednesses,
Which hurt imaginations only see:—
   And from this nothing seen, tells news of devils,
   Which but expressions be of inward evils.

109: *Sion lies waste*

Sion lies waste, and thy Jerusalem,
O Lord, is fallen to utter desolation;
Against thy prophets and thy holy men
The sin hath wrought a fatal combination,
   Profaned thy name, thy worship overthrown,
   And made thee, living Lord, a God unknown.

Thy powerful laws, thy wonders of creation,
Thy Word incarnate, glorious heaven, dark hell,
Lie shadowed under Man's degeneration,
Thy Christ still crucified for doing well;
   Impiety, O Lord, sits on thy throne,
   Which makes thee, living Light, a God unknown.

Man's superstition hath thy truths entombed,
His atheism again her pomps defaceth;
That sensual unsatiable vast womb
Of thy seen church, thy unseen church disgraceth;
   There lives no truth with them that seem thine own,
   Which makes thee, living Lord, a God unknown.

Yet unto thee, Lord, (mirror of transgression)
We, who for earthly idols have forsaken
Thy heavenly Image (sinless, pure impression)
And so in nets of vanity lie taken,
    All desolate, implore that to thine own,
    Lord, thou no longer live a God unknown.

Yet, Lord, let Israel's plagues not be eternal,
Nor sin forever cloud thy sacred mountains,
Nor with false flames, spiritual but infernal,
Dry up thy mercy's ever-springing fountains;
    Rather, sweet Jesus, fill up time, and come
    To yield the sin her everlasting doom.

GEORGE PEELE: 1556–96

Peele was born in London and spent his early years in that city as a student at Christ's Hospital, a kind of orphanage for the very poor, where his father was a bookkeeper. He received an M.A. from Oxford, after which he returned to London, in 1581. For the next fifteen years he made a precarious living as a writer of court poetry, pageants, and plays. He was probably one of a coterie that included Marlowe, Green, and Thomas Nashe. Peele died at forty, impoverished and forgotten by his friends.

Peele is a minor dramatist, historically rather than intrinsically important. Because of his incessant struggles against poverty, his literary energies were directed away from the short poem; but of those that we have, most of which are songs from the plays, a few are remarkably delicate and moving.

TEXT:

The Works of Peele, in 2 vols., edited by A. H. Bullen (1888).

WHAT THING IS LOVE

What thing is love? for sure love is a thing.
It is a prick, it is a sting,
It is a pretty, pretty thing;
It is a fire, it is a coal,
Whose flame creeps in at every hole;
And as my wit doth best devise,
Love's dwelling is in ladies' eyes,

From whence do glance love's piercing darts,
That make such holes into our hearts;
And all the world herein accord,
Love is a great and mighty lord;
And when he list to mount so high,
With Venus he in heaven doth lie,
And evermore hath been a god,
Since Mars and she played even and odd.

HIS GOLDEN LOCKS

His golden locks time hath to silver turned;
  O time too swift, O swiftness never ceasing!
His youth 'gainst time and age hath ever spurned,
  But spurned in vain; youth waneth by increasing.
Beauty, strength, youth are flowers but fading seen;
Duty, faith, love are roots and ever green.

His helmet now shall make a hive for bees,
  And, lover's sonnets turned to holy psalms,
A man-at-arms must now serve on his knees,
  And feed on prayers, which are age's alms.
But though from court to cottage he depart,
His saint is sure of his unspotted heart.

And when he saddest sits in homely cell,
  He'll teach his swains this carol for a song:
Blessed be the hearts that wish my sovereign well,
  Cursed be the souls that think her any wrong.
Goddess, allow this aged man his right
To be your beadsman now that was your knight.

BETHSABE'S SONG

Hot sun, cool fire, tempered with sweet air,
Black shade, fair nurse, shadow my white hair;
Shine, sun; burn, fire; breathe, air, and ease me;
Black shade, fair nurse, shroud me and please me:
Shadow, my sweet nurse, keep me from burning,
Make not my glad cause cause of mourning.
      Let not my beauty's fire
      Inflame unstaid desire,
      Nor pierce any bright eye
      That wandereth lightly.

ROBERT GREENE: 1560?-92

Like Peele's, Greene's origins were middle class. He was born in Norwich and educated at Cambridge, where he received the B.A. and the M.A. degrees. He went to London and became a writer of plays, pamphlets, and "novels." For a few years he was quite successful; but like Peele, he died at an early age, in great poverty.

During his brief life, Greene was exceedingly prolific; his plays greatly influenced Shakespeare's romantic comedies, and were still popular after his death. Grosart's edition of his *Complete Works* is in fifteen volumes, and it is unlikely that Grosart discovered all that he had written. Most of Greene's poems appeared in his "novels," of which there are more than two dozen, and in his pamphlets, of which there are more.

TEXT:

The Plays and Poems of Robert Greene, in 2 vols., edited by J. Churton Collins (1905).

SEPHESTIA'S SONG TO HER CHILD

Weep not, my wanton, smile upon my knee;
When thou art old there's grief enough for thee.

    Mother's wag, pretty boy,
    Father's sorrow, father's joy.
    When thy father first did see
    Such a boy by him and me,

He was glad, I was woe:
Fortune changed made him so,
When he left his pretty boy,
Last his sorrow, first his joy.

Weep not, my wanton, smile upon my knee;
When thou art old there's grief enough for thee.

Streaming tears that never stint,
Like pearl drops from a flint,
Fell by course from his eyes,
That one another's place supplies:
Thus he grieved in every part,
Tears of blood fell from his heart,
When he left his pretty boy,
Father's sorrow, father's joy.

Weep not, my wanton, smile upon my knee;
When thou art old there's grief enough for thee.

The wanton smiled, father wept;
Mother cried, baby lept;
More he crowed, more we cried;
Nature could not sorrow hide.
He must go, he must kiss
Child and mother, baby bliss;
For he left his pretty boy,
Father's sorrow, father's joy.

Weep not, my wanton, smile upon my knee;
When thou art old there's grief enough for thee.

THE PALMER'S ODE

Old Menalcas on a day,
As in field this shepherd lay,
Tuning of his oaten pipe,
Which he hit with many a stripe,

Said to Coridon that he
Once was young and full of glee:
"Blithe and wanton was I then;
Such desires follow men.
As I lay and kept my sheep,
Came the God that hateth sleep,
Clad in armor all of fire,
Hand in hand with Queen Desire;
And with a dart that wounded nigh,
Pierced my heart as I did lie;
That when I woke I 'gan swear,
Phyllis' beauty palm did bear.
Up I start, forth went I,
With her face to feed mine eye:
There I saw Desire sit
That my heart with love had hit,
Laying forth bright beauty's hooks
To entrap my gazing looks.
Love I did and 'gan to woo,
Pray, and sigh; all would not do.
Women, when they take the toy,
Covet to be counted coy.
Coy she was, and I 'gan court;
She thought love was but a sport.
Profound hell was in my thought;
Such a pain Desire had wrought
That I sued with sighs and tears.
Still ingrate she stopped her ears,
Till my youth I had spent.
Last a passion of Repent
Told me flat that Desire
Was a brand of love's fire,
Which consumeth men in thrall,
Virtue, youth, wit, and all.
At this saw back I start,
Beat Desire from my heart,
Shook off love and made an oath
To be enemy to both.

Old I was when thus I fled
Such fond toys as cloyed my head.
But this I learned at Virtue's gate:
The way to good is never late."

THOMAS LODGE: 1558–1625

Lodge's father was a wealthy merchant and lord mayor of London. Educated at Trinity College, Oxford, Lodge early entered the study of law at Lincoln's Inn; but he soon turned from law to literature. During the fifteen years of his literary career, he wrote two plays, one in collaboration with Robert Greene; several prose tales under the influence of John Lyly, the best known of which is *Rosalynde*; a long mythological narrative poem; a collection of sonnets and lyrics titled *Phillis*; and a book of verse containing satires, eclogues, and epistles. Somewhat late in life, he took up the study of medicine, and became a successful physician.

In the sonnets that make up most of *Phillis*, Lodge is an imitator of Sidney; but his best work, the songs from the plays and prose works, are purer and less affected. His rhythms, especially, are interesting and skillful; it is not surprising that several of his poems were put to music, for his work clearly presages the delicacy of the Madrigalists and Lutenists.

TEXT:

The Complete Works of Thomas Lodge, in 4 vols., edited by E. W. Gosse (1883).

ODE

Now I find thy looks were feigned,
Quickly lost and quickly gained;
Soft thy skin like wool of wethers,
Heart unstable, light as feathers,

Tongue untrusty, subtle sighted,
Wanton will with change delighted.
　　Siren pleasant, foe to reason,
　　Cupid plague thee for this treason!

Of thine eyes I made my mirror,
From thy beauty came mine error;
All thy words I counted witty,
All thy smiles I deemëd pretty;
Thy false tears that me aggrievëd
First of all my trust deceivëd.
　　Siren pleasant, foe to reason,
　　Cupid plague thee for this treason!

Feigned acceptance when I asked,
Lovely words with cunning masked,
Holy vows but heart unholy.
Wretched man! my trust was folly.
Lily-white and pretty winking,
Solemn vows but sorry thinking.
　　Siren pleasant, foe to reason,
　　Cupid plague thee for this treason!

Now I see, O seemly cruel,
Others warm them at my fuel.
Wit shall guide me in this durance,
Since in love is no assurance.
Change thy pasture, take thy pleasure,
Beauty is a fading treasure.
　　Siren pleasant, foe to reason,
　　Cupid plague thee for this treason!

Prime youth lasts not, age will follow
And make white these tresses yellow;
Wrinkled face for looks delightful
Shall acquaint the dame despiteful;
And when time shall eat thy glory,
Then too late thou wilt be sorry.
　　Siren pleasant, foe to reason,
　　Cupid plague thee for thy treason.

SONG

Pluck the fruit and taste the pleasure,
  Youthful lordings, of delight;
Whilst occasion gives you seizure,
  Feed your fancies and your sight:
    After death, when you are gone,
    Joy and pleasure is there none.

Here on earth nothing is stable,
  Fortune's changes well are known;
Whilst as youth doth then enable,
  Let your seeds of joy be sown:
    After death, when you are gone,
    Joy and pleasure is there none.

Feast it freely with your lovers,
  Blithe and wanton sweets do fade;
Whilst that lovely Cupid hovers
  Round about this lovely shade,
    Sport it freely one to one;
    After death is pleasure none.

Now the pleasant spring allureth,
  And both place and time invites:
Out, alas! what heart endureth
  To disclaim his sweet delights?
    After death, when we are gone,
    Joy and pleasure is there none.

ROSALIND'S MADRIGAL

Love in my bosom like a bee
  Doth suck his sweet;
Now with his wings he plays with me,
  Now with his feet.

Within mine eyes he makes his nest,
His bed amidst my tender breast;
My kisses are his daily feast,
And yet he robs me of my rest.
    Ah, wanton, will ye?

And if I sleep, then percheth he
    With pretty flight,
And makes his pillow of my knee
    The livelong night.
Strike I my lute, he tunes the string;
He music plays if so I sing;
He lends me every lovely thing;
Yet cruel he my heart doth sting.
    Whist, wanton, still ye!

Else I with roses every day
    Will whip you hence,
And bind you, when you long to play,
    For your offense.
I'll shut my eyes to keep you in,
I'll make you fast it for your sin,
I'll count your power not worth a pin.
Alas! what hereby shall I win
    If he gainsay me?

What if I beat the wanton boy
    With many a rod?
He will repay me with annoy,
    Because a god.
Then sit thou safely on my knee,
And let thy bower my bosom be;
Lurk in mine eyes, I like of thee.
O Cupid, so thou pity me,
    Spare not, but play thee!

SAMUEL DANIEL: 1562–1619

Daniel was the son of a musician. He attended Oxford, and became tutor to the Countess of Pembroke's son, hence gaining access to the so-called "Pembroke Circle," one of the most important literary groups of the time. It was through this circle that he got to know Fulke Greville, who was an early patron and to whom he dedicated *Musophilus*, a philosophical poem about human knowledge and learning. When James I came to the throne, Daniel was made a groom of Queen Anne's privy chamber, and he held various offices in the Queen's household until shortly before his death.

With Spenser and Sidney, Daniel is one of the most representative of the Petrarchists, especially in his sequence *Delia*, in which he acknowledges his debt to Sidney. Daniel was admired in his own day, and he is especially important to the history of literary method, in that he serves as a link between the Petrarchism of the sixteenth century and the Romanticism of the nineteenth century; he was admired by Gray, Coleridge, and Wordsworth, and was in some respects influential upon their work.

Text:

Samuel Daniel, Poems and a Defence of Ryme, edited by A. C. Sprague (1930).

SONNETS FROM DELIA

6: *Fair is my love*

Fair is my love, and cruel as she's fair:
  Her brow shades frowns, although her eyes are sunny,
  Her smiles are lightning, though her pride despair,
  And her disdains are gall, her favors honey.
A modest maid, decked with a blush of honor,
  Whose feet do tread green paths of youth and love;
  The wonder of all eyes that look upon her,
  Sacred on earth, designed a saint above.
Chastity and beauty, which were deadly foes,
  Live reconcilëd friends within her brow;
  And had she pity to conjoin with those,
  Then who had heard the plaints I utter now?
For had she not been fair and thus unkind,
My muse had slept, and none had known my mind.

34: *When winter snows*

When winter snows upon thy sable hairs,
  And frost of age hath nipped thy beauties near,
  When dark shall seem thy day that never clears,
  And all lies withered that was held so dear,
Then take this picture which I here present thee,
  Limnëd with a pencil not all unworthy;
  Here see the gifts that God and nature lent thee,
  Here read thyself and what I suffered for thee.
This may remain thy lasting monument,
  Which happily posterity may cherish;
  These colors with thy fading are not spent,
  These may remain when thou and I shall perish.
If they remain, then thou shalt live thereby;
They will remain, and so thou canst not die.

39: *Read in my face*

Read in my face a volume of despairs,
    The wailing Iliads of my tragic woe
    Drawn with my blood and printed with my cares,
    Wrought by her hand, that I have honored so;
Who, whilst I burn, she sings at my soul's wrack,
    Looking aloft from turret of her pride;
    There my soul's tyrant joys her, in the sack
    Of her own seat, whereof I made her guide.
There do these smokes that from affliction rise
    Serve as an incense to a cruel Dame—
    A sacrifice thrice grateful to her eyes,
    Because their power serve to exact the same.
Thus ruins she, to satisfy her will,
The Temple where her name was honored still.

42: *Beauty, sweet love*

Beauty, sweet love, is like the morning dew,
    Whose short refresh upon the tender green
    Cheers for a time, but till the sun doth shew,
    And straight 'tis gone as it had never been.
Soon doth it fade that makes the fairest flourish,
    Short is the glory of the blushing rose;
    The hue which thou so carefully dost nourish,
    Yet which at length thou must be forced to lose,
When thou, surcharged with burthen of thy years,
    Shalt bend thy wrinkles homeward to the earth,
    And that in beauty's lease expired appears
    The date of age, the kalends of our death.
But, ah! no more; this must not be foretold,
For women grieve to think they must be old.

45: *Care-charmer sleep*

Care-charmer sleep, son of the sable night,
　Brother to death, in silent darkness born,
　Relieve my languish and restore the light;
　With dark forgetting of my care, return
And let the day be time enough to mourn
　The shipwreck of my ill-adventured youth;
　Let waking eyes suffice to wail their scorn
　Without the torment of the night's untruth.
Cease, dreams, the images of day-desires,
　To model forth the passions of the morrow;
　Never let rising sun approve you liars,
　To add more grief to aggravate my sorrow.
Still let me sleep, embracing clouds in vain,
And never wake to feel the day's disdain.

ULYSSES AND THE SIREN

Siren: Come, worthy Greek; Ulysses, come
Possess these shores with me:
The winds and seas are troublesome,
And here we may be free.
　Here may we sit and view their toil
That travail in the deep,
And joy the day in mirth the while,
And spend the night in sleep.

Ulysses: Fair nymph, if fame or honor were
To be attained with ease,
Then would I come and rest me there
And leave such toils as these.
　But here it dwells, and here must I
With danger seek it forth;
To spend the time luxuriously
Becomes not men of worth.

Siren: Ulysses, O be not deceived
With that unreal name:
This honor is a thing conceived,
And rests on others' fame,
 Begotten only to molest
Our peace, and to beguile
The best thing of our life, our rest,
And give us up to toil.

Ulysses: Delicious nymph, suppose there were
Nor honor nor report,
Yet manliness would scorn to wear
The time in idle sport.
 For toil doth give a better touch
To make us feel our joy;
And ease finds tediousness as much
As labor yields annoy.

Siren: Then pleasure likewise seems the shore,
Whereto tends all your toil,
Which you forego to make it more,
And perish oft the while.
 Who may disport them diversely
Find never tedious day,
And ease may have variety
As well as action may.

Ulysses: But natures of the noblest frame
These toils and dangers please,
And they take comfort in the same,
As much as you in ease,
 And with the thought of actions past
Are recreated still,
When pleasure leaves a touch at last,
To show that it was ill.

Siren: That doth opinion only cause,
That's out of custom bred,
Which makes us many other laws
Than ever Nature did.

No widows wail for our delights;
Our sports are without blood;
The world we see by warlike wights
Receives more hurt than good.

Ulysses: But yet the state of things require
These motions of unrest,
And these great spirits of high desire
Seem born to turn them best,
    To purge the mischiefs that increase,
And all good order mar;
For oft we see a wicked peace
To be well changed for war.

Siren: Well, well, Ulysses, then I see
I shall not have thee here,
And therefore I will come to thee
And take my fortunes there.
    I must be won that cannot win,
Yet lost were I not won;
For beauty hath created been
To undo or be undone.

EPISTLE TO HENRY WRIOTHESLEY,
EARL OF SOUTHAMPTON

He who hath never warred with misery,
Nor ever tugged with Fortune and Distress,
Hath had no occasion nor no field to try
The strength and forces of his worthiness:
Those parts of judgment which felicity
Keeps as concealed, affliction must express;
And only men show their abilities,
And what they are, in their extremities.

The world had never taken so full note
Of what thou art, hadst thou not been undone,
And only thy affliction hath begot
More fame than thy best fortunes could have done:

For ever by adversity are wrought
The greatest works of admiratión,
And all the fair examples of renown
Out of distress and misery are grown.
Mutius the fire, the tortures Regulus
Did make the miracles of faith and zeal;
Exile renowned and graced Rutilius;
Imprisonment and poison did reveal
The worth of Socrates; Fabricius'
Poverty did grace that common-weal
More than all Syllae's riches, got with strife;
And Cato's death did vie with Caesar's life.

Not to be unhappy is unhappiness,
And misery not to have known misery;
For the best way unto discretion is
The way that leads us by adversity:
And men are better showed what is amiss
By the expert finger of calamity

Mutius: Gaius Mucius Scaevola, a Roman hero who lost the use of his right hand by thrusting it upon an altar of burning coals, so impressing the Etrurian king by his fortitude that the king made peace with the Romans and withdrew from the city.

Regulus: a Roman consul horribly tortured to death by his Carthaginian captors, to whom, according to his promise, he voluntarily returned after having been sent to Rome to offer terms of peace that were refused.

Rutilius: a Roman consul, celebrated for his virtue; Sulla banished him from Rome, and he retired to Smyrna, amid the acclamations of the people.

Fabricius: a Roman consul and soldier, victorious over the Samnites and Lucanians, who, offered great wealth, refused it with contempt. He lived and died in great poverty.

Syllae: i.e., Sulla, the Roman dictator, the poverty of whose early years gave way to great inherited wealth, which gave him great power and influence.

Cato: the Roman censor, exceedingly wise, courageous, prudent, and kind, beloved by the people: he died in extreme old age, in his late eighties.

Than they can be with all that Fortune brings,
Who never shows them the true face of things.

How could we know that thou couldst have endured
With a reposëd cheer wrong and disgrace,
And with a heart and countenance assured
Have looked stern death and horror in the face?
How should we know thy soul had been secured
In honest counsels and in ways unbase,
Hadst thou not stood to show us what thou wert
By thy affliction, that descried thy heart?

It is not but the tempest that doth show
The seaman's cunning; but the field that tries
The captain's courage: and we come to know
Best what men are in their worst jeopardies.
For lo, how many have we seen to grow
To high renown from lowest miseries,
Out of the hands of death, and many a one
To have been undone, had they not been undone.

He that endures for what his conscience knows
Not to be ill, doth from a patience high
Look only on the cause whereto he owes
Those sufferings, not on his misery;
The more he endures, the more his glory grows,
Which never grows from imbecility:
Only the best composed and worthiest hearts
God sets to act the hard'st and constant'st parts.

TO THE RIGHT WORTHY KNIGHT SIR FULKE GREVILLE

If I have erred or run a course unfit
To vent my understanding in this kind,
Your approbation hath been cause of it
That fed this grateful error of my mind;

For your most worthy and judicious Knight
Did first draw forth from close obscurity
My unpresuming verse into the light
And graced the same, and made me known thereby:
And every man we see is easily
Confirmed in that wherein he takes delight,
But chiefly when he finds his industry
Allowed by him he knows can judge aright.
Though praise, I fear me, is not virtue's friend
So much as we would make it seem to be;
For more undone than raised thereby we see,
Whereas themselves men cannot comprehend.
And for my part, I have been oft constrained
To re-examine this my course herein
And question with my self what is contained
Or what solidity there was therein.
And then in casting it with that account
And reckonings of the world, I therein found
It came far short, and neither did amount
In value with those hopes I did propound
Nor answered the expenses of my time,
Which made me much distrust my self and rime.
And I was flying from my heart and from
The station I was set in, to remain;
And had left all, had not fresh forces come
And brought me back unto my self again,
And furnished my distrusts with this defense,
This armor wherewith all the best I could
I have made good, against the difference
Of fortune and the world, that which I told;
    And have maintained your honor in the same,
    Who herein holds an interest in my fame.

MICHAEL DRAYTON: 1563-1631

The son of a tanner, Drayton was brought up as a page in the household of Sir Henry Goodere in Warwickshire, to whose daughter, Anne, later Lady Rainsford, Drayton remained devoted all of his bachelor life. It is said that when he was "scarce ten years of age" Drayton conceived the ambition to be a poet; whether so early or not, it is certain that as a very young man Drayton devoted himself to this ambition. Goodere, who had been a friend of Sidney and had seen him die at Zutphen, indulged Drayton's ambition, and arranged patronage for him. For the rest of his rather uneventful life, except for a brief period he had to spend as one of Henslowe's hacks, Drayton was able to devote much of his time to his poetry.

Drayton wrote in virtually every poetic form that had any degree of popularity in his time. He apparently considered himself a professional poet, one for whom poetry was a public duty. His sonnet sequence is titled *Idea*, and many of the poems reflect the easy and conventional Platonism suggested by the title; but a few of them transcend that fashion and are genuine poems. Drayton's best works are probably the two patriotic Odes, poems in which the Petrarchism of much of *Idea* is hardly present at all. Though an incipient Petrarchism mars most of his work, Drayton seems not really at ease with the tradition; there is a curious and awkward struggle between an early Native practice and the fashionable ornateness of the Petrarchan manner. But the struggle is never resolved, as it is in Greville; and it harms Drayton's verse more than it gives it interest and tension.

TEXT: *The Works of Michael Drayton*, in 5 vols., edited by J. W. Hebel and others (1931–41).
Poems of Michael Drayton, in 2 vols., edited by John Buxton (1953). The Buxton volumes do not contain the complete poems.

SONNETS FROM IDEA:
TO THE READER OF THESE SONNETS

Into these loves, who but for passion looks,
At this first sight, here let him lay them by
And seek elsewhere, in turning other books,
Which better may his labor satisfy.
No far-fetched sigh shall ever wound my breast,
Love from mine eye a tear shall never wring,
Nor in "Ah, me's!" my whining sonnets dressed;
A libertine, fantastically I sing.
My verse is the true image of my mind,
Ever in motion, still desiring change;
And as thus to variety inclined,
So in all humors sportively I range:
    My muse is rightly of the English strain,
    That cannot long one fashion entertain.

6: How many paltry, foolish, painted things

How many paltry, foolish, painted things,
That now in coaches trouble every street,
Shall be forgotten, whom no poet sings,
Ere they be well wrapped in their winding-sheet?
Where I to thee eternity shall give,
When nothing else remaineth of these days,
And queens hereafter shall be glad to live
Upon the alms of thy superfluous praise.
Virgins and matrons, reading these my rimes,
Shall be so much delighted with thy story
That they shall grieve they lived not in these times,
To have seen thee, their sex's only glory:
    So shalt thou fly above the vulgar throng,
    Still to survive in my immortal song.

17: *Stay, speedy time*

Stay, speedy time; behold, before thou pass
From age to age, what thou hast sought to see:
One, in whom all the excellencies be,
In whom heaven looks itself as in a glass.
Time, look thou too, in this tralucent glass,
And thy youth past in this pure mirror see,
As the world's beauty in his infancy,
What it was then, and thou before it was.
Pass on, and to posterity tell this—
Yet see thou tell but truly what hath been:
Say to our nephews, that thou once hast seen
In perfect human shape all heavenly bliss,
    And bid them mourn, nay more, despair with thee,
    That she is gone, her like again to see.

26: *Cupid, dumb idol*

Cupid, dumb idol, peevish saint of love,
No more shalt thou nor saint nor idol be;
No God art thou, a Goddess she doth prove
Of all thine honor she hath robbèd thee.
Thy bow, half broke, is pieced with old desire;
Her bow is beauty, with ten thousand strings
Of purest gold, tempered with virtue's fire,
The least able to kill an host of kings.
Thy shafts be spent, and she (to war appointed)
Hides in those crystal quivers of her eyes
More arrows with heart-piercing metal pointed
Than there be stars at midnight in the skies.
    With these, she steals men's hearts for her relief,
    Yet happy he that's robbed of such a thief.

30: *Three sorts of serpents do resemble thee*

Three sorts of serpents do resemble thee:
That dangerous eye-killing cockatrice,
The enchanting siren, which doth so entice,
The weeping crocodile—these vile pernicious three.
The basilisk his nature takes from thee,
Who for my life in secret wait dost lie,
And to my heart sendst poison from thine eye:
Thus do I feel the pain, the cause, yet cannot see.
Fair-maid no more, but Mer-maid be thy name,
Who with thy sweet alluring harmony
Hast played the thief, and stolen my heart from me,
And like a tryant makst my grief thy game:
    Thou crocodile, who when thou hast me slain,
    Lamentst my death, with tears of thy disdain.

51: *Calling to mind since first my love begun*

Calling to mind since first my love begun,
The uncertain times oft varying in their course,
How things still unexpectedly have run,
As it please the fates, by their resistless force;
Lastly, mine eyes amazedly have seen
Essex' great fall, Tyrone his peace to gain,
The quiet end of that long-living Queen,
This King's fair entrance, and our peace with Spain,
We and the Dutch at length ourselves to sever.
Thus the world doth, and evermore shall reel;
Yet to my goddess am I constant ever,
Howe'er blind fortune turn her giddy wheel.
    Though heaven and earth prove both to me untrue,
    Yet am I still inviolate to you.

61: *Since there's no help*

Since there's no help, come, let us kiss and part—
Nay, I have done: you get no more of me;
And I am glad, yea, glad with all my heart
That thus so cleanly I myself can free.
Shake hands forever, cancel all our vows,
And when we meet at any time again,
Be it not seen in either of our brows
That we one jot of former love retain.
Now at the last gasp of love's latest breath,
When, his pulse failing, Passion speechless lies,
When Faith is kneeling by his bed of death,
And Innocence is closing up his eyes,—
    Now, if thou wouldst, when all have given him over,
    From death to life thou mightst him yet recover.

TO THE VIRGINIAN VOYAGE

You brave, heroic minds
Worthy your country's name,
    That honor still pursue,
    Go, and subdue,
Whilst loitering hinds
Lurk here at home, with shame.

Britons, you stay too long;
Quickly aboard bestow you,
    And with a merry gale
    Swell your stretched sail,
With vows as strong
As the winds that blow you.

Your course securely steer,
West and by South forth keep;
 Rocks, lee-shores, nor shoals,
 When Aeolus scowls,
You need not fear,
So absolute the deep.

And cheerfully at sea,
Success you still entice,
 To get the pearl and gold,
 And ours to hold,
Virginia,
Earth's only paradise,

Where nature hath in store
Fowl, venison, and fish,
 And the fruitful'st soil
 Without your toil
Three harvests more,
All greater than you wish.

And the ambitious vine
Crowns with his purple mass
 The cedar reaching high
 To kiss the sky,
The cypress, pine,
And useful sassafras.

To whose, the golden age
Still nature's laws doth give,
 No other cares that tend,
 But them to defend
From winter's age
That long there doth not live.

Whenas the luscious smell
Of that delicious land,
 Above the seas that flows,
 The clear wind throws,
Your hearts to swell
Approaching the dear strand,

In kenning of the shore,
Thanks to God first given,
 O you, the happiest men,
 Be frolic then;
Let cannons roar,
Frighting the wide heaven.

And in regions far,
Such heroes bring ye forth
 As those from whom we came,
 And plant our name
Under that star
Not known unto our north.

And as there plenty grows
Of laurel everywhere,
 Apollo's sacred tree,
 You it may see
A poet's brows
To crown, that may sing there.

Thy voyages attend,
Industrious Hakluyt,
 Whose reading shall inflame
 Men to seek fame,
And much commend
To after times thy wit.

THE BALLAD OF AGINCOURT

Fair stood the wind for France,
When we our sails advance,
Nor now to prove our chance,
 Longer will tarry;
But putting to the main
At Kaux, the mouth of Seine,
With all his martial train,
 Landed King Harry.

And taking many a fort,
Furnished in warlike sort,
Marcheth towards Agincourt,
    In happy hour;
Skirmishing day by day
With those that stopped his way,
Where the French general lay
    With all his power.

Which in his height of pride,
King Henry to deride,
His ransom to provide
    To the King sending;
Which he neglects the while
As from a nation vile,
Yet with an angry smile,
    Their fall portending.

And turning to his men,
Quoth our brave Henry then:
"Though they to one be ten,
    Be not amazèd.
Yet have we well begun;
Battles so bravely won
Have ever to the sun
    By fame been raisèd.

"And for my self," quoth he,
"This my full rest shall be,
England ne'er mourn for me,
    Nor more esteem me;
Victor I will remain,
Or on this earth lie slain,
Never shall she sustain
    Loss to redeem me."

Poiters and Crécy tell,
When most their pride did swell,
Under our swords they fell;
    No less our skill is

Than when our grandsire great,
Claiming the regal seat
By many a warlike feat,
    Lopped the French lilies.

The Duke of York so dread
The eager vaward led;
With the main Henry sped
    Amongst his henchmen.
Excester had the rear,
A braver man not there;
O Lord, how hot they were
    On the false Frenchmen!

They now to fight are gone,
Armor on armor shone,
Drum now to drum did groan;
    To hear was wonder,
That with cries they make
The very earth did shake,
Trumpet to trumpet spake,
    Thunder to thunder.

Well it thine age became,
O noble Erpingham,
Which didst the signal aim
    To our hid forces;
When from a meadow by,
Like a storm suddenly,
The English archery
    Stuck the French horses.

With Spanish yew so strong,
Arrows a cloth-yard long,
That like to serpents stung,
    Piercing the weather;
None from his fellow starts,
But playing manly parts,
And like true English hearts,
    Stuck close together.

When down their bows they threw,
And forth their bilboes drew,
And on the French they flew,
    Not one was tardy;
Arms were from shoulders sent,
Scalps to the teeth were rent,
Down the French peasants went;
    Our men were hardy.

This while our noble King,
His broad sword brandishing,
Down the French host did ding,
    As to o'er-whelm it;
And many a deep wound lent,
His arms with blood besprent,
And many a cruel dent
    Bruisëd his helmet.

Gloster, that Duke so good,
Next of the royal blood,
For famous England stood
    With his brave brother;
Clarence, in steel so bright,
Though but a maiden knight,
Yet in that furious fight,
    Scarce such another.

Warwick in blood did wade,
Oxford the foe invade,
And cruel slaughter made,
    Still as they ran up;
Suffolk his axe did ply,
Beaumont and Willoughby
Bare them right doughtily,
    Ferrers and Fanhope.

Upon Saint Crispin's day
Fought was this noble fray,
Which fame did not delay
    To England to carry;

O, when shall English men
With such acts fill a pen,
Or England breed again,
   Such a King Harry?

SO WELL I LOVE THEE

So well I love thee, as without thee I
Love nothing; if I might choose, I'd rather die
Than be one day debarred thy company.

Since beasts and plants do grow, and live and move,
Beasts are those men that such a life approve:
He only lives that deadly is in love.

The corn that in the ground is sown first dies,
And of one seed do many ears arise:
Love, this world's corn, by dying multiplies.

The seeds of love first by thy eyes were thrown
Into a ground untilled, a heart unknown
To bear such fruit, till by thy hands 'twas sown.

Look, as your looking glass by chance may fall,
Divide, and break in many pieces small,
And yet shows forth the self-same face in all,

Proportions, features, graces just the same,
And in the smallest piece as well the name
Of fairest one deserves as in the richest frame,

So all my thoughts are pieces but of you,
Which put together makes a glass so true
As I therein no other's face but yours can view.

ENGLISH MADRIGAL VERSE

The dozens of song books published between 1588 and 1622 attest to the vigor and popularity of the song tradition in the latter part of the English Renaissance. The rise of the song as an art form is roughly parallel to the rise of the Petrarchan movement; both had run their courses by the third decade of the seventeenth century, and the two movements are intimately related.

A musical distinction should be made between the work of the Madrigalists and the work of the Lutenists. The madrigal is an unaccompanied song for at least three but seldom more than six voices. It is constructed of short musical phrases, each phrase being taken up consecutively by the several voice parts; the verbal phrases, controlled by the musical, are several times reiterated and varied; each voice part has an equal share in the melodic interest, though occasionally all the voices move together in solid masses of harmony. Because of the elaborately repetitive nature of the madrigal, it seldom uses more than a single stanza of poetry. The Lutenists, who commonly described their compositions as Airs, wrote music for solo parts, using several verbal stanzas, for each of which the music was the same.

But this musical distinction is not important to the poetry. Frequently the same poems were set and performed both as madrigals and as solos sung to the accompaniment of lute or viol or both.

The composers got their poems from a variety of sources. They set to music poems that were already established in the English poetic tradition; they gathered and often refined a variety of folk poetry; a few of them wrote some of their own poems; and all except Campion probably at one time or another hired other poets to write original poems for them. Of the more than fifteen hundred poems gathered by E. H. Fellowes in his monumental *English Madrigal Verse*, fewer than two hundred may be assigned with any certainty to particular authors. Yet among these anonymous poems are some of the finest examples of Petrarchan art, and some of the purest examples of style in our language. Though the source of this poetry was consciously Italian (a few songs were even written and sung in that language), in the best poems the elaborately decorative detail complicated by an equally elaborate syntax is subdued, so that the lines are relatively clean units and so that the details, even when decorative, are relatively ordered and simple. This technical simplicity was no doubt necessitated by the elaborate music, especially of the Madrigal; but the technique can be deceiving. These are not simply "songs" in the usual sense of that word, or simply lovely objects like toys or jewels; they are genuine poems, and they carry their significance within themselves.

TEXT:

The poems that follow are printed in the order decided upon by E. H. Fellowes in his collection of *English Madrigal Verse: 1588–1632;* the names heading them are not of the authors of the poems but of the composers in whose song books they first appear. The authors of the poems themselves are unknown.

[THOMAS BATESON]

I heard a noise

I heard a noise and wishëd for a sight.
I looked aside and did a shadow see,
Whose substance was the sum of my delight;
It came unseen, and so it went from me.

But yet conceit persuaded my intent
There was a substance where the shadow went.
I did not play Narcissus in conceit,
I did not see my shadow in a spring;
I knew my eyes were dimmed with no deceit,
I saw the shadow of some worthy thing;
For as I saw the shadow passing by,
I had a glance of something in my eye.
Shadow, or she, or both, or choose you whether,
Blest be the thing that brought the shadow hither.

[WILLIAM BYRD]

When younglings first

When younglings first on Cupid fix their sight,
And see him naked, blindfold, and a boy,
Though bow and shafts and firebrand be his might,
Yet ween they he can work them none annoy.
And therefore with his purple wings they play,
For glorious seemeth Love, though light as feather,
And when they've done, they ween to 'scape away,
For blind men, say they, shoot they know not whither.
But when by proof they find that he did see,
And that his wound did rather dim their sight,
They wonder more how such a lad as he
Should be of such surpassing power and might.
But ants have galls, so hath the bee his sting.
Then shield me, heavens, from such a subtle thing.

Is Love a boy?

Is Love a boy? What means he then to strike?
Or is he blind? Why will he be a guide?
Is he a man? Why doth he hurt his like?
Is he a god? Why doth he men deride?

Not one of these, but one compact of all:
A wilful boy, a man still dealing blows,
Of purpose blind to lead men to their thrall,
A god that rules unruly, God He knows!
Boy, pity me that am a child again;
Blind, be no more my guide to make me stray;
Man, use thy might to force away my pain;
God, do me good and lead me to my way.
And if thou beest a power to me unknown,
Power of my life, let here thy grace be shown.

Penelope, that longëd for the sight

Penelope, that longëd for the sight
Of her Ulysses, wandering all too long,
Felt never joy wherein she took delight,
Although she lived in greatest joys among.
So I, poor wretch, possessing that I crave,
Both live and lack by wrong of that I have.
Then blame me not, although to heavens I cry,
And pray the gods that shortly I might die.

What is life

What is life or worldly pleasure?
Seeming shadows quickly sliding.
What is wealth or golden treasure?
Borrowed fortune never biding.
What is grace or princes' smiling?
Hopëd honor, time beguiling.

What are all in one combined,
Which divided so displease?
Apish toys and vain delights,
Mind's unrest and soul's disease.

Come, woeful Orpheus

Come, woeful Orpheus, with thy charming lyre,
And tune my voice unto thy skilful wire;
Some strange chromatic notes do you devise,
That best with mournful accents sympathise;
Of sourest sharps and uncouth flats make choice,
And I'll thereto compassionate my voice.

[ORLANDO GIBBONS]

The silver swan

The silver swan, who living had no note,
When death approached unlocked her silent throat;
Leaning her breast against the reedy shore,
Thus sung her first and last, and sung no more:
Farewell, all joys; O death, come close mine eyes;
More geese than swans now live, more fools than wise.

Lais now old

Lais now old, that erst attempting lass,
To goddess Venus consecrates her glass;
For she herself hath now no use of one,
No dimpled cheeks hath she to gaze upon.
She cannot see her springtime damask grace,
Nor dare she look upon her winter face.

[THOMAS MORLEY]

In nets of golden wires

In nets of golden wires,
With pearl and ruby spangled,
My heart entangled
Cries and help requires.
Sweet love, from out those briars
But thou vouchsafe to free me,
Ere long, alive, alas, thou shalt not see me.

Sing we and chant it

Sing we and chant it
While love doth grant it.
Not long youth lasteth,
And old age hasteth.
Now is best leisure
To take our pleasure.

All things invite us
Now to delight us.
Hence, care, be packing!
No mirth be lacking!
Let spare no treasure
To live in pleasure.

No, no, Nigella!

No, no, Nigella!
Let who list prove thee,
I cannot love thee.
Have I deserved
Thus to be served?
Well then, content thee,
If thou repent thee.

No, no, Nigella!
In sign I spite thee,
Lo, I requite thee,
Henceforth complaining
Thy love's disdaining,
Sit, thy hands wringing,
Whilst I go singing.

You black bright stars

You black bright stars, that shine while daylight lasteth,
Ah! why haste you away when night time hasteth?
In darker nights the stars still seem the lighter.
On me then shine a-nights with your beams brighter.
Beams that are cause my heart hath so aspired,
Fire mounts aloft, and they my heart have fired.

Ladies, you see time flieth

Ladies, you see time flieth,
And beauty too, it dieth.
Then take your pleasure,
While you have leisure.
Nor be so dainty
Of that which you have plenty.

[MARTIN PEERSON]

Since just disdain

Since just disdain began to rise,
And cry revenge for spiteful wrong,
What erst I praised I now despise,
And think my love was all too long.

I tread in dust that scornful pride
Which in thy looks I have descried.
Thy beauty is a painted skin
For fools to see their faces in.

Thine eyes that some as stars esteem,
From whence themselves, they say, take light,
Like to the foolish fire I deem,
That leads men to their death by night.
Thy words and oaths are light as wind,
And yet far lighter is thy mind.
Thy friendship is a broken reed
That fails thy friend in greatest need.

The spring of joy is dry

The spring of joy is dry
That ran into my heart;
And all my comforts fly.
My love and I must part.
Farewell, my love, I go,
If fate will have it so.
Yet to content us both
Return again, as doth
The shadow to the hour,
The bee unto the flower,
The fish unto the hook,
The cattle to the brook,
That we may sport our fill
And love continue still.

Where shall a sorrow great

Where shall a sorrow great enough be sought
For this sad ruin which the Fates have wrought,
Unless the Fates themselves should weep and wish
Their curbless powers had been controlled in this?

For thy loss, worthiest lord, no mourning eye
Has flood enough; no Muse nor elegy
Enough expression to thy worth can lend;
No, though thy Sidney had survived his friend.
Dead, noble Brooke shall be to us a name
Of grief and honor still, whose deathless fame
And virtue purchased as makes us to be
Unjust to Nature in lamenting thee,
Wailing an old man's fate, as if in pride
And heat of youth he had untimely died.

[FRANCIS PILKINGTON]

Stay, nymph

Stay, nymph, the ground seeks but to kiss thy feet.
Hark, hark, how Philomela sweetly sings;
Whilst water-wanton fishes, as they meet,
Strike crotchet-time amidst these crystal springs,
And Zephyrus 'mongst the leaves sweet murmur rings.
Stay but a while, Phoebe no tell-tale is,
She her Endymion, I'll my Phoebe kiss.

Have I found her

Have I found her (O rich finding!)
Goddess-like for to behold,
Her fair tresses seemly binding
In a chain of pearl and gold?
Chain me, chain me, O most fair,
Chain me to thee with that hair.

Brooke: the poet Fulke Grev-
ille, first Lord Brooke, who
was Sir Philip Sidney's clos-
est friend.

Wake, sleepy Thyrsis

Wake, sleepy Thyrsis, wake
For Love and Venus' sake.
Come, let us mount the hills,
Which Zephyrus' cool breath fills;
Or let us tread new alleys
In yonder shady valleys.
Rise, rise, rise,
Lighten thy heavy eyes;
See how the streams do glide,
And the green meads divide.
But stream nor fire shall part
This and this joinèd heart.

[THOMAS VAUTOR]

Sweet Suffolk owl

Sweet Suffolk owl, so trimly dight
With feathers like a lady bright,
Thou singest alone, sitting by night,
Te whit, te whoo, te whit, te whit.
Thy note, that forth so freely rolls,
With shrill command the mouse controls,
And sings a dirge for dying souls,
Te whit, te whoo, te whit, te whit.

Dainty sweet bird

Dainty sweet bird, who art encagèd there,
Alas, how like thine and my fortunes are.
Both prisoners, both sing, and both singing thus
Strive to please her, who hath imprisoned us.
Only in this we differ, thou and I,
Thou livest singing, but I singing die.

[JOHN WARD]

Come, sable night

Come, sable night, put on thy mourning stole,
And help Amyntas sadly to condole.
Behold, the sun hath shut his golden eye,
The day is spent, and shades fair lights supply.
All things in sweet repose
Their labors close;
Only Amyntas wastes his hours in wailing,
Whilst all his hopes do faint, and life is failing.

[THOMAS WEELKES]

The gods have heard my vows

The gods have heard my vows,
Fond Lycë, whose fair brows
Wont scorn with such disdain
My love, my tears, my pain.

But now those Spring-tide roses
Are turned to Winter posies,
To rue and thyme and sage,
Fitting that shrivelled age.

Now, youths with hot desire,
See, see that flameless fire,
Which erst your hearts so burned,
Quick into ashes turned.

[JOHN ATTEY]

Vain Hope, adieu

Vain Hope, adieu! thou life-consuming moth,
Which frets my soul in pieces with delay;
My well-spun threads will make no cloth
To shroud me from the tempest of decay;
For storms of fortune drench me like a flood,
Whilst rancor's frost nips merit in her bud.

[WILLIAM BARLEY]

Flow forth, abundant tears

Flow forth, abundant tears,
Bedew this doleful face,
Disorder now thy hairs,
That lives in such disgrace.

Ah! death exceedeth far
This life which I endure,
That still keeps me in war
Who can no peace procure.

I love whom I should hate.
She flies; I follow fast.
Such is my bitter state,
I wish no life to last.

Alas, affection strong
To whom I must obey,
My reason so doth wrong
As it can bear no sway.

My field of flint I find;
My harvest vain desire;
For he that sowëd wind
Now reapeth storm for hire.

Alas, like flowers of spine
Thy graces rosy be;
I prick these hands of mine
For haste to gather thee.

But now shall sorrow slack;
I yield to mortal strife,
To die; this for thy sake
Shall honor all my life.

Short is my rest

Short is my rest, whose toil is over long;
My joys are dark, but clear is seen my woe;
In safety small, great wracks I bide through wrong;
Whose time is swift, and yet my hope but slow.
Each grief and wound in my poor soul appears
That laugheth hours and weepeth many years.

Deeds of the day are fables for the night;
Sighs of desire are smokes of thoughtful tears;
My steps are false although my path is right;
Disgrace is bold, my favor full of fears.
Disquiet sleep keeps audit of my life,
Where rare content doth make displeasure rife.

The doleful clock, which is the voice of Time,
Calls on my end before my hap is seen;
Thus falls my hopes, whose harms have power to climb,
Not come to have which long in wish have been.
I trust your love, and fear not others' hate;
Be you with me and I have Caesar's fate.

[JOHN COOPER]

Oft thou hast with greedy ear

Oft thou hast with greedy ear
Drunk my notes and words of pleasure;
In affection's equal measure
Now my songs of sorrow hear,
Since from thee my griefs do grow,
Whom alive I prized so dear.
The more my joy, the more my woe.

Music, though it sweetens pain,
Yet no whit impairs lamenting,
But in passions like consenting
Makes them constant that complain,
And enchants their fancies so
That all comforts they disdain,
And fly from joy to dwell with woe.

[WILLIAM CORKINE]

Sweet Cupid, ripen her desire

Sweet Cupid, ripen her desire,
Thy joyful harvest may begin;
If age approach a little nigher,
'Twill be too late to get it in.

Cold winter storms lay standing corn,
Which once too ripe will never rise,
And lovers wish themselves unborn
When all their joys lie in their eyes.

Then, sweet, let us embrace and kiss.
Shall beauty shale upon the ground?
If age bereave us of this bliss,
Then will no more such sport be found.

Shall a frown

Shall a frown or angry eye,
Shall a word unfitly placed,
Shall a shadow make me fly,
As I were with tigers chased?
Love must not be so disgraced.

Shall I woo her in despite?
Shall I turn her from her flying?
Shall I tempt her with delight?
Shall I laugh out her denying?
No! Beware of lovers' crying.

Shall I then with patient mind
Still attend her wayward pleasure?
Time will make her prove more kind.
Let her coyness then take leisure.
Pains are worthy such a treasure.

My dearest mistress

My dearest mistress, let us live and love,
And care not what old doting fools reprove.
Let us not fear their censures nor esteem,
What they of us and of our loves shall deem.
Old Age's critic and censorious brow
Cannot of youthful dalliance allow,
Nor never could endure that we should taste
Of those delights which they themselves are past.

[JOHN DOWLAND]

Dear, if you change

Dear, if you change, I'll never choose again;
Sweet, if you shrink, I'll never think of love;
Fair, if you fail, I'll judge all beauty vain;
Wise, if too weak, moe wits I'll never prove.
Dear, Sweet, Fair, Wise, change, shrink, nor be not weak;
And, on my faith, my faith shall never break!

Earth with her flowers shall sooner heaven adorn;
Heaven her bright stars through earth's dim globe shall
      move;
Fire heat shall lose, and frosts of flames be born;
Air, made to shine, as black as hell shall prove.
Earth, Heaven, Fire, Air, the world transformed shall
      view,
Ere I prove false to faith, or strange to you.

Come away, come, sweet love

Come away, come, sweet love!
The golden morning breaks;
All the earth, all the air
Of love and pleasure speaks.
Teach thine arms then to embrace,
And sweet rosy lips to kiss,
And mix our souls in mutual bliss;
Eyes were made for beauty's grace,
Viewing, rueing love-long pain
Procured by beauty's rude disdain.

Come away, come, sweet love!
The golden morning wastes,
While the sun from his sphere
His fiery arrows casts,
Making all the shadows fly,
Playing, staying in the grove
To entertain the stealth of love.
Thither, sweet love, let us hie,
Flying, dying in desire
Winged with sweet hopes and heavenly fire.

Come away, come, sweet love!
Do not in vain adorn
Beauty's grace, that should rise
Like to the naked morn.
Lilies on the riverside
And fair Cyprian flowers new-blown
Desire no beauties but their own.
Ornament is nurse of pride;
Pleasure, measure, love's delight.
Haste then, sweet love, our wishèd flight!

Sleep, wayward thoughts

Sleep, wayward thoughts, and rest you with my love.
Let not my Love be with my love displeased.
Touch not, proud hands, lest you her anger move,
But pine you with my longings long diseased.
Thus while she sleeps I sorrow for her sake,
So sleeps my Love, and yet my love doth wake.

But O the fury of my restless fear;
The hidden anguish of my flesh desires;
The glories and the beauties, that appear
Between her brows near Cupid's closèd fires.
Thus while she sleeps moves sighing for her sake.
So sleeps my Love, and yet my love doth wake.

My love doth rage, and yet my Love doth rest.
Fear in my love, and yet my Love secure.
Peace in my Love, and yet my love oppressed,
Impatient yet of perfect temperature.
Sleep, dainty Love, while I sigh for thy sake.
So sleeps my Love, and yet my love doth wake.

Fine knacks for ladies

Fine knacks for ladies, cheap, choice, brave and new!
Good pennyworths! but money cannot move.
I keep a fair but for the fair to view;
A beggar may be liberal of love.
Though all my wares be trash, the heart is true.

Great gifts are guiles and look for gifts again;
My trifles come as treasures from my mind.
It is a precious jewel to be plain;
Sometimes in shell the Orient's pearls we find.
Of others take a sheaf, of me a grain.

Within this pack pins, points, laces, and gloves,
And divers toys fitting a country fair.
But in my heart, where duty serves and loves,
Turtles and twins, court's brood, a heavenly pair.
Happy the heart that thinks of no removes!

Flow not so fast

Flow not so fast, ye fountains;
What needeth all this haste?
Swell not above your mountains,
Nor spend your time in waste.
Gentle springs, freshly your salt tears
Must still fall dropping from their spheres.

Weep they apace whom Reason
Or lingering Time can ease.
My sorrow can no Season,
Nor aught besides, appease.
Gentle springs, freshly your salt tears
Must still fall dropping from their spheres.

Time can abate the terror
Of every common pain;
But common grief is error,
True grief will still remain.
Gentle springs, freshly your salt tears
Must still fall dropping from their spheres.

Go, nightly Cares

Go, nightly Cares, the enemy to rest,
Forbear awhile to vex my grievëd sprite.
So long your weight hath lain upon my breast
That, lo, I live of life bereavëd quite.
O give me time to draw my weary breath,
Or let me die, as I desire the death.
Welcome, sweet Death! O Life no life, a hell!
Then thus and thus I bid the world farewell.

False world, farewell! the enemy to rest,
Now do thy worst, I do not weigh thy spite;
Free from thy cares I live for ever blest,
Enjoying peace, and heavenly true delight,
Delight whom woes nor sorrows shall amate;
Nor fears nor tears disturb her happy state.
And thus I leave thy hopes, thy joys untrue;
And thus and thus, vain world, again adieu.

amate: cast down.

[ROBERT JONES]

My love is neither young nor old

My love is neither young nor old,
Not fiery hot, nor frozen cold;
But fresh and fair as springing briar,
Blooming the fruit of love's desire.

Not snowy white nor rosy red,
But fair enough for shepherd's bed;
And such a love was never seen
On hill or dale or country green.

Shall I look

Shall I look to ease my grief?
No, my sight is lost with eyeing.
Shall I speak and beg relief?
No, my voice is hoarse with crying.
What remains but only dying?

Love and I of late did part,
But the boy my peace envying,
Like a Parthian threw his dart
Backward, and did wound me flying.
What remains but only dying?

She whom then I lookëd on,
My remembrance beautifying,
Stays with me though I am gone,
Gone and at her mercy lying.
What remains but only dying?

Shall I try her thoughts and write?
No, I have no means of trying.
If I should, yet at first sight
She would answer with denying.
What remains but only dying?

Thus my vital breath doth waste,
And my blood with sorrow drying;
Sighs and tears make life to last,
For a while their place supplying.
What remains but only dying?

WILLIAM SHAKESPEARE: 1564–1616

Though Shakespeare's reputation as a dramatist has certainly intensified his reputation as a poet, the one does not depend upon the other. Nevertheless, the profound originality of the dramatist sometimes obscures the essential conventionality of the poet.

Shakespeare began his poetic career with two narrative poems, *Venus and Adonis* and *The Rape of Lucrece*. The first is the kind of poem most fashionable at the height of the Petrarchan flourishing, an erotic retelling of a story from Ovid's *Metamorphoses*; the second has its source in those Latin writers approved by the "new" learning, principally Ovid and Livy. Both poems make use of the familiar Petrarchan machinery: they are highly ornate, decorative, and rhetorical; they are artificial to an extreme degree; and they forbid the reader to take them very seriously. These poems were very popular in the early 1600s, and they have remained fairly popular in our own time; but it is unlikely that they would be read now were it not for Shakespeare's other achievements.

In most of the *Sonnets*, Shakespeare is a conventional and skillful Petrarchist, though the rhetoric is less flamboyant than that of his earlier narrative poems and more finished than that of any Petrarchist save Sidney at his best and some of the song writers. Shakespeare seems at ease in the Petrarchan tradition, but he also seems at ease in an earlier, plainer tradition; note especially sonnets 62: *Sin of self-love*, 129: *The expense of spirit*, and 146: *Poor soul, the center of my sinful earth.* In other poems, such as 116: *Let me not to the marriage of true minds*, the two methods, the plain and the ornate, exist side by side, yet without violent conflict or awkwardness. In the poems noted here, in several others, and in the remarkable *The Phoenix and the Turtle,* Shakespeare is at his best, and squarely in the major tradition of the short English poem.

Text:

A *New Variorium Edition of Shakespeare: The Poems,* edited by H. E. Rollins (1938).
Shakespeare's Songs and Poems, edited by Edward Hubler (1959).

THE SONNETS

3: *Look in thy glass*

Look in thy glass, and tell the face thou viewest
Now is the time that face should form another,
Whose fresh repair if now thou not renewest,
Thou dost beguile the world, unbless some mother.
For where is she so fair whose uneared womb
Disdains the tillage of thy husbandry?
Or who is he so fond will be the tomb
Of his self-love, to stop posterity?
Thou art thy mother's glass, and she in thee
Calls back the lovely April of her prime.
So thou through windows of thine age shalt see,
Despite of wrinkles, this thy golden time.
    But if thou live remembered not to be,
    Die single, and thine image dies with thee.

unbless: i.e., not bless with motherhood.   *uneared:* unplowed.
fond: foolish.

12: *When I do count the clock*

When I do count the clock that tells the time,
And see the brave day sunk in hideous night;
When I behold the violet past prime,
And sable curls all silvered o'er with white;
When lofty trees I see barren of leaves,
Which erst from heat did canopy the herd,
And summer's green all girded up in sheaves
Borne on the bier with white and bristly beard—
Then of thy beauty do I question make,
That thou among the wastes of time must go,
Since sweets and beauties do themselves forsake
And die as fast as they see others grow.
  And nothing 'gainst Time's scythe can make defense
  Save breed, to brave him when he takes thee hence.

30: *When to the sessions*

When to the sessions of sweet silent thought
I summon up remembrance of things past,
I sigh the lack of many a thing I sought
And with old woes new wail my dear time's waste.
Then can I drown an eye unused to flow
For precious friends hid in death's dateless night,
And weep afresh love's long since cancelled woe,
And moan the expense of many a vanished sight.
Then can I grieve at grievances foregone,
And heavily from woe to woe tell o'er
The sad account of fore-bemoanëd moan,
Which I new pay as if not paid before:
    But if the while I think on thee, dear friend,
    All losses are restored and sorrows end.

brave him: taunt or defy Time.

53: *What is your substance*

What is your substance, whereof are you made,
That millions of strange shadows on you tend?
Since every one hath, every one, one shade,
And you, but one, can every shadow lend.
Describe Adonis, and the counterfeit
Is poorly imitated after you;
On Helen's cheek all art of beauty set,
And you in Grecian tires are painted new;
Speak of the spring and foison of the year,
The one doth shadow of your beauty show,
The other as your bounty doth appear;
And you in every blessèd shape we know.
    In all external grace you have some part,
    But you like none, none you, for constant heart.

55: *Not marble nor the gilded monuments*

Not marble nor the gilded monuments
Of princes shall outlive this powerful rime,
But you shall shine more bright in these contents
Than unswept stone, besmeared with sluttish time.
When wasteful war shall statues overturn,
And broils root out the work of masonry,
Nor Mars his sword nor war's quick fire shall burn
The living record of your memory.
'Gainst death and all oblivious enmity
Shall you pace forth, your praise shall still find room
Even in the eyes of all posterity
That wear this world out to the ending doom.
    So, till the judgment that yourself arise,
    You live in this, and dwell in lovers' eyes.

tires: attire.
foison: harvest, i.e., autumn.

stone: i.e., the slab over the
grave on a church floor.

60: *Like as the waves*

Like as the waves make towards the pebbled shore,
So do our minutes hasten to their end,
Each changing place with that which goes before,
In sequent toil all forwards do contend.
Nativity, once in the main of light,
Crawls to maturity, wherewith being crowned,
Crookèd eclipses 'gainst his glory fight,
And Time that gave doth now his gift confound.
Time doth transfix the flourish set on youth
And delves the parallels in beauty's brow,
Feeds on the rarities of nature's truth,
And nothing stands but for his scythe to mow.
    And yet to times in hope my verse shall stand,
    Praising thy worth, despite his cruel hand.

62: *Sin of self-love*

Sin of self-love possesseth all mine eye
And all my soul and all my every part;
And for this sin there is no remedy,
It is so grounded inward in my heart.
Methinks no face so gracious is as mine,
No shape so true, no truth of such account,
And for myself mine own worth do define
As I all other in all worths surmount.
But when my glass shows me myself indeed,
Beated and chopped with tanned antiquity,
Mine own self-love quite contrary I read:
Self so self-loving were iniquity.
    'Tis thee, myself, that for myself I praise,
    Painting my age with beauty of thy days.

Nativity: i.e., the newborn   *chopped:* lined, aged.
child.

64: *When I have seen*

When I have seen by Time's fell hand defaced
The rich proud cost of outworn buried age,
When sometime lofty towers I see down-razed,
And brass eternal slave to mortal rage;
When I have seen the hungry ocean gain
Advantage on the kingdom of the shore,
And the firm soil win of the watery main,
Increasing store with loss and loss with store;
When I have seen such interchange of state,
Or state itself confounded to decay,
Ruin hath taught me thus to ruminate
That Time will come and take my love away.
    This thought is as a death, which cannot choose
    But weep to have that which it fears to lose.

65: *Since brass nor stone*

Since brass, nor stone, nor earth, nor boundless sea,
But sad mortality o'er-sways their power,
How with this rage shall beauty hold a plea,
Whose action is no stronger than a flower?
O how shall summer's honey breath hold out
Against the wrackful siege of battering days,
When rocks impregnable are not so stout,
Nor gates of steel so strong, but Time decays?
O fearful meditation! Where, alack,
Shall Time's best jewel from Time's chest lie hid?
Or what strong hand can hold his swift foot back,
Or who his spoil of beauty can forbid?
    O none, unless this miracle have might,
    That in black ink my love may still shine bright.

71: *No longer mourn for me*

No longer mourn for me when I am dead
Than you shall hear the surly sullen bell
Give warning to the world that I am fled
From this vile world, with vilest worms to dwell.
Nay, if you read this line, remember not
The hand that writ it; for I love you so
That I in your sweet thoughts would be forgot,
If thinking on me then should make you woe.
O if, I say, you look upon this verse
When I, perhaps, compounded am with clay,
Do not so much as my poor name rehearse,
But let your love even with my life decay,
    Lest the wise world should look into your moan,
    And mock you with me after I am gone.

73: *That time of year*

That time of year thou mayst in me behold
When yellow leaves, or none, or few, do hang
Upon those boughs which shake against the cold,
Bare ruined choirs, where late the sweet birds sang;
In me thou seest the twilight of such day
As after sunset fadeth in the west,
Which by and by black night doth take away,
Death's second self, that seals up all in rest;
In me thou seest the glowing of such fire
That on the ashes of his youth doth lie,
As the death-bed whereon it must expire,
Consumed with that which it was nourished by.
    This thou perceiv'st, which makes thy love more strong,
    To love that well which thou must leave ere long.

choir. that part of the church in which services were sung. The image suggests a church fallen to ruins, with only the high roofless choir of the abbey remaining.

77: *Thy glass will show thee*

Thy glass will show thee how thy beauties wear,
Thy dial how thy precious minutes waste;
The vacant leaves thy mind's imprint will bear,
And of this book this learning mayst thou taste.
The wrinkles which thy glass will truly show
Of mouthèd graves will give thee memory;
Thou by thy dial's shady stealth mayst know
Time's thievish progress to eternity.
Look! what thy memory cannot contain
Commit to these waste blanks, and thou shalt find
Those children nursed, delivered from thy brain,
To take a new acquaintance of thy mind.
   These offices, so oft as thou wilt look,
   Shall profit thee and much enrich thy book.

97: *How like a winter*

How like a winter hath my absence been
From thee, the pleasure of the fleeting year!
What freezings have I felt, what dark days seen,
What old December's bareness every where!
And yet this time removed was summer's time;
The teeming autumn, big with rich increase,
Bearing the wanton burden of the prime,
Like widowed wombs after their lord's decease.
Yet this abundant issue seemed to me
But hope of orphans and unfathered fruit;
For summer and his pleasures wait on thee,
And, thou away, the very birds are mute,
   Or, if they sing, 'tis with so dull a cheer
   That leaves look pale, dreading the winter's near.

Sonnet 77: intended to accompany a gift of a book of blank pages, which was to be used to record thoughts, observations, etc.

104: *To me fair friend*

To me, fair friend, you never can be old,
For as you were when first your eye I eyed,
Such seems your beauty still. Three winters cold
Have from the forests shook three summers' pride,
Three beauteous springs to yellow autumn turned
In process of the seasons have I seen,
Three April perfumes in three hot Junes burned,
Since first I saw you fresh, which yet are green.
Ah, yet doth beauty, like a dial hand
Steal from his figure, and no pace perceived;
So your sweet hue, which methinks still doth stand,
Hath motion, and mine eye may be deceived:
    For fear of which, hear this, thou age unbred;
    Ere you were born was beauty's summer dead.

106: *When in the chronicle of wasted time*

When in the chronicle of wasted time
I see descriptions of the fairest wights,
And beauty making beautiful old rime
In praise of ladies dead and lovely knights,
Then in the blazon of sweet beauty's best,
Of hand, of foot, of lip, of eye, of brow,
I see their antique pen would have expressed
Even such a beauty as you master now.
So all their praises are but prophecies
Of this our time, all you prefiguring;
And, for they looked but with divining eyes,
They had not still enough your worth to sing:
    For we which now behold these present days
    Have eyes to wonder, but lack tongues to praise.

wights: men, a poetical word.

116: *Let me not to the marriage of true minds*

Let me not to the marriage of true minds
Admit impediments. Love is not love
Which alters when it alteration finds,
Or bends with the remover to remove:
O no! it is an ever fixëd mark,
That looks on tempests and is never shaken;
It is the star to every wandering bark,
Whose worth's unknown, although his height be taken.
Love's not Time's fool, though rosy lips and cheeks
Within his bending sickle's compass come;
Love alters not with his brief hours and weeks,
But bears it out even to the edge of doom.
    If this be error and upon me proved,
    I never writ, nor no man ever loved.

129: *The expense of spirit*

The expense of spirit in a waste of shame
Is lust in action; and till action, lust
Is perjured, murderous, bloody, full of blame,
Savage, extreme, rude, cruel, not to trust;
Enjoyed no sooner, but despisëd straight;
Past reason hunted and no sooner had,
Past reason hated as a swallowed bait
On purpose laid to make the taker mad:
Mad in pursuit, and in possession so;
Had, having, and in quest to have, extreme;
A bliss in proof, and proved, a very woe;
Before, a joy proposed; behind, a dream.
    All this the world well knows; yet none knows well
    To shun the heaven that leads men to this hell.

146: Poor soul, the center of my sinful earth

Poor soul, the center of my sinful earth,
Fooled by these rebel powers that thee array,
Why dost thou pine within and suffer dearth,
Painting thy outward walls so costly gay?
Why so large cost, having so short a lease,
Dost thou upon thy fading mansion spend?
Shall worms, inheritors of this excess,
Eat up thy charge? Is this thy body's end?
Then, soul, live thou upon thy servant's loss,
And let that pine to aggravate thy store;
By terms divine in selling hours of dross;
Within be fed, without be rich no more.
    So shalt thou feed on Death that feeds on men,
    And Death once dead, there's no more dying then.

SONGS FROM THE PLAYS

Who is Silvia?

Who is Silvia? what is she,
    That all our swains commend her?
Holy, fair, and wise is she;
    The heaven such grace did lend her,
That she might admirèd be.

Is she kind as she is fair?
    For beauty lives with kindness:
Love doth to her eyes repair
    To help him of his blindness;
And being helped, inhabits there.

Fooled by: this is an emendation suggested by Edmund Malone, to correct an obvious error by the printer of the 1609 Quarto.

Then to Silvia let us sing
  That Silvia is excelling;
She excels each mortal thing
  Upon the dull earth dwelling.
To her let us garlands bring.

Take, O take those lips away

Take, O take those lips away,
  That so sweetly were forsworn;
And those eyes, the break of day,
  Lights that do mislead the morn:
But my kisses bring again,
    Bring again,
Seals of love, but sealed in vain,
    Sealed in vain.

When daisies pied

When daisies pied and violets blue
  And lady-smocks all silver-white
And cuckoo-buds of yellow hue
  Do paint the meadows with delight,
The cuckoo then, on every tree,
Mocks married men; for thus sings he,
    Cuckoo,
Cuckoo, cuckoo! O word of fear
Unpleasing to a married ear!

When shepherds pipe on oaten straws,
  And merry larks are ploughmen's clocks,
When turtles tread, and rooks, and daws,
  And maidens bleach their summer smocks,
The cuckoo then, on every tree,
Mocks married men; for thus sings he,
    Cuckoo,
Cuckoo, cuckoo! O word of fear,
Unpleasing to a married ear!

When icicles hang by the wall,
   And Dick the shepherd blows his nail,
And Tom bears logs into the hall,
   And milk comes frozen home in pail,
When blood is nipped, and ways be foul,
Then nightly sings the staring owl,
     Tu-whit, to-who,
     A merry note,
While greasy Joan doth keel the pot.

When all aloud the wind doth blow,
   And coughing drowns the parson's saw,
And birds sit brooding in the snow,
   And Marian's nose looks red and raw,
When roasted crabs hiss in the bowl,
Then nightly sings the staring owl,
     Tu-whit, to-who,
     A merry note,
While greasy Joan doth keel the pot.

Now the hungry lion

Now the hungry lion roars,
   And the wolf behowls the moon;
Whilst the heavy ploughman snores,
   All with weary task fordone.
Now the wasted brands do glow,
   Whilst the screech owl, screeching loud,
Puts the wretch that lies in woe
   In remembrance of a shroud.
Now it is the time of night
   That the graves, all gaping wide,
Every one lets forth his sprite,
   In the churchway paths to glide;
And we fairies, that do run
   By the triple Hecate's team
From the presence of the sun,
   Following darkness like a dream,

Now are frolic. Not a mouse
Shall disturb this hallowed house.
I am sent, with broom, before,
To sweep the dust behind the door.

Tell me where is fancy bred

Tell me where is fancy bred,
Or in the heart or in the head?
How begot, how nourishëd?
        Reply, reply!
It is engendered in the eyes,
With gazing fed; and fancy dies
In the cradle where it lies.
        Let us all ring fancy's knell:
        I'll begin it—Ding, dong, bell.
        Ding, dong, bell.

Under the greenwood tree

Under the greenwood tree
Who loves to lie with me,
And turn his merry note
Unto the sweet bird's throat,
Come hither, come hither, come hither:
        Here shall he see
        No enemy
But winter and rough weather.

Who doth amibition shun
And loves to live in the sun,
Seeking the food he eats,
And pleased with what he gets,
Come hither, come hither, come hither:
        Here shall he see
        No enemy
But winter and rough weather.

Blow, blow, thou winter wind

Blow, blow, thou winter wind,
Thou are not so unkind
   As man's ingratitude;
Thy tooth is not so keen
Because thou art not seen,
   Although thy breath be rude.
Heigh-ho! sing heigh-ho, unto the green holly:
Most friendship is feigning, most loving mere folly:
   Then heigh-ho! the holly!
    This life is most jolly.

Freeze, freeze, thou bitter sky
That dost not bite so nigh
   As benefits forgot:
Though thou the waters warp,
Thy sting is not so sharp
   As friend remembered not.
Heigh-ho! sing heigh-ho, unto the green holly:
Most friendship is feigning, most loving mere folly:
   Then heigh-ho! the holly!
    This life is most jolly.

O mistress mine

O mistress mine, where are you roaming?
O, stay and hear; your true-love's coming,
   That can sing both high and low.
Trip no further, pretty sweeting;
Journeys end in lovers meeting,
   Every wise man's son doth know.

What is love? 'tis not hereafter;
Present mirth hath present laughter;
　　What's to come is still unsure:
In delay there lies no plenty;
Then come kiss me, sweet and twenty!
　　Youth's a stuff will not endure.

When that I was and a little tiny boy

When that I was and a little tiny boy,
　　With hey, ho, the wind and the rain,
A foolish thing was but a toy,
　　For the rain it raineth every day.

But when I came to man's estate,
　　With hey, ho, the wind and the rain,
'Gainst knaves and thieves men shut their gate,
　　For the rain it raineth every day.

But when I came, alas! to wive,
　　With hey, ho, the wind and the rain,
By swaggering could I never thrive,
　　For the rain it raineth every day.

But when I came unto my beds,
　　With hey, ho, the wind and the rain,
With tosspots still had drunken heads,
　　For the rain it raineth every day.

A great while ago the world begun,
　　With hey, ho, the wind and the rain;
But that's all one, our play is done,
　　And we'll strive to please you every day.

Hark, hark! the lark

Hark, hark! the lark at heaven's gate sings,
   And Phoebus 'gins arise,
His steeds to water at those springs
   On chaliced flowers that lies;
And winking Mary-buds begin
   To ope their golden eyes.
With every thing that pretty is
   My lady sweet, arise:
      Arise, arise!

Fear no more

Fear no more the heat o' the sun
   Nor the furious winter's rages;
Thou thy worldly task hast done,
   Home art gone, and ta'en thy wages;
Golden lads and girls all must,
As chimney-sweepers, come to dust.

Fear no more the frown o' the great,
   Thou art past the tyrant's stroke;
Care no more to clothe and eat,
   To thee the reed is as the oak:
The scepter, learning, physic, must
All follow this and come to dust.

Fear no more the lightning flash,
   Nor the all-dreaded thunder-stone;
Fear not slander, censure rash;
   Thou hast finished joy and moan:
All lovers young, all lovers must
Consign to thee and come to dust.

No exorciser harm thee!
>Nor no witchcraft charm thee!
Ghost unlaid forbear thee!
>Nothing ill come near thee!
Quiet consummation have,
And renownèd be thy grave.

Where the bee sucks

Where the bee sucks, there suck I:
>In a cowslip's bell I lie;
There I couch when owls do cry.
>On the bat's back I do fly
>After summer merrily.
>Merrily, merrily shall I live now
Under the blossom that hangs on the bough.

Orpheus with his lute

Orpheus with his lute made trees
And the mountain tops that freeze
>Bow themselves when he did sing:
To his music plants and flowers
Ever sprung, as sun and showers
>There had made a lasting spring.

Everything that heard him play,
Even the billows of the sea,
>Hung their heads, and then lay by:
In sweet music is such art
Killing care and grief of heart
>Fall asleep, or hearing, die.

THE PHOENIX AND THE TURTLE

Let the bird of loudest lay,
On the sole Arabian tree,
Herald sad and trumpet be,
To whose sound chaste wings obey.

But thou shrieking harbinger,
Foul precurrer of the fiend,
Augur of the fever's end,
To this troop come thou not near.

From this session interdict
Every fowl of tyrant wing,
Save the eagle, feathered king;
Keep the obsequy so strict.

Let the priest in surplice white,
That defunctive music can,
Be the death-divining swan,
Lest the requiem lack his right.

And thou treble-dated crow,
That thy sable gender mak'st,
With the breath thou giv'st and tak'st,
'Mongst our mourners shalt thou go.

Here the anthem doth commence:
Love and Constancy is dead;
Phoenix and the turtle fled
In a mutual flame from hence.

So they loved as love in twain
Had the essence but in one;
Two distincts, division none:
Number there in love was slain.

defunctive: i.c., funeral.　　　　*can*: knows.

Hearts remote, yet not asunder;
Distance, and no space was seen
Twixt this turtle and his queen:
But in them it were a wonder.

So between them love did shine
That the turtle saw his right
Flaming in the phoenix' sight;
Either was the other's mine.

Property was thus appalled,
That the self was not the same;
Single nature's double name
Neither two nor one was called.

Reason, in itself confounded,
Saw division grow together,
To themselves, yet either neither,
Simple were so well compounded

That it cried, "How true a twain
Seemeth this concordant one!
Love hath reason, Reason none,
If what parts can so remain."

Whereupon it made this threne
To the phoenix and the dove,
Co-supremes and stars of love,
As chorus to their tragic scene:

Beauty, Truth, and Rarity,
Grace in all simplicity,
Here enclosed in cinders lie.

Death is now the phoenix nest,
And the turtle's loyal breast
To eternity doth rest,

Leaving no posterity:
'Twas not their infirmity,
It was married chastity.

Truth may seem, but cannot be;
Beauty brag, but 'tis not she;
Truth and Beauty buried be.

To this urn let those repair
That are either true or fair;
For these dead birds sigh a prayer.

THOMAS CAMPION: 1567–1620

Campion's early devotion to music and poetry caused him
some difficulty in choosing a profession for a livelihood.
He studied at Cambridge, but did not take a degree; he
entered Gray's Inn for the study of law, but did not go
to the bar; finally, he took a degree in medicine and re-
turned to London to practice.

Campion was the only song writer of his day who
wrote both the words and music of his songs. Though he
was not so great a musician as some others, especially
Dowland, he is certainly the greatest poet of the song
tradition. Unlike many of his fellows, Campion did not
make a very firm distinction between the song and the
poem. In a note to the reader in *Two Books of Airs*, he
writes: "Short airs, if they be skillfully framed and natu-
rally expressed, are like quick and good epigrams in
poesy, many of them showing as much artifice, and breed-
ing as great difficulty as a larger poem."

Campion is among the purest stylists in the language.
Though by virtue of his immersion in the song tradition,
by his choice of subjects, and by the nature of some of
his detail, he must be accounted a Petrarchan, he is never-
theless a remarkably restrained one. He was aware of the
foreign source of the song: ". . . some there are who
admit only French or Italian airs, as if every country had
not his proper air. . . ." But he wished to go beyond the
prevailing practice. In a note to the *Fourth Book of Airs*,
he writes: "The apothecaries have books of gold, whose
leaves being opened are so light as that they are subject
to be shaken with the least breath; yet rightly handled,
they serve both ornament and use. . . ."

For both ornament and use, then, were Campion's airs composed and written. Gently moving, at once gay and profound, delicate and somber, his voice is one that lingers when others more strident have ceased.

TEXT:

Campion's Works, edited by Percival Vivian (1909).

MY SWEETEST LESBIA

My sweetest Lesbia, let us live and love;
And though the sager sort our deeds reprove,
Let us not weigh them: heaven's great lamps do dive
Into their west, and straight again revive:
But soon as once set is our little light,
Then must we sleep one ever-during night.

If all would lead their lives in love like me,
Then bloody swords and armor should not be;
No drum nor trumpet peaceful sleeps should move,
Unless alarm came from the camp of love:
But fools do live, and waste their little light,
And seek with pain their ever-during night.

When timely death my life and fortune ends,
Let not my hearse be vexed with mourning friends;
But let all lovers, rich in triumph, come
And with sweet pastimes grace my happy tomb:
And, Lesbia, close up thou my little light,
And crown with love my ever-during night.

THOUGH YOU ARE YOUNG

Though you are young, and I am old,
Though your veins hot, and my blood cold,
Though youth is moist, and age is dry;
Yet embers live, when flames do die.

The tender graft is easily broke,
But who shall shake the sturdy oak?
You are more fresh and fair than I;
Yet stubs do live when flowers do die.

Thou, that thy youth dost vainly boast,
Know buds are soonest nipped with frost:
Think that thy fortune still doth cry,
"Thou fool, tomorrow thou must die."

FOLLOW THY FAIR SUN

Follow thy fair sun, unhappy shadow;
Though thou be black as night,
And she made all of light,
Yet follow thy fair sun, unhappy shadow.

Follow her whose light thy light depriveth;
Though here thou livest disgraced,
And she in heaven is placed,
Yet follow her whose light the world reviveth.

Follow those pure beams whose beauty burneth,
That so have scorchëd thee,
As thou still black must be,
Till her kind beams thy black to brightness turneth.

Follow her, while yet her glory shineth.
There comes a luckless night
That will dim all her light,
And this the black unhappy shade divineth.

Follow still, since so thy fates ordainëd.
The sun must have his shade,
Till both at once do fade,
The sun still proud, the shadow still disdainëd.

WHEN TO HER LUTE

When to her lute Corinna sings,
Her voice revives the leaden strings,
And doth in highest notes appear,
As any challenged echo clear;
But when she doth of mourning speak,
Even with her sighs the strings do break.

And as her lute doth live or die,
Led by her passion, so must I.
For when of pleasure she doth sing,
My thoughts enjoy a sudden spring;
But if she doth of sorrow speak,
Even from my heart the strings do break.

FOLLOW YOUR SAINT

Follow your saint, follow with accents sweet;
Haste you, sad notes, fall at her flying feet:
There, wrapped in cloud of sorrow, pity move,
And tell the ravisher of my soul I perish for her love.
But if she scorns my never-ceasing pain,
Then burst with sighing in her sight, and ne'er return
        again.

All that I sung still to her praise did tend;
Still she was first, still she my songs did end.
Yet she my love and music both doth fly,
That music that her echo is and beauty's sympathy.
Then let my notes pursue her scornful flight:
It shall suffice that they were breathed and died for her
        delight.

THOU ART NOT FAIR

Thou art not fair, for all thy red and white,
For all those rosy ornaments in thee;
Thou art not sweet, though made of mere delight,
Nor fair nor sweet, unless thou pity me.
I will not soothe thy fancies: thou shalt prove
That beauty is no beauty without love.

Yet love not me, nor seek thou to allure
My thoughts with beauty, were it more divine:
Thy smiles and kisses I cannot endure;
I'll not be wrapped up in those arms of thine.
Now show it, if thou be a woman right,—
Embrace, and kiss, and love me, in despite!

WHEN THOU MUST HOME

When thou must home to shades of underground,
And there arrived, a new admirëd guest,
The beauteous spirits do engirt thee round,
White Iope, blithe Helen, and the rest,
To hear the stories of thy finished love
From that smooth tongue whose music hell can move;

Then wilt thou speak of banqueting delights,
Of masques and revels which sweet youth did make,
Of tourneys and great challenges of knights,
And all these triumphs for thy beauty's sake:
When thou hast told these honors done to thee,
Then tell, O tell, how thou didst murder me.

WHAT THEN IS LOVE BUT MOURNING

What then is love but mourning?
　　What desire, but a self-burning?
Till she, that hates, doth love return,
Thus will I mourn, thus will I sing:
　　Come away, come away, my darling.

Beauty is but a blooming,
　　Youth in his glory entombing;
Time hath a while, which none can stay;
Then come away, while thus I sing:
　　Come away, come away, my darling.

Summer in winter fadeth;
　　Gloomy night heavenly light shadeth;
Like to the morn are Venus' flowers;
Such are her hours. Then will I sing:
　　Come away, come away, my darling.

WHETHER MEN DO LAUGH OR WEEP

Whether men do laugh or weep,
Whether they do wake or sleep,
Whether they die young or old,
Whether they feel heat or cold;
There is, underneath the sun,
Nothing in true earnest done.

All our pride is but a jest;
None are worst, and none are best;
Grief and joy, and hope and fear,
Play their pageants everywhere:
Vain opinion all doth sway,
And the world is but a play.

Powers above in clouds do sit,
Mocking our poor apish wit,
That so lamely, with such state,
Their high glory imitate:
No ill can be felt but pain,
And that happy men disdain.

ROSE-CHEEKED LAURA

Rose-cheeked Laura, come,
Sing thou smoothly with thy beauties
Silent music, either other
    Sweetly gracing.

Lovely forms do flow
From consent divinely framëd;
Heaven is music, and thy beauty's
    Birth is heavenly.

These dull notes we sing
Discords need for helps to grace them;
Only beauty purely loving
    Knows no discord,

But still moves delight,
Like clear springs renewed by flowing,
Ever perfect, ever in them-
    selves eternal.

THE MAN OF LIFE UPRIGHT

The man of life upright,
  Whose cheerful mind is free
From weight of impious deeds
  And yoke of vanity;

The man whose silent days
In harmless joys are spent,
Whom hopes cannot delude
Nor sorrows discontent;

That man needs neither towers
Nor armor for defense,
Nor vaults his guilt to shroud
From thunder's violence:

He only can behold
With unaffrighted eyes
The horrors of the deep
And terrors of the skies.

Thus, scorning all the cares
That fate or fortune brings,
His book the Heavens he makes,
His wisdom heavenly things,

Good thoughts his surest friends,
His wealth a well-spent age,
The earth his sober inn
And quiet pilgrimage.

TO MUSIC BENT IS MY RETIRËD MIND

To music bent is my retirëd mind,
And fain would I some song of pleasure sing;
But in vain joys no comfort now I find:
From heavenly thoughts all true delight doth spring.
Thy power, O God, thy mercies, to record,
Will sweeten every note and every word.

All earthly pomp or beauty to express
Is but to carve in snow, on waves to write;
Celestial things, though men conceive them less,
Yet fullest are they in themselves of light.
Such beams they yield as know no means to die,
Such heat they cast as lifts the spirit high.

THE PEACEFUL WESTERN WIND

The peaceful western wind
The winter storms hath tamed,
And Nature in each kind
The kind heat hath inflamed:
The forward buds so sweetly breathe
Out of their earthy bowers,
That heaven, which views their pomp beneath,
Would fain be decked with flowers.

See how the morning smiles
On her bright eastern hill,
And with soft steps beguiles
Them that lie slumbering still.
The music-loving birds are come
From cliffs and rocks unknown,
To see the trees and briars bloom
That late were overflown.

What Saturn did destroy,
Love's Queen revives again;
And now her naked boy
Doth in the fields remain,
Where he such pleasing change doth view
In every living thing,
As if the world were born anew
To gratify the spring.

If all things life present,
Why die my comforts then?
Why suffers my content?
Am I the worst of men?
O, Beauty, be not thou accused
Too justly in this case:
Unkindly if true love be used,
'Twill yield thee little grace.

NOW WINTER NIGHTS ENLARGE

Now winter nights enlarge
The number of their hours,
And clouds their storms discharge
Upon the airy towers.
Let now the chimneys blaze
And cups o'erflow with wine;
Let well-tuned words amaze
With harmony divine!
Now yellow waxen lights
Shall wait on honey love
While youthful revels, masques and Courtly sights,
Sleep's leaden spells remove.

This time doth well dispense
With lovers' long discourse;
Much speech hath some defence,
Though beauty no remorse.
All do not all things well;
Some measures comely tread,
Some knotted riddles tell,
Some poems smoothly read.
The summer hath his joys,
And winter his delights;
Though love and all his pleasures are but toys,
They shorten tedious nights.

SHALL I COME, SWEET LOVE

Shall I come, sweet love, to thee,
    When the evening beams are set?
Shall I not excluded be?
    Will you find no feignëd let?
Let me not, for pity, more
Tell the long hours at your door.

feignëd let: i.e., pretended hin-
    drance.

Who can tell what thief or foe,
   In the covert of the night,
For his prey will work my woe,
   Or through wicked foul despite?
So may I die unredressed,
Ere my long love be possessed.

But to let such dangers pass,
   Which a lover's thoughts disdain,
'Tis enough in such a place
   To attend love's joys in vain.
Do not mock me in thy bed,
While these cold nights freeze me dead.

SLEEP, ANGRY BEAUTY

Sleep, angry beauty, sleep, and fear not me;
For who a sleeping lion dares provoke?
It shall suffice me here to sit and see
Those lips shut up that never kindly spoke.
   What sight can more content a lover's mind
   Than beauty seeming harmless, if not kind?

My words have charmed her, for secure she sleeps,
Though guilty much of wrong done to my love;
And in her slumber, see! she, close-eyed, weeps;
Dreams often more than waking passions move.
   Plead, Sleep, my cause, and make her soft like thee,
   That she in peace may wake and pity me.

THERE IS A GARDEN IN HER FACE

There is a garden in her face,
Where roses and white lilies grow;
A heavenly paradise is that place,
Wherein all pleasant fruits do flow.
There cherries grow, which none may buy
Till "Cherry ripe" themselves do cry.

Those cherries fairly do enclose
Of orient pearl a double row,
Which when her lovely laughter shows,
They look like rosebuds filled with snow.
Yet them nor peer nor prince can buy
Till "Cherry ripe" themselves do cry.

Her eyes like angels watch them still;
Her brows like bended bows do stand,
Threatening with piercing frowns to kill
All that attempt, with eye or hand,
Those sacred cherries to come nigh
Till "Cherry ripe" themselves do cry.

COME, FOLLOW ME

Come, follow me, my wandering mates,
Sons and daughters of the Fates:
Friends of night, that oft have done
Homage to the hornëd moon,
Fairly march and shun not light
With such stars as these made bright.
Yet bend you low your curlëd tops,
Touch the hallowed earth, and then
Rise again with antic hops
Unused of men.
Here no danger is, nor fear,
For true honor harbors here,
Whom grace attends.
Grace can make our foes our friends.

WHAT IF A DAY

What if a day, or a month, or a year
Crown thy delights with a thousand sweet contentings?
Cannot a chance of a night or an hour
Cross thy desires with as many sad tormentings?

Fortune, honor, beauty, youth
Are but blossoms dying;
Wanton pleasure, doting love,
Are but shadows flying.
All our joys are but toys,
Idle thoughts deceiving;
None have power of an hour
In their lives' bereaving.

Earth's but a point to the world, and a man
Is but a point to the world's comparèd censure;
Shall then the point of a point be so vain
As to triumph in a silly point's adventure?
All is hazard that we have,
There is nothing biding;
Days of pleasure are like streams
Through fair meadows gliding.
Weal and woe, time doth go,
Time is never turning:
Secret fates guide our states,
Both in mirth and mourning.

THOMAS NASHE: 1567–1601

Nashe's personal life and career are often linked with those of Peele, Greene, and Marlowe. He was educated at Cambridge, toured France and Italy as a very young man, and settled in London. Like the other University Wits with whom his name is associated, his personal life was uncertain, his fortunes often low, and his professional career prolific. In this career Nashe wrote a masque, a satire, and an allegorical pamphlet; he collaborated with Ben Jonson on a play; and he wrote an early English "novel."

He is best known for this picaresque, historical fiction, *The Unfortunate Traveler*, or *the Life of Jack Wilton*. He wrote few poems. The best of these appear in his satirical masque, *Summer's Last Will and Testament*.

Text:

The Works of Thomas Nashe, in 5 vols., edited by R. B. McKerrow (1904–10).

AUTUMN HATH ALL THE SUMMER'S FRUITFUL TREASURE

Autumn hath all the summer's fruitful treasure;
Gone is our sport, fled is poor Croydon's pleasure.
Short days, sharp days, long nights come on apace,—
Ah, who shall hide us from the winter's face?
Cold doth increase, the sickness will not cease,
And here we lie, God knows, with little ease.
  From winter, plague, and pestilence, good Lord deliver
    us!

London doth mourn, Lambeth is quite forlorn;
Trades cry, Woe worth that ever they were born.
The want of term is town and city's harm;
Close chambers we do want to keep us warm.
Long banished must we live from our friends;
This low-built house will bring us to our ends.
    From winter, plague, and pestilence, good Lord deliver
        us!

IN TIME OF PLAGUE

Adieu, farewell, earth's bliss!
This world uncertain is:
Fond are life's lustful joys,
Death proves them all but toys.
None from his darts can fly;
I am sick, I must die—
    Lord, have mercy on us.

Rich men, trust not in wealth,
Gold cannot buy you health;
Physic himself must fade;
All things to end are made;
The plague full swift goes by;
I am sick, I must die—
    Lord, have mercy on us.

Beauty is but a flower
Which wrinkles will devour;
Brightness falls from the hair;
Queens have died young and fair;
Dust hath closed Helen's eye;
I am sick, I must die—
    Lord, have mercy on us.

hair: the usual reading of this word, "air," is almost certainly incorrect. See J. V. Cunningham, *Tradition and Poetic Structure* (Denver, 1960), p. 57; and Nashe's *Works*, ed. R. B. McKerrow (London, 1904–10), IV, p. 440.

Strength stoops unto the grave,
Worms feed on Hector brave;
Swords may not fight with fate;
Earth still holds ope her gate;
Come, come! the bells do cry—
I am sick, I must die—
    Lord, have mercy on us.

Wit with his wantonness
Tasteth death's bitterness;
Hell's executioner
Hath no ears for to hear
What vain art can reply;
I am sick, I must die—
    Lord, have mercy on us.

Haste, therefore, each degree
To welcome destiny;
Heaven is our heritage;
Earth but a player's stage;
Mount we unto the sky;
I am sick, I must die—
    Lord, have mercy on us.

JOHN DONNE: 1572–1631

Donne was born a Catholic, educated at Oxford and Cambridge, toured the continent, and in 1592 was admitted to Lincoln's Inn for the study of law. In 1596 he volunteered to accompany Essex on the expedition to Cadiz and to the Azores. Returning to London, he gave himself to the pursuit of the pleasures that the city could afford. In 1601 he secretly married Anne More, the daughter of his employer and a descendent of Sir Thomas More; for this he was dismissed from his post, and he spent the next years in great poverty. He had slowly grown away from the Roman Catholic Church; and in 1615, partly because of the urging of his friends, he was ordained into the Church of England. In 1621 he was made dean of St. Paul's; his death prevented his advancement to a bishopric.

Donne published only a few of his poems in his own lifetime, and regretted the appearance even of these. His poems did, however, circulate very widely in manuscript. They were collected and published two years after his death, in 1633.

Donne's verse has been tremendously admired in the twentieth century, and few modern poets have altogether escaped his influence. He began writing at the height of the Petrarchan movement, and his verse demonstrates the method, if not the manner, of that movement. That is to say, the detail of his poetry is typically decorative, hyperbolic, metaphoric, and excessive; but his style is rough, harsh, nervous, and conversational in the manner of the earlier Native poets. It is the collision of the Petrarchan method and the Native manner, joined by Donne's peculiar temperament and genius, that gives the poems their unique force, that makes for their greatest triumphs and their greatest failures.

TEXT:

Donne's Poetical Works, in 2 vols., edited by H. J. C. Grierson (1912).

THE GOOD-MORROW

I wonder, by my troth, what thou and I
Did till we loved? Were we not weaned till then,
But sucked on country pleasures childishly?
Or snorted we in the seven sleepers' den?
'Twas so; but this, all pleasures fancies be.
If ever any beauty I did see
Which I desired, and got, 'twas but a dream of thee.

And now good morrow to our waking souls,
Which watch not one another out of fear;
For love all love of other sights controls,
And makes one little room an everywhere.
Let sea-discoverers to new worlds have gone,
Let maps to other, worlds on worlds have shown,
Let us possess one world: each hath one, and is one.

My face in thine eye, thine in mine appears,
And true plain hearts do in the faces rest.
Where can we find two better hemispheres,
Without sharp North, without declining West?
Whatever dies was not mixed equally;
If our two loves be one, or thou and I
Love so alike that none do slacken, none can die.

seven sleepers: seven Christian youths of Ephesus, walled in a cave by the tyrant Decius, where they slept for more than 200 years.

SONG

Go and catch a falling star,
 Get with child a mandrake root,
Tell me where all past years are,
 Or who cleft the devil's foot,
Teach me to hear mermaids singing,
Or to keep off envy's stinging,
  And find
  What wind
Serves to advance an honest mind.

If thou be'st born to strange sights,
 Things invisible to see,
Ride ten thousand days and nights
 Till age snow white hairs on thee;
Thou, when thou return'st, wilt tell me
All strange wonders that befell thee,
  And swear
  Nowhere
Lives a woman true, and fair.

If thou find'st one, let me know;
 Such a pilgrimage were sweet—
Yet do not; I would not go,
 Though at next door we might meet.
Though she were true when you met her,
And last till you write your letter,
  Yet she
  Will be
False ere I come, to two or three.

THE SUN RISING

Busy old fool, unruly sun,
　　Why dost thou thus
Through windows and through curtains call on us?
Must to thy motions lovers' seasons run?
　　Saucy, pedantic wretch, go chide
　　Late schoolboys and sour prentices,
　Go tell court huntsmen that the king will ride,
　Call country ants to harvest offices.
Love, all alike, no season knows nor clime,
Nor hours, days, months, which are the rags of time.

Thy beams so reverend and strong,
　　Why shouldst thou think?
I could eclipse and cloud them with a wink,
But that I would not lose her sight so long.
　　If her eyes have not blinded thine,
　　Look, and tomorrow late tell me
　Whether both the Indias of spice and mine
　Be where thou left'st them, or lie here with me;
Ask for those kings whom thou saw'st yesterday,
And thou shalt hear: All here in one bed lay.

She's all states, and all princes I;
　　Nothing else is.
Princes do but play us; compared to this,
All honor's mimic, all wealth alchemy.
　　Thou, sun, art half as happy as we,
　　In that the world's contracted thus;
　Thine age asks ease, and since thy duties be
　To warm the world, that's done in warming us.
Shine here to us, and thou art everywhere;
This bed thy center is, these walls thy sphere.

THE CANONIZATION

For God's sake, hold your tongue and let me love!
   Or chide my palsy or my gout,
My five gray hairs or ruined fortune flout;
     With wealth your state, your mind with arts improve,
       Take you a course, get you a place,
       Observe his Honor or his Grace,
Or the King's real, or his stampèd face
   Contemplate, what you will, approve—
   So you will let me love.

Alas, alas, who's injured by my love?
   What merchant's ships have my sighs drowned?
Who says my tears have overflowed his ground?
     When did my colds a forward spring remove?
       When did the heats which my veins fill
       Add one more to the plaguy bill?
Soldiers find wars, and lawyers find out still
   Litigious men which quarrels move,
   Though she and I do love.

Call us what you will, we are made such by love:
   Call her one, me another fly;
We're tapers, too, and at our own cost die;
     And we in us find the eagle and the dove.
       The phoenix riddle hath more wit
       By us; we two, being one, are it.
So to one neutral thing both sexes fit;
   We die and rise the same, and prove
   Mysterious by this love.

real: literally, a small silver
coin; also, a pun on "royal."

We can die by it, if not live by love;
    And if unfit for tombs and hearse
Our legend be, it will be fit for verse;
    And if no piece of chronicle we prove,
        We'll build in sonnets pretty rooms
        (As well a well-wrought urn becomes
The greatest ashes, as half-acre tombs),
    And by these hymns all shall approve
    Us canonized for love,

And thus invoke us: "You whom reverend love
    Made one another's hermitage,
You to whom love was peace that now is rage,
    Who did the whole world's soul contract, and drove
        Into the glasses of your eyes
        (So made such mirrors and such spies
That they did all to you epitomize),
    Countries, towns, courts beg from above
    A pattern of your love!"

SONG

Sweetest love, I do not go
    For weariness of thee,
Nor in hope the world can show
    A fitter love for me;
        But since that I
Must die at last, 'tis best
To use myself in jest
    Thus by feigned deaths to die.

Yesternight the sun went hence,
    And yet is here today;
He hath no desire nor sense,
    Nor half so short a way.
        Then fear not me,
But believe that I shall make
Speedier journeys, since I take
    More wings and spurs than he.

O how feeble is man's power,
    That if good fortune fall,
Cannot add another hour,
    Nor a lost hour recall!
        But come bad chance,
And we join to it our strength,
And we teach it art and length,
    Itself o'er us to advance.

When thou sigh'st, thou sigh'st not wind,
    But sigh'st my soul away;
When thou weep'st, unkindly kind,
    My life's blood doth decay.
        It cannot be
That thou lov'st me as thou say'st,
If in thine my life thou waste.
    Thou art the best of me.

Let not thy divining heart
    Forethink me any ill;
Destiny may take thy part,
    And may thy fears fulfill;
        But think that we
Are but turned aside to sleep.
They who one another keep
    Alive, ne'er parted be.

AIR AND ANGELS

Twice or thrice had I loved thee
Before I knew thy face or name;
So in a voice, so in a shapeless flame
Angels affect us oft, and worshipped be.
    Still, when to where thou wert I came,
Some lovely glorious nothing I did see.

But since my soul, whose child love is,
Takes limbs of flesh, and else could nothing do,
    More subtile than the parent is,
Love must not be, but take a body too;
        And therefore what thou wert, and who,
            I bid love ask, and now
That it assume thy body, I allow,
And fix itself in thy lip, eye, and brow.

Whilst thus to ballast love I thought,
And so more steadily to have gone,
With wares which would sink admiratión,
I saw I had love's pinnace overfraught;
        Every thy hair for love to work upon
Is much too much; some fitter must be sought.
        For nor in nothing, nor in things
Extreme and scattering bright can love inhere.
        Then, as an angel, face and wings
Of air not pure as it, yet pure, doth wear,
            So thy love may be my love's sphere.
                Just such disparity
As is twixt air and angels' purity,
Twixt women's love and men's will ever be.

BREAK OF DAY

'Tis true, 'tis day; what though it be?
O wilt thou therefore rise from me?
Why should we rise because 'tis light?
Did we lie down because 'twas night?
Love which in spite of darkness brought us hither
Should in despite of light keep us together.

Light hath no tongue, but is all eye;
If it could speak as well as spy,
This were the worst that it could say:
That being well, I fain would stay,
And that I loved my heart and honor so
That I would not from him that had them go.

Must business thee from hence remove?
Oh, that's the worst disease of love;
The poor, the foul, the false, love can
Admit, but not the busied man.
He which hath business and makes love doth do
Such wrong as when a married man doth woo.

A VALEDICTION: OF MY NAME IN THE WINDOW

I

My name engraved herein
Doth contribute my firmness to this glass,
    Which, ever since that charm, hath been
    As hard as that which graved it was;
Thine eye will give it price enough to mock
    The diamonds of either rock.

II

'Tis much that glass should be
As all-confessing and through-shine as I;
    'Tis more, that it shows thee to thee
    And clear reflects thee to thine eye.
But all such rules, love's magic can undo;
    Here you see me, and I am you.

III

As no one point nor dash,
Which are but accessaries to this name,
    The showers and tempests can outwash,
    So shall all times find me the same;
You this entireness better may fulfil,
    Who have the pattern with you still.

IV

Or if too hard and deep
This learning be for a scratched name to teach,
  It as a given death's head keep
  Lovers' mortality to preach,
Or think this ragged bony name to be
    My ruinous anatomy.

V

Then, as all my souls be
Emparadised in you (in whom alone
  I understand and grow and see),
  The rafters of my body, bone
Being still with you, the muscle, sinew, and vein
    Which tile this house will come again.

VI

Till my return, repair
And recompact my scattered body so.
  As all the virtuous powers which are
  Fixed in the stars are said to flow
Into such characters as gravëd be
    When these stars have supremacy,

VII

So, since this name was cut
When love and grief their exaltation had,
  No door 'gainst this name's influence shut.
  As much more loving as more sad
'Twill make thee; and thou shouldst, till I return,
    Since I die daily, daily mourn.

VIII

When thy inconsiderate hand
Flings ope this casement with my trembling name
  To look on one whose wit or land
  New battery to thy heart may frame,
Then think this name alive, and that thou thus
  In it offendst my Genius.

IX

And when thy melted maid,
Corrupted by thy lover's gold and page,
  His letter at thy pillow hath laid,
  Disputed it, and tamed thy rage,
And thou beginst to thaw towards him, for this,
  May my name step in and hide his.

X

And if this treason go
To an overt act, and that thou write again,
  In superscribing, this name flow
  Into thy fancy from the pane.
So, in forgetting thou remembrest right,
  And unaware to me shall write.

XI

But glass and lines must be
No means our firm substantial love to keep;
  Near death inflicts this lethargy,
  And this I murmur in my sleep:
Impute this idle talk to that I go,
  For dying men talk often so.

A VALEDICTION: OF WEEPING

Let me pour forth
My tears before thy face, whilst I stay here;
For thy face coins them, and thy stamp they bear,
And by this mintage they are something worth,
 For thus they be
 Pregnant of thee;
Fruits of much grief they are, emblems of more:
When a tear falls, that *thou* falls which it bore;
So thou and I are nothing then, when on a divers shore.

On a round ball
A workman that hath copies by, can lay
An Europe, Afric, and an Asia,
And quickly make that which was nothing, all;
 So doth each tear
 Which thee doth wear,
A globe, yea world, by that impression grow,
Till thy tears mixed with mine do overflow
This world, by waters sent from thee, my heaven dissolvèd
  so.

O more than moon,
Draw not up seas to drown me in thy sphere,
Weep me not dead in thine arms, but forbear
To teach the sea what it may do too soon.
 Let not the wind
 Example find
To do me more harm than it purposeth;
Since thou and I sigh one another's breath,
Whoe'er sighs most is cruelest, and hastes the other's
  death.

A NOCTURNAL UPON ST. LUCY'S DAY,
BEING THE SHORTEST DAY

'Tis the year's midnight, and it is the day's,
Lucy's, who scarce seven hours herself unmasks;
   The sun is spent, and now his flasks
   Send forth light squibs, no constant rays;
     The world's whole sap is sunk;
The general balm the hydroptic earth hath drunk,
Whither, as to the bed's feet, life is shrunk,
Dead and interred; yet all these seem to laugh
Compared with me, who am their epitaph.

Study me then, you who shall lovers be
At the next world—that is, at the next spring—
   For I am every dead thing
   In whom Love wrought new alchemy;
     For his art did express
A quintessence even from nothingness,
From dull privations and lean emptiness.
He ruined me, and I am re-begot
Of absence, darkness, death: things which are not.

All others from all things draw all that's good:
Life, soul, form, spirit, whence they being have;
   I, by love's limbeck, am the grave
   Of all that's nothing. Oft a flood
     Have we two wept, and so
Drowned the whole world—us two. Oft did we grow
To be two Chaoses when we did show
Care to aught else; and often absences
Withdrew our souls and made us carcasses.

limbeck: alembic, i.e., distilla-
tion.

But I am by her death (which word wrongs her)
Of the first nothing the elixir grown;
    Were I a man, that I were one
    I needs must know; I should prefer,
        If I were any beast,
Some ends, some means; yea plants, yea stones detest
And love; all, all some properties invest;
If I an ordinary nothing were,
As shadow, a light and body must be here.

But I am none, nor will my Sun renew.
You lovers, for whose sake the lesser sun
    At this time to the Goat is run
    To fetch new lust and give it you,
        Enjoy your summer all;
Since she enjoys her long night's festival,
Let me prepare towards her, and let me call
This hour her vigil and her eve, since this
Both the year's and the day's deep midnight is.

THE APPARITION

When by thy scorn, O murderess, I am dead,
    And that thou think'st thee free
From all solicitatión from me,
Then shall my ghost come to thy bed,
And thee, feigned vestal, in worse arms shall see;
Then thy sick taper will begin to wink,
And he whose thou art then, being tired before,
Will, if thou stir or pinch to wake him, think
    Thou call'st for more,
And in false sleep will from thee shrink,
And then, poor aspen wretch, neglected, thou
Bathed in a cold, quicksilver sweat wilt lie
    A verier ghost than I.
What I will say, I will not tell thee now,
Lest that preserve thee; and since my love is spent,
I'd rather thou shouldst painfully repent
Than by my threatenings rest still innocent.

A VALEDICTION: FORBIDDING MOURNING

As virtuous men pass mildly away,
　　And whisper to their souls to go,
Whilst some of their sad friends do say,
　　The breath goes now; and some say, No;

So let us melt and make no noise,
　　No tear-floods nor sigh-tempests move;
'Twere profanation of our joys
　　To tell the laity our love.

Moving of the earth brings harms and fears;
　　Men reckon what it did and meant;
But trepidation of the spheres,
　　Though greater far, is innocent.

Dull sublunary lovers' love,
　　Whose soul is sense, cannot admit
Absence, because it doth remove
　　Those things which elemented it.

But we by a love so much refined
　　That ourselves know not what it is,
Interassurèd of the mind,
　　Care less eyes, lips, and hands to miss.

Our two souls, therefore, which are one,
　　Though I must go, endure not yet
A breach, but an expansión,
　　Like gold to airy thinness beat.

If they be two, they are two so
　　As stiff twin compasses are two;
Thy soul, the fixed foot, makes no show
　　To move, but doth if the other do.

And though it in the center sit,
   Yet when the other far doth roam,
It leans and hearkens after it,
   And grows erect as that comes home.

Such wilt thou be to me, who must,
   Like the other foot, obliquely run;
Thy firmness makes my circle just,
   And makes me end where I begun.

THE ECSTASY

Where, like a pillow on a bed,
   A pregnant bank swelled up to rest
The violet's reclining head,
   Sat we two, one another's best.
Our hands were firmly cementéd
   With a fast balm which thence did spring;
Our eye-beams twisted and did thread
   Our eyes upon one double string;
So to intergraft our hands, as yet
   Was all the means to make us one,
And pictures in our eyes to get
   Was all our propagatión.
As twixt two equal armies Fate
   Suspends uncertain victory,
Our souls, which to advance their state
   Were gone out, hung twixt her and me.
And whilst our souls negotiate there,
   We like sepulchral statues lay;
All day the same our postures were
   And we said nothing all the day.
If any (so by love refined
   That he soul's language understood,
And by good love were grown all mind)
   Within convenient distance stood,

He (though he knew not which soul spake,
    Because both meant, both spake the same)
Might thence a new concoction take,
    And part far purer than he came.
This Ecstasy doth unperplex,
    We said, and tell us what we love;
We see by this it was not sex,
    We see we saw not what did move;
But as all several souls contain
    Mixture of things, they know not what,
Love these mixcd souls doth mix again
    And makes both one, each this and that.
A single violet transplant,
    The strength, the color, and the size
(All which before was poor and scant)
    Redoubles still and multiplies.
When love with one another so
    Interinanimates two souls,
That abler soul, which thence doth flow,
    Defects of loneliness controls.
We then, who are this new soul, know
    Of what we are composed and made,
For the atomies of which we grow
    Are souls, whom no change can invade.
But O, alas, so long, so far
    Our bodies why do we forbear?
They're ours, though they're not we; we are
    The intelligences, they the sphere.
We owe them thanks because they thus
    Did us to us at first convey,
Yielded their forces, sense, to us,
    Nor are dross to us, but allay.
On man heaven's influence works not so,
    But that it first imprints the air;
So soul into the soul may flow,
    Though it to body first repair.

allay: alloy.

As our blood labors to beget
   Spirits as like souls as it can,
Because such fingers need to knit
   That subtle knot which makes us man,
So must pure lovers' souls descend
   To affections and to faculties
Which sense may reach and apprehend,
   Else a great prince in prison lies.
To our bodies turn we then, that so
   Weak men on love revealed may look;
Love's mysteries in souls do grow,
   But yet the body is his book.
And if some lover, such as we,
   Have heard this dialogue of one,
Let him still mark us; he shall see
   Small change when we're to bodies gone.

LOVE'S DEITY

I long to talk with some old lover's ghost
   Who died before the god of love was born.
I cannot think that he who then loved most
   Sunk so low as to love one which did scorn.
But since this god produced a destiny,
And that vice-nature, custom, lets it be,
   I must love her that loves not me.

Sure, they which made him god meant not so much,
   Nor he in his young godhead practiced it.
But when an even flame two hearts did touch,
   His office was indulgently to fit
Actives to passives. Correspondency
Only his subject was. It cannot be
   Love, till I love her that loves me.

But every modern god will now extend
    His vast prerogative as far as Jove.
To rage, to lust, to write to, to commend,
    All is the purlieu of the god of love.
O were we wakened by this tyranny
To ungod this child again, it could not be
    I should love her who loves not me.

Rebel and atheist too, why murmur I
    As though I felt the worst that love could do?
Love might make me leave loving, or might try
    A deeper plague, to make her love me too,
Which, since she loves before, I'm loath to see.
Falsehood is worse than hate, and that must be
    If she whom I love should love me.

THE FUNERAL

Whoever comes to shroud me, do not harm
    Nor question much
That subtle wreath of hair which crowns my arm;
The mystery, the sign, you must not touch,
    For 'tis my outward soul,
Viceroy to that, which then to heaven being gone,
    Will leave this to control
And keep these limbs, her provinces, from dissolution.

For if the sinewy thread my brain lets fall
    Through every part
Can tie those parts and make me one of all,
These hairs, which upward grew, and strength and art
    Have from a better brain,
Can better do it; except she meant that I
    By this should know my pain,
As prisoners then are manacled, when they're condemned
    to die.

Whate'er she meant by it, bury it with me,
           For since I am
Love's martyr, it might breed idolatry
If into others' hands these relics came.
           As 'twas humility
To afford to it all that a soul can do,
           So 'tis some bravery
That since you would save none of me, I bury some of you.

THE RELIC

When my grave is broke up again
Some second guest to entertain
(For graves have learned that womanhead
To be to more than one a bed),
           And he that digs it spies
A bracelet of bright hair about the bone,
           Will he not let us alone,
And think that there a loving couple lies,
Who thought that this device might be some way
To make their souls at the last busy day
Meet at this grave, and make a little stay?

If this fall in a time or land
Where mis-devotion doth command,
Then he that digs us up will bring
Us to the bishop and the king
           To make us relics; then
Thou shalt be a Mary Magdalen, and I
           A something else thereby.
All women shall adore us, and some men;
And since at such time miracles are sought,
I would have that age by this paper taught
What miracles we harmless lovers wrought.

First, we loved well and faithfully,
Yet knew not what we loved, nor why;
Difference of sex no more we knew
Than our guardian angels do;
 Coming and going, we
Perchance might kiss, but not between those meals;
 Our hands ne'er touched the seals
Which nature, injured by late law, sets free.
These miracles we did; but now, alas,
All measure and all language I should pass,
Should I tell what a miracle she was.

A LECTURE UPON THE SHADOW

Stand still, and I will read to thee
A lecture, Love, in love's philosophy.
 These three hours that we have spent
 Walking here, two shadows went
Along with us, which we ourselves produced;
But, now the sun is just above our head,
 We do those shadows tread,
 And to brave clearness all things are reduced.
So whilst our infant loves did grow,
Disguises did, and shadows, flow
From us and our cares; but now 'tis not so.

That love hath not attained the highest degree
Which is still diligent lest others see.

Except our loves at this noon stay,
We shall new shadows make the other way.
 As the first were made to blind
 Others, these which come behind
Will work upon ourselves and blind our eyes.
If our loves faint and westwardly decline,
 To me thou falsely thine,
 And I to thee mine actions shall disguise.

The morning shadows wear away,
But these grow longer all the day.
But O, love's day is short if love decay!

Love is a growing, or full constant light,
And his first minute after noon is night.

ELEGY V: HIS PICTURE

Here, take my picture; though I bid farewell,
Thine in my heart, where my soul dwells, shall dwell.
'Tis like me now, but I dead, 'twill be more,
When we are shadows both, than 'twas before.
When weather-beaten I come back, my hand
Perhaps with rude oars torn, or sunbeams tanned,
My face and breast of haircloth, and my head
With care's rash sudden storms being o'erspread,
My body a sack of bones, broken within,
And powder's blue stains scattered on my skin;
If rival fools tax thee to have loved a man
So foul and coarse as, O, I may seem then,
This shall say what I was, and thou shalt say:
"Do his hurts reach me? doth my worth decay?
Or do they reach his judging mind that he
Should now love less what he did love to see?
That which in him was fair and delicate
Was but the milk which in love's childish state
Did nurse it, who now is grown strong enough
To feed on that which to disusèd tastes seems tough."

ELEGY XIX: GOING TO BED

Come, Madam, come! All rest my powers defy;
Until I labor, I in labor lie.
The foe ofttimes, having the foe in sight,
Is tired with standing though he never fight.
Off with that girdle, like heaven's zones glittering,
But a far fairer world encompassing.

Unpin that spangled breastplate, which you wear
That the eyes of busy fools may be stopped there.
Unlace yourself, for that harmonious chime
Tells me from you that now it is bedtime.
Off with that happy busk, which I envý,
That still can be, and still can stand so nigh.
Your gown going off, such beauteous state reveals
As when from flowery meads the hill's shadow steals.
Off with that wiry coronet, and show
The hairy diadem which on you doth grow.
Now off with those shoes, and then safely tread
In this Love's hallowed temple, this soft bed.
In such white robes heaven's angels used to be
Received by men; thou, angel, bringst with thee
A heaven like Mahomet's paradise. And though
Ill spirits walk in white, we easily know
By this these angels from an evil sprite:
Those set our hairs, but these our flesh upright.
    License my roving hands, and let them go
Before, behind, between, above, below.
O my America! my new-found-land,
My kingdom, safeliest when with one man manned,
My mine of precious stones, my empery,
How blest am I in this discovering thee!
To enter in these bonds is to be free;
Then where my hand is set, my seal shall be.
    Full nakedness! All joys are due to thee!
As souls unbodied, bodies unclothed must be
To taste whole joys. Gems which you women use
Are as Atlanta's balls, cast in men's views
That when a fool's eye lighteth on a gem,
His earthly soul may covet theirs, not them.
Like pictures, or like books' gay coverings made
For laymen, are all women thus arrayed;
Themselves are mystic books, which only we,
Whom their imputed grace will dignify,
Must see revealed. Then, since that I may know,
As liberally as to a midwife, show

Thyself; cast all, yea, this white linen hence;
Here is no penance due to innocence.
    To teach thee, I am naked first. Why, then,
What needst thou have more covering than a man?

HOLY SONNETS:

1.

Thou hast made me; and shall thy work decay?
Repair me now, for now mine end doth haste;
I run to death, and death meets me as fast,
And all my pleasures are like yesterday.
I dare not move my dim eyes any way;
Despair behind, and death before doth cast
Such terror, and my feeble flesh doth waste
By sin in it, which it towards hell doth weigh.
Only thou art above, and when towards thee
By thy leave I can look, I rise again;
But our old subtle foe so tempteth me
That not one hour myself I can sustain.
Thy Grace may wing me to prevent his art,
And thou like Adamant draw mine iron heart.

5.

I am a little world made cunningly
Of elements and an angelic sprite,
But black sin hath betrayed to endless night
My world's both parts, and, O, both parts must die.
You which beyond that heaven which was most high
Have found new spheres, and of new lands can write,
Pour new seas in mine eyes that so I might
Drown my world with my weeping earnestly,

Adamant: a legendary rock of   magnetic powers.
    impregnable hardness, with

Or wash it, if it must be drowned no more.
But O, it must be burnt! Alas, the fire
Of lust and envy have burnt it heretofore
And made it fouler. Let their flames retire,
And burn me, O Lord, with a fiery zeal
Of thee and thy house, which doth in eating heal.

7.

At the round earth's imagined corners, blow
Your trumpets, angels, and arise, arise
From death, you numberless infinities
Of souls, and to your scattered bodies go,
All whom the flood did, and fire shall o'erthrow,
All whom war, dearth, age, agues, tyrannies,
Despair, law, chance hath slain, and you whose eyes
Shall behold God and never taste death's woe.
But let them sleep, Lord, and me mourn a space,
For if above all these my sins abound,
'Tis late to ask abundance of thy grace
When we are there. Here on this lowly ground
Teach me how to repent, for that's as good
As if thou'dst sealed my pardon with thy blood.

9.

If poisonous minerals, and if that tree
Whose fruit threw death on else immortal us,
If lecherous goats, if serpents envious
Cannot be damned, alas, why should I be?
Why should intent or reason, born in me,
Make sins, else equal, in me more heinous?
And mercy being easy and glorious
To God, in his stern wrath why threatens he?

But who am I that dare dispute with thee,
O God? Oh! of thine only worthy blood
And my tears, make a heavenly Lethean flood,
And drown in it my sins' black memory.
That thou remember them, some claim as debt;
I think it mercy if thou wilt forget.

10.

Death, be not proud, though some have callèd thee
Mighty and dreadful, for thou art not so;
For those whom thou think'st thou dost overthrow
Die not, poor Death; nor yet canst thou kill me.
From rest and sleep, which but thy pictures be,
Much pleasure; then, from thee much more must flow,
And soonest our best men with thee do go,
Rest of their bones and soul's delivery.
Thou art slave to fate, chance, kings, and desperate men,
And dost with poison, war, and sickness dwell;
And poppy or charms can make us sleep as well,
And better than thy stroke. Why swell'st thou then?
One short sleep passed, we wake eternally,
And death shall be no more. Death, thou shalt die.

14.

Batter my heart, three-personed God; for you
As yet but knock, breathe, shine, and seek to mend.
That I may rise and stand, o'erthrow me and bend
Your force to break, blow, burn, and make me new.
I, like an usurped town to another due,
Labor to admit you, but Oh, to no end!
Reason, your viceroy in me, me should defend,
But is captived, and proves weak or untrue.

Yet dearly I love you and would be lovëd fain,
But am betrothed unto your enemy.
Divorce me, untie, or break that knot again;
Take me to you, imprison me, for I,
Except you enthrall me, never shall be free,
Nor ever chaste except you ravish me.

GOOD FRIDAY, 1613. RIDING WESTWARD

Let man's soul be a sphere, and then in this
The intelligence that moves, devotion is;
And as the other spheres, by being grown
Subject to foreign motions, lose their own,
And being by others hurried every day,
Scarcé in a year their natural form obey;
Pleasure or business, so, our souls admit
For their first mover, and are whirled by it.
Hence is it that I am carried towards the West
This day, when my soul's form bends toward the East.
There I should see a Sun by rising set,
And by that setting endless day beget;
But that Christ on this cross did rise and fall,
Sin had eternally benighted all.
Yet dare I almost be glad I do not see
That spectacle of too much weight for me.
Who sees God's face, that is self-life, must die;
What a death were it then to see God die!
It made his own lieutenant, Nature, shrink;
It made his footstool crack, and the sun wink.
Could I behold those hands which span the poles
And tune all spheres at once, pierced with those holes?
Could I behold that endless height which is
Zenith to us, and our antipodes,
Humbled below us? or that blood which is
The seat of all our souls, if not of his,
Made dirt of dust, or that flesh which was worn
By God for his apparel, ragg'd and torn?

If on these things I durst not look, durst I
Upon his miserable mother cast mine eye,
Who was God's partner here, and furnished thus
Half of that sacrifice which ransomed us?
Though these things as I ride be from mine eye,
They're present yet unto my memory.
For that looks towards them; and thou look'st towards me,
O Saviour, as thou hang'st upon the tree.
I turn my back to thee but to receive
Corrections, till thy mercies bid thee leave.
O think me worth thine anger, punish me,
Burn off my rusts and my deformity,
Restore thine Image so much, by thy grace,
That thou mayst know me, and I'll turn my face.

A HYMN TO CHRIST, AT THE AUTHOR'S LAST GOING INTO GERMANY

In what torn ship soever I embark,
That ship shall be my emblem of thy Ark;
What sea soever swallow me, that flood
Shall be to me an emblem of thy blood.
Though thou with clouds of anger do disguise
Thy face, yet through that mask I know those eyes,
    Which, though they turn away sometimes,
        They never will despise.

I sacrifice this island unto thee,
And all whom I loved there, and who loved me;
When I have put our seas twixt them and me,
Put thou thy sea betwixt my sins and thee.
As the tree's sap doth seek the root below
In winter, in my winter now I go
    Where none but thee, the eternal root
        Of true love, I may know.

Nor thou nor thy religion dost control
The amorousness of an harmonious soul,
But thou wouldst have that love thyself. As thou
Art jealous, Lord, so am I jealous now;
Thou lov'st not, till from loving more, thou free
My soul. Whoever gives, takes liberty.
   O, if thou car'st not whom I love,
      Alas, thou lov'st not me.

Seal then this bill of my divorce to all
On whom those fainter beams of love did fall;
Marry those loves which in youth scattered be
On Fame, Wit, Hopes (false mistresses), to thee.
Churches are best for prayer that have least light;
To see God only, I go out of sight;
   And to 'scape stormy days, I choose
      An everlasting night.

HYMN TO GOD, MY GOD,
IN MY SICKNESS

Since I am coming to that holy room
   Where with thy choir of saints for evermore
I shall be made thy music, as I come
   I tune the instrument here at the door,
   And what I must do then, think here before.

Whilst my physicians by their love are grown
   Cosmographers, and I their map, who lie
Flat on this bed, that by them may be shown
   That this is my Southwest discovery
   Per fretum febris, by these straits to die,

I joy that in these straits I see my West.
   For though their currents yield return to none,
What shall my West hurt me? As West and East
   In all flat maps (and I am one) are one,
   So death doth touch the resurrection.

Per fretum febris: through the
raging of fever.

Is the Pacific Sea my home? Or are
    The Eastern riches? Is Jerusalem?
Anyan and Magellán and Gibraltár,
    All straits, and none but straits, are ways to them,
    Whether where Japhet dwelt, or Cham or Shem.

We think that Paradise and Calvary,
    Christ's Cross and Adam's tree, stood in one place.
Look, Lord, and find both Adams met in me;
    As the first Adam's sweat surrounds my face,
    May the last Adam's blood my soul embrace.

So, in his purple wrapped, receive me, Lord;
    By these his thorns give me his other crown;
And as to others' souls I preached thy word,
    Be this my text, my sermon to mine own:
    Therefore that he may raise, the Lord throws down.

HYMN TO GOD THE FATHER

I

Wilt thou forgive that sin where I begun,
    Which was my sin though it were done before?
Wilt thou forgive that sin through which I run,
    And do run still, though still I do deplore?
        When thou hast done, thou hast not done,
        For I have more.

Anyan: Hakluyt in the *Principal Navigations* speaks of the "strait of Anian," conjectured to lie between America and Asia, allowing sea passage to Japan and the riches of the East; in 1728 this strait was "discovered" by Vitus Bering and afterwards named the Bering Strait.

II

Wilt thou forgive that sin by which I've won
  Others to sin, and made my sin their door?
Wilt thou forgive that sin which I did shun
  A year or two, but wallowed in a score?
      When thou hast done, thou hast not done,
        For I have more.

III

I have a sin of fear, that when I've spun
  My last thread, I shall perish on the shore;
But swear by thyself that at my death thy son
  Shall shine as he shines now, and heretofore;
      And having done that, Thou hast done;
        I fear no more.

BEN JONSON: 1572–1637

Jonson went to school at Westminster, where one of his teachers was the antiquarian and classicist, William Camden. Jonson did not attend a university, though he became one of the most learned men of his time. He worked for a while as a bricklayer, which was the trade of his stepfather; he enlisted for military service in Flanders; upon his return from the wars he married; and he became associated with a company of players. By the end of the century he was one of Henslowe's playwrights. In 1598 he killed an actor in a duel and escaped the gallows by claiming right of clergy. As his reputation as poet and dramatist grew, he became a most active and sought after writer of masques for the court. In 1616 he was made "King's Poet" by James I, and was given a pension; in the same year he collected his plays, masques, and poems for publication. His last years were spent in illness and poverty.

Jonson's training was vigorously classical, but his genius was native. He wrote one of the earliest and best English grammars, and his own verse regulated and fixed the language into a fluent yet powerful instrument of thought and expression. The discussion of literary and other problems in his commonplace book, *Timber: or Discoveries*, shows him to possess a stubborn common sense that is a kind of genius. It is this common sense that made it possible for his classical training to comprehend the two dominant opposing practices of his century, the Native and the Petrarchan, to reconcile them, and by that reconciliation to establish most firmly the major tradition of English poetry.

TEXT: *Ben Jonson*, in 11 vols., edited by C. H. Herford and Percy and Evelyn Simpson (1925–52).

ON MY FIRST DAUGHTER

Here lies, to each her parents' ruth,
Mary, the daughter of their youth:
Yet, all heavens' gifts, being heavens' due,
It makes the father less to rue.
At six months' end, she parted hence
With safety of her innocence;
Whose soul heaven's Queen, (whose name she bears)
In comfort of her mother's tears,
Hath placed amongst her virgin-train;
Where, while that severed doth remain,
This grave partakes the fleshly birth—
Which cover lightly, gentle earth.

ON MY FIRST SON

Farewell, thou child of my right hand, and joy;
   My sin was too much hope of thee, loved boy.
Seven years thou wert lent to me, and I thee pay,
   Exacted by thy fate, on the just day.
O, could I lose all father, now! For why
   Will man lament the state he should envý?
To have so soon 'scaped world's and flesh's rage,
   And, if no other misery, yet age!
Rest in soft peace; and, asked, say: Here doth lie
   Ben Jonson his best piece of poetry—
For whose sake, henceforth, all his vows be such,
   As what he loves may never like too much.

ON LUCY, COUNTESS OF BEDFORD

This morning, timely rapt with holy fire,
   I thought to form unto my zealous Muse
What kind of creature I could most desire
   To honor, serve, and love, as poets use.

I meant to make her fair and free and wise,
    Of greatest blood, and yet more good than great;
I meant the day-star should not brighter rise,
    Nor lend like influence from his lucent seat.
I meant she should be courteous, facile, sweet,
    Hating that solemn vice of greatness, pride;
I meant each softest virtue there should meet,
    Fit in that softer bosom to reside.
Only a learnèd and a manly soul
    I purposed her, that should, with even powers,
The rock, the spindle, and the shears control
    Of destiny, and spin her own free hours.
Such when I meant to feign, and wished to see,
    My Muse bade: Bedford write. And that was she.

INVITING A FRIEND TO SUPPER

Tonight, grave sir, both my poor house and I
Do equally desire your company;
Not that we think us worthy such a guest,
But that your worth will dignify our feast
With those that come, whose grace may make that seem
Something which else could hope for no esteem.
It is the fair acceptance, sir, creates
The entertainment perfect, not the cates.
Yet shall you have, to rectify your palate,
An olive, capers, or some bitter salad
Ushering the mutton; with a short-legged hen,
If we can get her, full of eggs; and then,
Lemons, and wine for sauce: to these, a cony
Is not to be despaired of for our money;
And though fowl now be scarce, yet there are clerks,
The sky not falling, think we may have larks.
I'll tell you of more, and lie, so you will come:
Of partridge, pheasant, woodcock, of which some
May yet be there; and godwit if we can;
Gnat, rail, and ruff, too. Howsoe'er, my man

Shall read a piece of Virgil, Tacitus,
Livy, or of some better book to us,
Of which we'll speak our minds, amidst our meat;
And I'll profess no verses to repeat:
To this if aught appear, which I not know of,
That will the pastry, not my paper, show of.
Digestive cheese, and fruit there sure will be;
But that which most doth take my muse and me,
Is a pure cup of rich Canary wine,
Which is the Mermaid's now, but shall be mine:—
Of which had Horace, or Anacreon tasted,
Their lives, as do their lines, till now had lasted.
Tobacco, nectar, or the Thespian spring,
Are all but Luther's beer, to this I sing.
Of this we will sup free, but moderately,
And we will have no Pooly or parrot by;
Nor shall our cups make any guilty men,
But at our parting, we will be as when
We innocently met. No simple word
That shall be uttered at our mirthful board
Shall make us sad next morning, or affright
The liberty that we'll enjoy tonight.

EPITAPH ON S. P., A CHILD OF QUEEN ELIZABETH'S CHAPEL

Weep with me all you that read
    This little story;
And know, for whom a tear you shed,
    Death's self is sorry.
'Twas a child, that so did thrive
    In grace and feature,
As Heaven and Nature seemed to strive
    Which owned the creature.

godwit, gnat, rail, ruff: small, choice game birds for the table.

Pooly: A pun upon Robert Pooly, a spy present at Marlowe's death.

Years he numbered scarce thirteen
    When Fates turned cruel,
Yet three filled zodiacs had he been
    The stage's jewel;
And did act, what now we moan,
    Old men so duly,
As, sooth, the Parcae thought him one,
    He played so truly.
So, by error, to his fate
    They all consented;
But viewing him since (alas, too late)
    They have repented.
And have sought, to give new birth,
    In baths to steep him;
But, being so much too good for earth,
    Heaven vows to keep him.

EPITAPH ON ELIZABETH, L. H.

Wouldst thou hear what man can say
    In a little? Reader, stay.
Underneath this stone doth lie
    As much beauty as could die,
Which in life did harbor give
    To more virtue than doth live.
If, at all, she had a fault,
    Leave it buried in this vault.
One name was Elizabeth;
    The other—let it sleep with death.
Fitter, where it died, to tell,
    Than that it lived at all. Farewell.

Parcae: Parca was the Roman goddess of birth; the plural form of her name, Parcae, was used for the Fates, i.e., the divinities of the duration of human life.

TO THE WORLD:
A FAREWELL FOR A GENTLEWOMAN,
VIRTUOUS AND NOBLE

False world, good-night: since thou hast brought
  That hour upon my morn of age,
Henceforth I quit thee from my thought;
  My part is ended on thy stage.
Do not once hope that thou canst tempt
  A spirit so resolved to tread
Upon thy throat, and live exempt
  From all the nets that thou canst spread.
I know thy forms are studied arts,
  Thy subtle ways be narrow straits,
Thy courtesy but sudden starts,
  And what thou call'st thy gifts are baits.
I know, too, though thou strut and paint,
  Yet art thou both shrunk up and old,
That only fools make thee a saint,
  And all thy good is to be sold.
I know thou whole art but a shop
  Of toys and trifles, traps and snares,
To take the weak or make them stop:
  Yet art thou falser than thy wares.
And, knowing this, should I yet stay,
  Like such as blow away their lives,
And never will redeem a day,
  Enamoured of their golden gyves?
Or, having 'scaped, shall I return
  And thrust my neck into the noose
From whence, so lately, I did burn,
  With all my powers, my self to loose?
What bird or beast is known so dull,
  That fled his cage or broke his chain,
And tasting air and freedom, will
  Render his head in there again?

If these, who have but sense, can shun
  The engines that have them annoyed,
Little for me had reason done,
  If I could not thy 'gins avoid.
Yes, threaten, do. Alas, I fear
  As little as I hope from thee;
I know thou canst nor show nor bear
  More hatred than thou hast to me.
My tender, first, and simple years
  Thou didst abuse, and then betray;
Since, stirred'st up jealousies and fears,
  When all the causes were away.
Then, in a soil hast planted me
  Where breathe the basest of thy fools;
Where envious arts professëd be,
  And pride and ignorance the schools;
Where nothing is examined, weighed,
  But as 'tis rumored, so believed;
Where every freedom is betrayed,
  And every goodness taxed or grieved.
But what we're born for, we must bear:
  Our frail condition, it is such
That, what to all may happen here,
  If it chance to me, I must not grutch;
Else I my state should much mistake
  To harbor a divided thought
From all my kind—that for my sake,
  There should a miracle be wrought.
No, I do know that I was born
  To age, misfortune, sickness, grief:
But I will bear these with that scorn
  As shall not need thy false relief.
Nor for my peace will I go far,
  As wanderers do, that still do roam,
But make my strengths, such as they are,
  Here in my bosom, and at home.

TO CELIA

Kiss me, sweet: the wary lover
Can your favors keep, and cover,
When the common courting jay
All your bounties will betray.
Kiss again: no creature comes.
Kiss, and score up wealthy sums
On my lips, thus hardly sundered,
While you breathe. First give a hundred,
Then a thousand, then another
Hundred, then unto the other
Add a thousand, and so more;
Till you equal with the store
All the grass that Rumney yields,
Or the sands in Chelsea fields,
Or the drops in silver Thames,
Or the stars that gild his streams
In the silent summer-nights
When youths ply their stolen delights—
That the curious may not know
How to tell 'em as they flow,
And the envious, when they find
What their number is, be pined.

SONG: TO CELIA

Drink to me only with thine eyes,
    And I will pledge with mine;
Or leave a kiss but in the cup,
    And I'll not look for wine.
The thirst that from the soul doth rise
    Doth ask a drink divine;
But might I of Jove's nectar sup,
    I would not change for thine.

I sent thee late a rosy wreath,
    Not so much honoring thee,
As giving it a hope that there
    It could not withered be.
But thou thereon didst only breathe,
    And sent'st it back to me—
Since when it grows and smells, I swear,
    Not of itself, but thee.

TO HEAVEN

Good and great God, can I not think of Thee,
But it must straight my melancholy be?
Is it interpreted in me disease,
That, laden with my sins, I seek for ease?
O, be thou witness, that the reins dost know
And hearts of all, if I be sad for show;
And judge me after, if I dare pretend
To aught but grace, or aim at other end.
As thou art all, so be thou all to me,
First, midst, and last, converted One and Three;
My faith, my hope, my love; and in this state,
My judge, my witness, and my advocate.
Where have I been this while exiled from thee?
And whither rapt, now thou but stoop'st to me?
Dwell, dwell here still! O, being everywhere,
How can I doubt to find Thee ever here?
I know my state, both full of shame and scorn,
Conceived in sin, and unto labor born,
Standing with fear, and must with horror fall,
And destined unto judgement, after all.
I feel my griefs too, and there scarce is ground
Upon my flesh to inflict another wound.
Yet dare I not complain or wish for death
With holy Paul, lest it be thought the breath
Of discontent; or that these prayers be
For weariness of life, not love of thee.

A HYMN TO GOD THE FATHER

Hear me, O God!
A broken heart
Is my best part:
Use still thy rod,
That I may prove
Therein thy Love.

If thou hadst not
Been stern to me,
But left me free,
I had forgot
My self and thee.

For sin's so sweet
As minds ill bent
Rarely repent,
Until they meet
Their punishment.

Who more can crave
Than thou hast done,
That gav'st a Son
To free a slave?—
First made of nought,
With all since bought.

Sin, Death, and Hell
His glorious Name
Quite overcame;
Yet I rebel
And slight the same.

But I'll come in
Before my loss
Me farther toss,
As sure to win
Under His cross.

A CELEBRATION OF CHARIS

I. *His excuse for loving*

Let it not your wonder move,
Less your laughter, that I love.
Though I now write fifty years,
I have had, and have my peers:
Poets, though divine, are men;
Some have loved as old again.
And it is not always face,
Clothes, or fortune gives the grace,
Or the feature, or the youth;
But the language and the truth,
With the ardor and the passion,
Gives the lover weight and fashion.
If you then will read the story,
First, prepare you to be sorry
That you never knew till now
Either whom to love, or how;
But be glad, as soon with me,
When you know that this is she
Of whose beauty it was sung,
She shall make the old man young,
Keep the middle age at stay,
And let nothing high decay,
Till she be the reason why
All the world for love may die.

II. *How he saw her*

I beheld her on a day
When her look out-flourished May,
And her dressing did out-brave
All the pride the fields then have;

Far I was from being stupid,
For I ran and called on Cupid:
"Love, if thou wilt ever see
Mark of glory, come with me;
Where's thy quiver? Bend thy bow;
Here's a shaft; thou art too slow!"
And, withal, I did untie
Every cloud about his eye;
But he had not gained his sight
Sooner than he lost his might
Or his courage; for away
Straight he ran, and durst not stay,
Letting bow and arrow fall;
Nor for any threat or call
Could be brought once back to look.
I, fool-hardy, there uptook
Both the arrow he had quit
And the bow, with thought to hit
This my object. But she threw
Such a lightning as I drew
At my face, that took my sight
And my motion from me quite;
So that, there, I stood a stone,
Mocked of all; and called of one
(Which with grief and wrath I heard)
Cupid's statue with a beard,
Or else one that played his ape,
In a Hercules's shape.

THE HOUR-GLASS

Do but consider this small dust
  Here running in the glass,
    By atoms moved;
Could you believe that this
  The body, ever, was
    Of one that loved?

And in his mistress' flame, playing like a fly,
    Turned to cinders by her eye?
    Yes; and in death, as life, unblessed,
        To have't expressed,
    Even ashes of lovers find no rest.

MY PICTURE LEFT IN SCOTLAND

I now think Love is rather deaf than blind,
    For else it could not be
        That she
Whom I adore so much should so slight me,
    And cast my love behind.
I'm sure my language to her was as sweet,
    And every close did meet
    In sentence of as subtle feet
        As hath the youngest he
That sits in shadow of Apollo's tree.

    Oh, but my conscious fears
        That fly my thoughts between,
        Tell me that she hath seen
        My hundred of gray hairs,
        Told seven and forty years,
    Read so much waste, as she cannot embrace
    My mountain belly and my rocky face;
And all these through her eyes have stopped her ears.

A LITTLE SHRUB GROWING BY

Ask not to know this man. If fame should speak
    His name in any metal, it would break.
Two letters were enough the plague to tear
    Out of his grave, and poison every ear.
A parcel of court-dirt, a heap, and mass
    Of all vice hurled together, there he was,

Proud, false, and treacherous, vindictive, all
   That thought can add, unthankful, the lay-stall
Of putrid flesh alive! of blood, the sink!
   And so I leave to stir him, lest he stink.

AN ELEGY

Though beauty be the mark of praise,
   And yours of whom I sing be such
   As not the world can praise too much,
Yet is't your virtue now I raise.

A virtue, like allay, so gone
   Throughout your form, as though that move,
   And draw, and conquer all men's love,
This subjects you to love of one,

Wherein you triumph yet: because
   'Tis of your self, and that you use
   The noblest freedom, not to choose
Against or faith, or honor's laws.

But who should less expect from you,
   In whom alone love lives again?
   By whom he is restored to men,
And kept, and bred, and brought up true.

His falling temples you have reared,
   The withered garlands ta'en away,
   His altars kept from the decay
That envy wished and nature feared;

And on them burn so chaste a flame
   With so much loyalty's expense,
   As Love, to acquit such excellence,
Is gone himself into your name.

And you are he: the deity
  To whom all lovers are designed,
  That would their better objects find—
Among which faithful troop am I,

Who as an offering at your shrine
  Have sung this hymn, and here entreat
  One spark of your diviner heat
To light upon a love of mine,

Which, if it kindle not, but scant
  Appear, and that to shortest view,
  Yet give me leave to adore in you
What I, in her, am grieved to want.

AN ODE: TO HIMSELF

Where dost thou careless lie,
  Buried in ease and sloth?
Knowledge that sleeps doth die;
And this security,
  It is the common moth
That eats on wits and arts, and so destroys them both.

Are all the Aonian springs
  Dried up? lies Thespia waste?
Doth Clarius' harp want strings,
That not a nymph now sings?
  Or droop they as disgraced
To see their seats and bowers by chattering pies defaced?

If hence thy silence be,
  As 'tis too just a cause,
Let this thought quicken thee:
Minds that are great and free
  Should not on fortune pause;
'Tis crown enough to virtue still, her own applause.

pies: i.e., magpies.

What though the greedy fry
  Be taken with false baits
Of worded balladry
And think it poesy?
  They die with their conceits,
And only piteous scorn upon their folly waits.

Then take in hand thy lyre,
  Strike in thy proper strain;
With Japhet's line, aspire
Sol's chariot for new fire,
  To give the world again:
Who aided him, will thee, the issue of Jove's brain.

And since our dainty age
  Cannot endure reproof,
Make not thy self a page
To that strumpet, the stage,
  But sing high and aloof,
Safe from the wolves' black jaw and the dull asses' hoof.

AN EPITAPH: ON ELIZABETH CHUTE

What beauty would have lovely styled,
What manners pretty, nature mild,
What wonder perfect—all were filed
Upon record in this blest child;
    And till the coming of the soul
    To fetch the flesh, we keep the roll.

AN ELEGY

Since you must go, and I must bid farewell,
Hear, Mistress, your departing servant tell
What it is like; and do not think they can
Be idle words, though of a parting man.

It is as if a night should shade noon-day,
Or that the sun was here, but forced away,
And we were left under that hemisphere
Where we must feel it dark for half a year.
What fate is this, to change men's days and hours,
To shift their seasons, and destroy their powers!
Alas, I've lost my heat, my blood, my prime;
Winter is come a quarter ere his time,
My health will leave me; and when you depart,
How shall I do, sweet Mistress, for my heart?
You would restore it? No, that's worth a fear,
As if it were not worthy to be there.
O, keep it still; for it had rather be
Your sacrifice than here remain with me.
And so I spare it. Come what may become
Of me, I'll softly tread unto my tomb,
Or like a ghost walk silent amongst men,
Till I may see both it and you again.

TO THE READER

This figure that thou here seest put,
It was for gentle Shakespeare cut,
Wherein the graver had a strife
With nature, to out-do the life.
O, could he but have drawn his wit
As well in brass as he hath hit
His face—the print would then surpass
All that was ever writ in brass.
But since he cannot, Reader, look
Not on his picture, but his book.

TO THE MEMORY OF MY BELOVED WILLIAM SHAKESPEARE AND WHAT HE HATH LEFT US

To draw no envy, Shakespeare, on thy name,
Am I thus ample to thy book and fame,
While I confess thy writings to be such
As neither man nor muse can praise too much.
'Tis true, and all men's suffrage. But these ways
Were not the paths I meant unto thy praise;
For silliest ignorance on these may light,
Which, when it sounds at best, but echoes right;
Or blind affection, which doth ne'er advance
The truth, but gropes, and urgeth all by chance;
Or crafty malice might pretend this praise,
And think to ruin, where it seemed to raise.
These are, as some infamous bawd or whore
Should praise a matron; what could hurt her more?
But thou art proof against them, and indeed
Above the ill fortune of them, or the need.
I, therefore will begin. Soul of the Age!
The applause, delight, the wonder of our stage!
My Shakespeare, rise; I will not lodge thee by
Chaucer or Spenser, or bid Beaumont lie
A little further, to make thee a room:
Thou art a monument without a tomb,
And art alive still, while thy book doth live,
And we have wits to read, and praise to give.
That I not mix thee so, my brain excuses;
I mean with great but disproportioned Muses.
For, if I thought my judgment were of years,
I should commit thee surely with thy peers,
And tell how far thou didst our Lyly out-shine,
Or sporting Kyd, or Marlowe's mighty line.
And though thou hadst small Latin and less Greek,
From thence to honor thee, I would not seek
For names; but call forth thundering Æschylus,
Euripides, and Sophocles to us,

Pacuvius, Accius, him of Cordoba dead,
To life again, to hear thy buskin tread,
And shake a stage; or when thy socks were on,
Leave thee alone, for the comparison
Of all, that insolent Greece or haughty Rome
Sent forth, or since did from their ashes come.
Triumph, my Britain, thou hast one to show,
To whom all scenes of Europe homage owe.
He was not of an age, but for all time!
And all the Muses still were in their prime,
When like Apollo he came forth to warm
Our ears, or like a Mercury to charm!
Nature herself was proud of his designs,
And joyed to wear the dressing of his lines!
Which were so richly spun, and woven so fit,
As, since, she will vouchsafe no other wit.
The merry Greek, tart Aristophanes,
Neat Terence, witty Plautus, now not please,
But antiquated and deserted lie
As they were not of Nature's family.
Yet must I not give Nature all: thy art,
My gentle Shakespeare, must enjoy a part.
For though the Poet's matter nature be,
His art doth give the fashion. And, that he
Who casts to write a living line, must sweat,
(Such as thine are) and strike the second heat
Upon the Muses' anvil, turn the same,
And himself with it, that he thinks to frame—
Or for the laurel, he may gain a scorn;
For a good poet's made, as well as born.
And such wert thou. Look how the father's face
Lives in his issue; even so the race
Of Shakespeare's mind and manners brightly shines
In his well turnëd, and true-filëd lines,
In each of which he seems to shake a lance,
As brandished at the eyes of Ignorance.

him of Cordoba dead: i.e.,
  Seneca.

Sweet swan of Avon! what a sight it were
To see thee in our waters yet appear,
And make those flights upon the banks of Thames
That so did take Eliza and our James!
But stay, I see thee in the hemisphere
Advanced, and made a constellation there!
Shine forth, thou star of poets, and with rage,
Or influence, chide, or cheer the drooping stage,
Which, since thy flight from hence, hath mourned like
       night,
And despair's day, but for thy volume's light.

SONGS FROM THE MASQUES AND PLAYS

Love's Triumph

Joy, joy to mortals! The rejoicing fires
    Of gladness smile in your dilated hearts,
Whilst Love presents a world of chaste desires,
    Which may produce a harmony of parts!

Love is the right affection of the mind,
    The noble appetite of what is best,
Desire of union with the thing designed;
    But in fruition of it, cannot rest.

The Father plenty is, the Mother want;
    Plenty the beauty, which it wanteth, draws;
Want yields itself, affording what is scant:
    So, both affections are the union's cause.

But rest not here. For Love hath larger scopes,
    New joys, new pleasures, of as fresh a date
As are his minutes; and in him no hopes
    Are pure, but those he can perpetuate.

To you that are by excellence a Queen,
    The top of beauty! but of such an air
As only by the mind's eye may be seen
    Your interwoven lines of good and fair!

Vouchsafe to grace Love's triumph here tonight
  Through all the streets of your Callipolis,
Which by the splendor of your rays made bright
  The seat and region of all beauty is.

Love in perfection longeth to appear,
  But prays, of favor, he be not called on,
Till all the suburbs and the skirts be clear
  Of perturbations, and the infection gone.

Then will he flow forth, like a rich perfume
  Into your nostrils! or some sweeter sound
Of melting music that shall not consume
  Within the ear, but run the mazes round.

Meantime, we make lustration of the place,
  And with our solemn fires and waters prove
To have frighted hence the weak diseasëd race
  Of those were tortured on the wheel of love.

The glorious, whining, the adventurous fool,
  Fantastic, bribing, and the jealous ass,
The sordid, scornful, and the angry mule,
  The melancholic, dull, and envious mass,

With all the rest that in the sensual school
  Of lust for their degree of brute may pass—
    All which are vapored hence.
    No love, but slaves to sense:
    Mere cattle, and not men.
  Sound, sound, and treble all our joys again,
Who had the power and virtue to remove
Such monsters from the labyrinth of love.

Song

Slow, slow, fresh fount, keep time with my salt tears;
   Yet slower, yet; O faintly gentle springs;
List to the heavy part the music bears,
   Woe weeps out her division when she sings:
      Droop herbs and flowers;
      Fall grief in showers;
      Our beauties are not ours.
        O, I could still,
Like melting snow upon some craggy hill,
      Drop, drop, drop, drop,
Since nature's pride is now a withered daffodil.

Song

Still to be neat, still to be dressed
As you were going to a feast;
Still to be powdered, still perfumed:
Lady, it is to be presumed,
Though art's hid causes are not found,
All is not sweet, all is not sound.

Give me a look, give me a face
That makes simplicity a grace;
Robes loosely flowing, hair as free:
Such sweet neglect more taketh me
Than all the adulteries of art;
They strike mine eyes, but not my heart.

Song

Though I am young and cannot tell
Either what Death or Love is well,
Yet I have heard they both bear darts
And both do aim at human hearts;

And then again, I have been told,
Love wounds with heat, as Death with cold,
So that I fear they do but bring
Extremes to touch, and mean one thing.

As in a ruin we it call
One thing to be blown up or fall,
Or to our end like way may have
By a flash of lightning or a wave,
So Love's inflaméd shaft or brand
May kill as soon as Death's cold hand,
Except Love's fires the virtue have
To fright the frost out of the grave.

Hymn to Diana

Queen and huntress, chaste and fair,
Now the sun is laid to sleep,
Seated in thy silver chair
State in wonted manner keep:
    Hesperus entreats thy light,
    Goddess excellently bright.

Earth, let not thy envious shade
Dare itself to interpose;
Cynthia's shining orb was made
Heaven to clear, when day did close;
    Bless us then with wishéd sight,
    Goddess excellently bright.

Lay thy bow of pearl apart,
And thy crystal shining quiver;
Give unto the flying hart
Space to breathe, how short soever,
    Thou that mak'st a day of night,
    Goddess excellently bright.

Song: to Celia

Come, my Celia, let us prove,
While we may, the sports of love.
Time will not be ours forever;
He, at length, our good will sever.
Spend not then his gifts in vain;
Suns that set may rise again,
But if once we lose this light,
'Tis with us perpetual night.
Why should we defer our joys?
Fame and rumor are but toys.
Cannot we delude the eyes
Of a few poor household spies?
Or his easier ears beguile,
So removèd by our wile?
'Tis no sin love's fruit to steal,
But the sweet theft to reveal:
To be taken, to be seen,
These have crimes accounted been.

INDEX OF TITLES AND FIRST LINES

THE NORTON LIBRARY

SEVENTEENTH-CENTURY SERIES

J. MAX PATRICK, *General Editor*